Ten Miles from Aspen

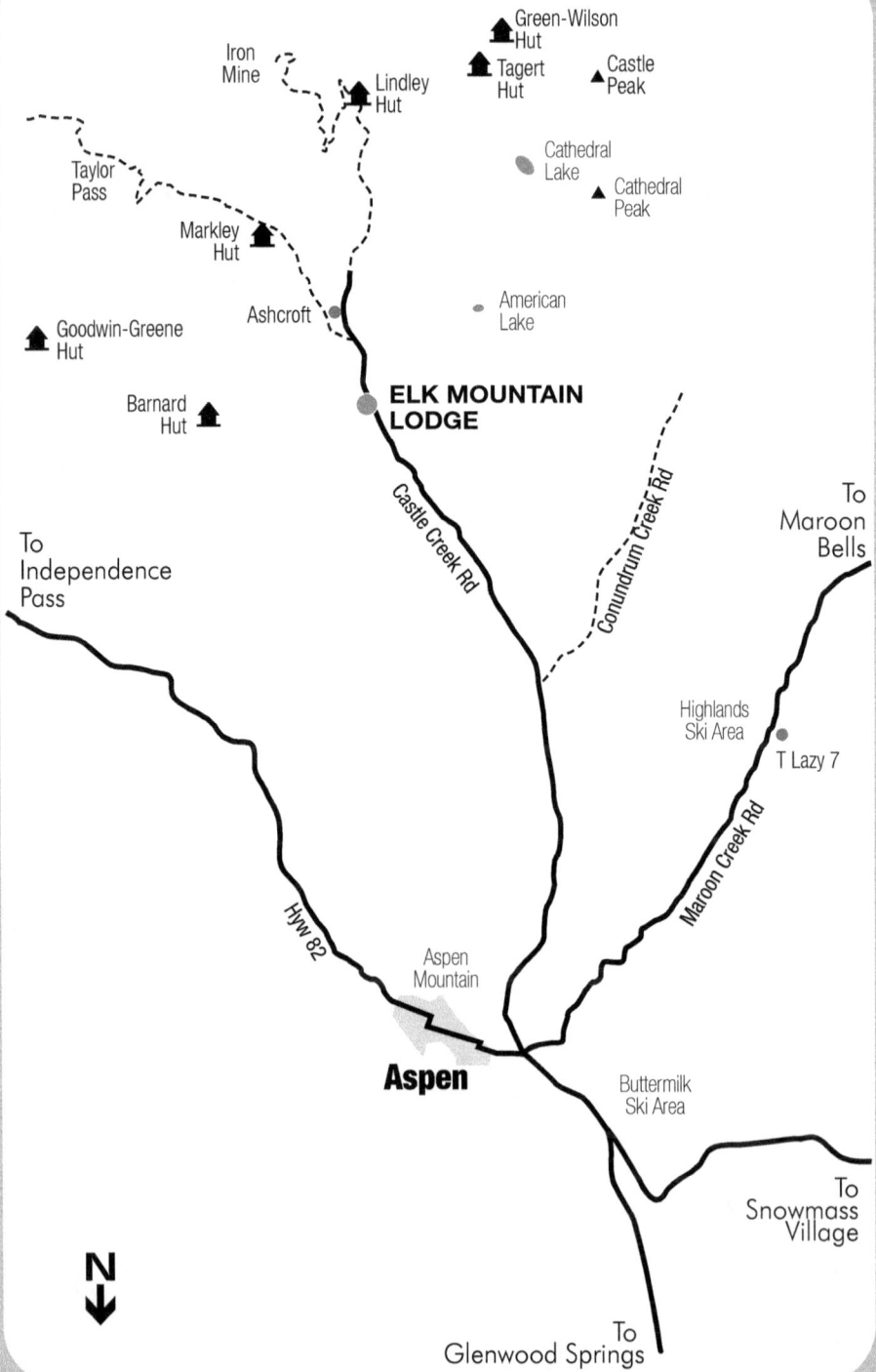

Green-Wilson
Hut

Iron
Mine

Tagert
Hut

Lindley
Hut

Castle
Peak

Taylor
Pass

Cathedral
Lake

Cathedral
Peak

Markley
Hut

Ashcroft

American
Lake

Goodwin-Greene
Hut

**ELK MOUNTAIN
LODGE**

Barnard
Hut

Castle Creek Rd

Conundrum Creek Rd

To
Maroon
Bells

To
Independence
Pass

Highlands
Ski Area

T Lazy 7

Maroon Creek Rd

Hyw 82

Aspen
Mountain

Aspen

Buttermilk
Ski Area

To
Snowmass
Village

N

To
Glenwood Springs

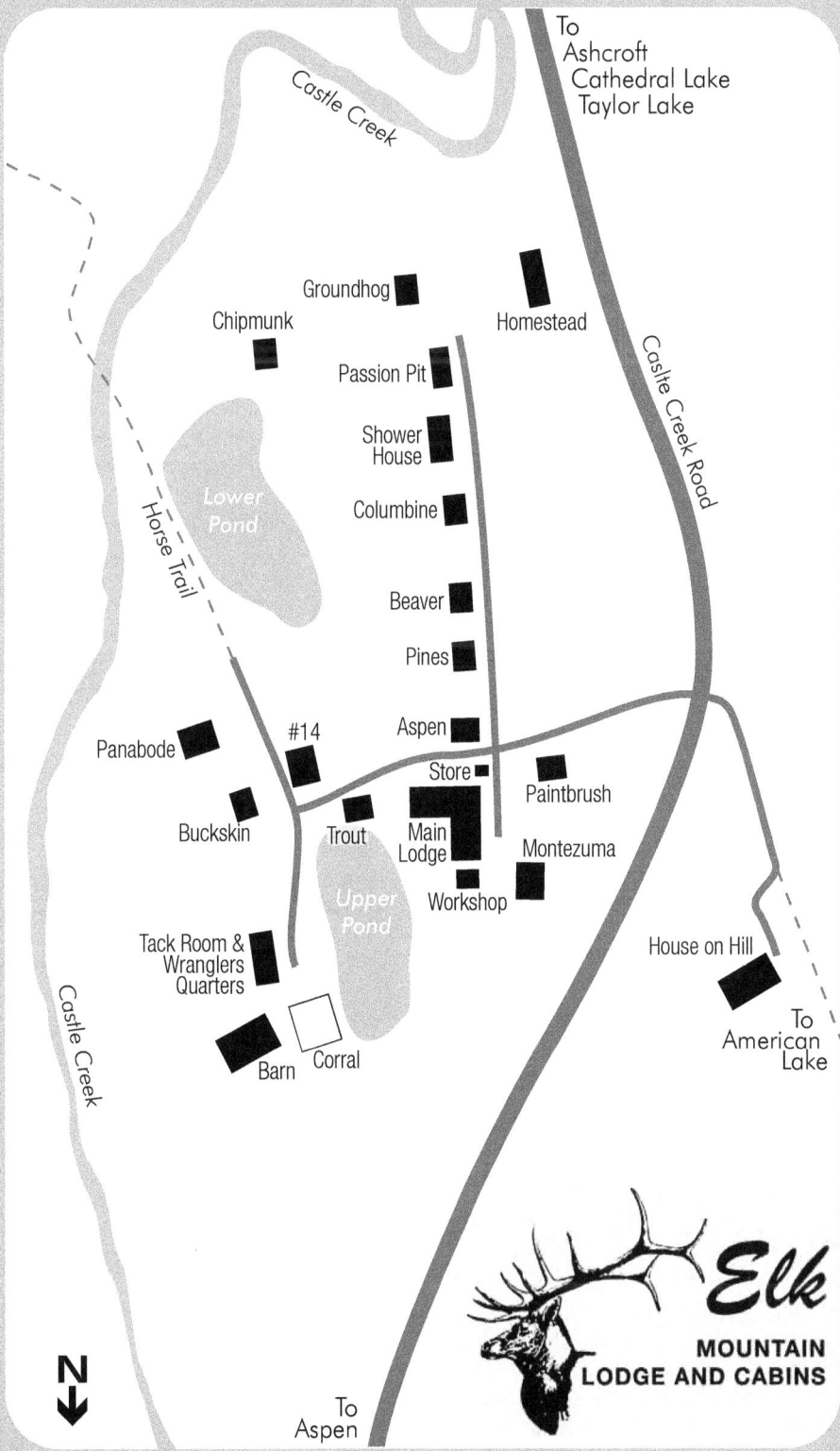

To
Ashcroft
Cathedral Lake
Taylor Lake

Castle Creek

Castle Creek Road

Groundhog

Chipmunk

Homestead

Passion Pit

Shower House

Lower Pond

Columbine

Horse Trail

Beaver

Pines

Aspen

Panabode

#14

Store

Paintbrush

Buckskin

Trout

Main Lodge

Montezuma

Upper Pond

Workshop

Tack Room & Wranglers Quarters

House on Hill

To American Lake

Castle Creek

Barn   Corral

N

To Aspen

Elk

MOUNTAIN LODGE AND CABINS

TEN MILES
from
ASPEN

Life at the Lodge in the 60s and 70s

Joanne Brand

Ms. LODGE
PUBLISHING

Contact @ tenmilesfromaspen.com

1st Edition
Copyright © 2010 by Joanne Brand
Photos, and Original Drawings Copyright © 2010 by Joanne Brand
TEN MILES from ASPEN   Life at the Lodge in the 60s and 70s

ISBN # 978-0-615-36393-6

Library of Congress Number 2010915313

Printed in the United States
Ms. Lodge Publishing
Aurora, Colorado
www. tenmilesfromaspen.com

Book Design: Tina Brand
Book Consultant: Pat Landaker

For quantity orders, please send request to tenmilesfromaspen.com

PREFACE

I wrote *Ten Miles from Aspen* to record my unique life on our guest ranch high in the Rocky Mountains of Colorado in the 1960s and 70s. My book tells my true life and how I observed the 13 years at our Elk Mountain Lodge, ten miles from the world-renowned ski resort of Aspen, Colorado. I was a city girl suddenly thrown into an unknown life high in the Rocky Mountains. I tell the other side of Aspen—not all glitz and glamour.

I have been writing this book since 1965 because of my brief entries in my diaries. This year I was ready to print my life during the years at our lodge near Aspen. I tell of the everyday struggles of living with summer tourist activity, wood-burning stoves, catastrophes including horse injuries, deaths, abuse, and dangerous horse rescues. Hilarious affairs with dynamite, critters and tenants give breaks from the serious sides. Fires and threats were fearful and some involved court cases. Mountain rescues involved the family in summer and winter, while TV documentaries and celebrity episodes kept life interesting. Conflicts came in the winter between snowmobiles and cross-country skiers, while more conflict came in the winter with hippie tenants and feisty Joanne. Off-seasons gave breaks from the hectic life with picnics in the Rockies, vacation, or dinners and partying in Aspen restaurants, lounges and clubs.

The 1960s and 70s were turbulent years in our country, which included the Vietnam War, war protests, the Civil Rights movement and, of course, the revolution of our culture and moral values. My family was affected by many changes during this time—not all good—not all bad.

Memories are now on paper
for my children
Life as I lived is now on paper
for my grandchildren

I dedicate this book to Michael H. and Lettie Lee Brand,
my mother and father-in-law,in honor of their years at
Elk Mountain Lodge and in Aspen, Colorado.
Without them, I would not have these experiences
or learned to love the Rocky Mountains.

About the Author

Joanne Brand met and married her husband, Larry, while working in Denver, and then moved to Elk Mountain Lodge, ten miles from Aspen, Colorado. She experienced unique struggles of guest ranch life mingled with the struggles of the country during the 1960s and 70s. She gradually transformed from a city girl to a lover of the Rocky Mountains.

Joanne is now retired and enjoying life. She loves to read and decided to write her story as well as poetry and fiction. She paints realistic scenery and has sold many paintings and note cards. Joanne also volunteers in helping others through her church organizations and also other volunteer work. Her greatest pleasure is being close to her children and grandchildren. She often has said that her best education has been life's experiences and the people she has met. Her love for the mountains is always present in her mind.

Acknowledgements

I am especially grateful to my children for all their help, support and encouragement. Tina, Greg and Susy have been right there with me in writing my book.

My Heather Gardens Writers Club encouraged me to write and I learned much from the group. I am grateful to Mary Jo Duckworth and Emelie Schmitz who had faith in me to write this book. I am grateful for my friends Jack, Dale and Neal for their information and encouragement. I appreciate the help from Pitkin County Library for sending me copies of archived Aspen Times articles.

Of course, I am most grateful to my husband, Larry Brand, who stood side by side with me while living through the years. He was an amazing man who had many talents and he was a gentle, even-tempered, humorous man who taught me how to laugh and to love the Rocky Mountains, especially the Elk Mountains and Castle Creek Valley.

Contents

The view from the front porch of Elk Mountain Lodge

Chapter 1

Leaving Elk Mountain Lodge (1978)

I sat on my favorite boulder in late August 1978, propped my elbows on my knees and my chin rested on my open hands. Behind me sat Elk Mountain Lodge, my home of the last 13 years. Our small guest ranch lay nestled between the tall pine and aspen trees in a narrow valley of the Rocky Mountains just 10 miles from the world-renowned ski resort of Aspen, Colorado. Castle Creek, in front of me, wound through our property and seemed to flow by with a whisper of music keeping time. I looked past the beaver ponds, the ghost town of Ashcroft, and up to the beautiful Elk Mountain Range which gave our lodge its name.

Memories of the last 13 years began to waltz in my mind…the same as the music of the creek flowing onward. *So much happened since I first moved here. What a time we had!*

Initiation (1965)

My husband, Larry, and I moved to Elk Mountain Lodge Guest Ranch in early spring of 1965. We arrived with our two small children, 3-year old Tina and 1½-year old Greg and another on the way. Mother Brand left the lodge and land to her four sons when she died the year before. Larry's father had been gone for years. We would help run the lodge with Larry's brother, Glenn. The other two brothers lived on the west coast.

I had no idea what mountain life would be like because I had always been a city girl surrounded by conveniences. The lodge felt so isolated, but I would always follow my husband wherever he went. Larry was my rock and my idol. He was always calm, even when I got frustrated or angry.

When we turned into the drive, off Castle Creek Road, I noticed our lodge had three-quarter log siding and the long porch railing had slanting pine limbs. I had been to the lodge once in 1962, but I couldn't remember what it looked like. When I saw it again, I realized that nothing looked like the exclusive resorts I had seen in travel brochures.

We began to unpack the trailer containing our meager possessions, hoping to beat the dark and the oncoming rain that cast an earthy scent. After all our belongings were inside, darkness began to creep through the valley. I checked the round-cornered refrigerator and the cupboards and found them well-stocked because Larry had been at the lodge a month prior to my arrival. In that month, he tore off the small bedroom and built three new bedrooms to accommodate us.

The kitchen's two outside walls contained six small 8-inch square windows with another row on top. Against one log wall sat a wood burning stove next to a small LP gas range. The refrigerator sat by the other log wall next to the

Front porch of Elk Mountain Lodge

back door. The kitchen was separated from the lobby by the massive fireplace and cupboards along one side. The almost colorless linoleum flooring in the kitchen looked as if it had about 30-years wear.

I opened the refrigerator and the tiny freezer compartment held nothing but two sets of metal ice cube trays. I didn't see anything for a meal, so I checked the cupboards for canned meat. I found some tuna and told Larry, "Okay, I'm using the gas range. I'm not going to attempt to use that wood stove tonight. I'll just use the gas oven for a casserole."

"Sounds fine to me…I'm starved." Unpacking took energy and he was ready to devour anything. He always ate hardily, but somehow stayed thin. Maybe because he was so tall it gave more room to spread evenly and higher. I was just the opposite: short and no room for extra weight except to spread out, which I now felt with our new baby scheduled to arrive in November.

Thunder, lightning and rain soon began to race through the valley. Bright jagged flashes licked the mountainsides and thunder quickly followed. Bolts of fire and deafening cracks, like a bullwhip, enveloped the valley. I jumped with each burst that hit nearby and that seemed to occur simultaneously.

I put the casserole in the oven and peeked out the window just as an explosion of thunder and blinding light burst too close. Immediately, the electricity went out and the house went dark as a cave, except for the flashes of fire-bolts outside.

My eyes widened. "Oh my God, what are we going to do now?"

"It's probably just a tree that fell on the power line, or lightening hit a transformer." Larry tried to minimize my anxiety. "Don't worry. I'll call REA—that's the Rural Electric Association. They'll fix the line in no time." He gave me a hug and smiled down at me as his brown eyes sparkled bright through his glasses with each lightening flash and his 6-foot frame and broad shoulders dwarfed me. He reminded me of an old-time Western movie star with his prominent square chin and high cheekbones. The difference was Larry did not wear a cowboy hat. He liked his fishing hat better.

I want to go back to Denver. This isn't for me, but Larry has always loved this place and Aspen. He grew up here and it's in his blood. But how can I live this way?

Larry stepped back and pulled down two kerosene lamps from the wall shelf and lit them. "Okay kids, let's play like old-time pioneers." He laughed, winked at them, and clapped his hands. Tina and Greg had no idea what pioneers were, but they laughed and clapped also. When the lamps were lit, he called REA.

After supper in the lamplight, I gave some leftovers to the cat and dog. We put the children to bed early and they soon fell asleep. They'd had a long, exciting day. Larry and I were exhausted and not far behind them. I couldn't get to sleep thinking of the storm and no electricity. I felt like this was another world and I worried if more surprises were in store for me.

Elk Mountain Lodge Tour

Morning brought the bright sun and electricity again. After breakfast, we toured the lodge and surrounding grounds. The lobby's large hanging wagon wheel light fixture impressed me and the tongue and groove pine paneling gave a rustic feeling. A native stone fireplace stood an impressive 10 feet wide and reached to the cathedral ceiling. On one side of the fireplace were bookshelves full of interesting books and on the other side stood a tall counter in front of our office, which led to the kitchen. The guests registered at the counter. The lobby doubled as our living room and in front of the sofa sat a large solid wood antique secretary desk that was made into a coffee table by cutting the legs short. It held a photo album with the story of Ashcroft, pictures and names of flowers, and had ads of restaurants or tourist attractions in the area. The two outside lobby walls held windows with four 12-inch square glass panes across and three high. Each pane sat puttied into wood frames painted red. I'd soon learn to hate to clean them of children and dog smears.

When Larry left Aspen for college, he decided to stay in Denver to work. He had not returned to Aspen except for quick visits. I knew Mother Brand lived at the lodge in the summers, but spent her winters in her large Victorian home in Aspen. It had been sold and we would now live at our guest ranch year-round, which caused me some panic. Even though Larry said the 10 miles to town would be well-plowed in the winter, the lodge still seemed to be too isolated and so far away from civilization.

We stood on the porch and looked around. I asked, "Where can the kids play? There's no fenced yard. The ponds and corral are too close and Castle Creek is so swift and dangerous…what if they fall in?" I held onto each child's hand protecting them from the wild outdoors I envisioned.

"Don't worry. We can keep the kids close, and there isn't much here that is dangerous or going to kill them. The water isn't deep in the ponds, and we'll teach the kids to stay away from the creek when it's high in the spring." Larry spent his summers as a little boy at the lodge and remembered adventure after childhood adventure, free of any dangers. He was eager for his children to discover and enjoy the alpine life that had given him so much pleasure.

"How much land do we have?"

"We've got around 90 acres, and we're sitting at an altitude of 9,500 feet. It's high, but it's sure pretty up here." His love for the mountains was evident in his voice and eyes. This is where he would always want to be.

I learned that the winters were about six frozen snowy months, spring two muddy and chilly ones, fall two shivering-cold ones, and that left summer with about two warm months and no higher than about 70°F. Sometimes there were a few more weeks in the spring or fall that stayed warm. Snow began to stack up in the mountains in October and continue until about the end of March or early April. There could still be a possible snow dusting at the lodge in the summer months, but it would melt quickly.

Larry explained to me that his father bought this land in 1933. The three original cabins, the Homestead, Groundhog and Tree Horn—which was renamed the Passion Pit—were built in 1907 and 1908. The ghost town of Ashcroft sat about a mile south of us and past it was the Sawtooth Range and Star Peak.

Our lodge was built later and the rest of the cabins were built about one a year after that. Each had a name like the Paintbrush, Montezuma, Trout, Pines, Buckskin, Columbine, Chipmunk and so forth. The House on the Hill sat across the road by the American Lake trailhead. All cabins were housekeeping meaning the guests did their own cooking and cleaning. We furnished the linens, dishes, pots, pans and silverware. Half were rustic with no running water and a wood burning stove for cooking and heat. A water spigot rose from the ground outside each rustic cabin and the shower house had a women's side and a men's

Tina and Greg by the back pond

side with showers, stools and sinks. The other half of the cabins were modern with electricity, running water, a bath and a full kitchen with a propane gas range. They had a gas wall heater and a Ben Franklin wood stove or a fireplace. A Ben Franklin is a free-standing fireplace-type wood stove.

I asked how I could tell which cabins were which. Larry answered that I would learn soon enough.

We walked around and he pointed to the other side of the pond behind us to show me the stables and the wrangler's quarters. The old barn sat just behind it. Turning back, he pointed again to the little building past the lodge and tall flag pole with the American flag waving in the breeze. It was our ranch store. We would keep food supplies and fishing gear on hand for the tourists.

There was so much to learn, but I had one more question: "Where's the closest neighbor, Larry?"

"There's only one and that's the Mace family across from the ghost town of Ashcroft up a mile. Stuart Mace doesn't like us being in his valley. They have the Toklot Lodge and run a restaurant, and he also runs his dog sled tours in the winter, but there's no lodging there. A separate building has the cross-country skiing headquarters which his son, Greg, runs." He paused a minute and then continued, "My brother gets along okay with Stuart and his son, Greg. Glenn and Greg, both, belong to the Aspen Mountain Rescue."

"Any other families close by?"

"The only other neighbors live 5 miles down valley toward Aspen. No one's in between."

Now I really felt isolated! That ended our tour and my mind whirled with anxiety.

Glenn's Back

The next day Larry's brother, Glenn, came back from a trip. He had been handling the lodge with his mother for several years. He went to Grand Junction to acquire some equipment for heating and roof repair along with other items that the lodge would need for the summer. He occupied the bedroom on the end of the new structure, which Larry had built. Larry and I occupied the middle room and the children occupied the third bedroom.

Soon Larry and Glenn worked side by side repairing roofs, cleaning cabins, painting porches and trim, opening the water lines and various other tasks. One day, they came in for a coffee break.

Glenn ambled over to the large wood kitchen table, stretched his long legs underneath, and picked up the newspaper on the counter and then threw it back down. "The paper is full of the Vietnam War and the anti-war demonstrations. Added to that, we have the fight for civil rights and the hippie movement. I don't want to read anymore of it."

Larry nodded and sat at the other end of the table and also stretched his long legs underneath. "Yeah, the war sure has created a huge cry of dissension and these hippie nuts want to do as they please."

I knew the hippies coincided with the new age of "ME," which was a growing number of people who thought only of themselves. They were the pioneers of an emerging new culture and would change the life of all Americans in one way or another. Change would also come through the peace marchers, draft dodgers and deserters, civil rights movement, women's liberation, and morality leniency. It came with a new way of life to the country—not all good, not all bad. I came from a good Christian background. The new loose morals flabbergasted me.

I also paid close attention to the news on the Vietnam War because my nephew enlisted and was over there. We were also aware of the plight of the Negroes—the name we used. Some used much worse names! As I recall, I think Aspen had only one Negro resident and he was treated with respect and liked. He was the only connection the area seemed to have with the South, as far I as I could tell.

I asked, "Did you read about the civil rights march at Selma, Alabama?"

"Yeah," Larry answered, "I read about the beatings the marchers received and they're calling March 7th 'Bloody Sunday.' The Negroes just want to be able to register to vote and have equal rights. The Alabama State Troopers and the police met them at the Pettus Bridge and attacked them. They gave no mercy to anyone, not even women or children with their billy clubs, tear gas and whips." He paused, shook his head in disbelief, sipped his coffee, and then continued. "When Martin Luther King organized the second march two days later the troopers and others were at the bridge again with their weapons. All the media was there ready to record the violence. Instead, they recorded a great event." He stopped and grinned. "I read that King stopped at the bridge and held a short prayer service and turned the march back around instead of receiving more beatings. It was great publicity showing King's power by peaceful means to further their cause."

Glenn added, "Many people consider them too illiterate to understand and vote the way they should…the way the whites want. It isn't right."

They drained their coffee cups and decided to get back to work. After they left, I thought about what else was happening in the world. It had become a time of technological and scientific advancement in the space industry. The United States and the Soviet Union were vying to be first in space technology to give them an edge as well as in the weapons field. The Russians were our strongest enemy and they wanted to rule the world.

About that time, I also realized I needed to get back to work.

Dandelion Potatoes and Horses (1965)

I gave a sigh of relief when I found out all the cabins were set up for cooking and I did not have to cook meals for the guests. Meals were sometimes experimental, especially when I ran out of an ingredient. I had to learn how to substitute. I couldn't run to the store 10 miles away on the spur of the moment. Improvisation and sometimes experimentation were needed. Thank goodness Larry and Glenn never complained about my cooking…maybe because of my standard remark to the children, if they complained: "What's on your plate is what you get. Take it or don't eat."

On a late sunny, warm afternoon I picked up a bucket and gathered the children. "We're going to pick dandelions for supper. I'm going to make dandelion potatoes and I want you to help me pick the leaves." Tina and Greg were eager and ran ahead. "Now, we only want to gather the leaves that don't have flowers yet. No flowers, just leaves."

"How's this, Mama?" Tina asked as she held up a dandelion with the roots still attached. Her eyes squinted in the sunlight, and her mouth twisted to one side, as if it would help shield her from the sun.

"Very good, sweetie, only don't pull the roots up. We just want the leaves."

"Here, Mama." Greg proudly held up a tuft of tall grass. Already his hands were dirty.

"Oh, that's good, Greg. But you know what? I'm going to need you to carry the pail, so I can have my hands free to pick. It may get heavy, but I think you can carry it. If the pail gets too heavy, I'll carry it."

"Okay, Mama," he said proudly in his toddler speech. He grabbed the pail with determination and waddled beside me.

It didn't take long before enough leaves were picked. Greg carried the pail high against his chest, leaning back for balance. He struggled to keep it upright as his little legs waddled from side to side.

When we got back to the house, I rinsed, sorted, drained the leaves, and chopped them fine. I fried a pound of bacon to a crisp and crumbled them. Potatoes were boiled and mashed. I placed the chopped dandelion leaves and bacon bits in a bowl. I mixed vinegar into the bacon grease and then drizzled the hot mixture over the leaves. The wilted dandelions became the "gravy" for the potatoes. Larry, Glenn and I loved this dish almost as much as a good steak.

The next day brought another adventure. I looked out the kitchen window and across the back pond. "Larry, there's a truck and trailer down at the stables, and I think there are horses in it. From here it looks like a cowboy getting out of the truck. Who is he?"

"That's Cal Bennett with the horses. He's a horse rancher from down valley and we lease them for the summer. We only lease 10, but someday we'll grow and have more horses. We rent them out by the hour, half-day, all day rides and for pack trips. I'm going down to check the horses." He grabbed the checkbook on his way out.

Tina jumped up and down. "I want to go see the horses."

"Me too," chimed in Greg. The two headed for the door.

I quickly wagged my finger up and down. "Now just a minute. You two aren't going down there by yourselves. Those horses are dangerous. I'll go with you, but you must stay back and only watch."

They bounced to the stables and I followed close behind. We watched Cal and Larry unload the horses and lead them to the corral. The two men finalized the deal with a hand shake. The rest of the 10 horses would arrive the next day. Larry invited Cal for coffee before he headed back down the road.

"Thanks, but I've got a thermos of coffee and I want to get back. I got a sick heifer. The wife has been watching her while I came up here." Cal waved out the window when he drove off with a whirlwind of dust from his tires, trying to catch up.

Larry got a pail and dipped it in a barrel full of oats. After he fed the horses, he let them out into the tall lush pasture.

"What kind of horses are they?" I asked. I didn't think they looked like pictures I'd seen in magazines of well-groomed thoroughbreds.

"They're just plain ol' dude horses. We call city folk "dudes" because they usually don't know anything about horses. These are gentle, reliable and they're good with kids too."

I fit in the category of a dude, I thought. I sure didn't know anything about horses.

Tina dragged behind and kept looking back at the horses. "They're beautiful. I want to ride one."

Wrangler Cathy

Our wrangler, Cathy, arrived a couple of days later. We hired a wrangler each summer to handle the horses and riders. The long building by the corral was the wrangler's living quarters next to the tack room holding the saddles and equipment.

Cathy's pleasant smile and easy manner won me over right away. Her jeans and western shirt showed her slender form and she wore her brown hair in a bobbed style that accentuated her tanned pleasant face.

Larry took her to the wrangler's quarters and showed her the stables and tack room. I tagged along to learn about the horses. He told her, "The county road splits our land and part of the pastureland is on this side and part on the other side. We begin pasturing the horses in the field by the stables. When it is eaten down, they are switched across the road, and when that's eaten down, the first side will have new grass again."

"Okay. I'll ride the fence to see if it all looks okay."

"Every adult and every parent must sign a release form. It protects us unless we're negligent. The riders can't run the horses up here, or they'll get wind-broke. They come from a lower altitude and are not used to this elevation. The rules are posted by the tack room door."

The tack room had plenty of saddles on the racks, storage for the pack trip gear, ponchos and meal ride equipment. The room smelled of well-used leather, canvas and dust. Riders would sign in at the counter against the wall by the door.

We saw from the first that she had plenty of experience with horses. Soft spoken, but in no way weak, she handled her duties well. Soon the stables became active with tourists from Aspen or cabin guests for rides. Mornings were busy with Cathy rounding up the horses and saddling them. She swung the saddles up and onto the backs of the horses with ease. If there were breaks in business, she polished saddles or groomed the horses.

When it came time to switch the horses to the other pasture, they galloped out the corral gate and Cathy pushed them through camp while she sat bareback on her favorite mount. She twirled her looped rope in the air beside her and moved back and forth behind the horses to keep them headed in the right direction through camp. They galloped across the road with their eyes on the new lush pasture awaiting them and went through the gate easily. Cathy halted, swung her right leg over her horse's neck, and slid off. She removed the bridle and gave a firm slap on his rump. He trotted off to be with his mates. Then she secured the gate with the gatepost placed in the wire loops attached to the fence post. Carrying the bridle over her shoulder, she strolled back to her quarters and made sure everything was ready for the next day.

Every day Tina ran to the stables and into the corral to pet the horses. They treated her like a new colt and just stepped around her. She wore her tiny cowboy boots to be just like Cathy and she had her cowboy hat dangling off her back.

Cathy asked Larry if she could teach Tina to ride. He said, "okay" and then broke the news to me.

The next day, Cathy sat Tina in the saddle, and then she mounted behind. She wrapped her arms around Tina while they both held the reins. I nervously stood close by.

Cathy began the lesson. "Okay, Tina. Let me show you how to rein a horse. You have to tell the horse what you want him to do. If you want him to go right, you pull just a bit on the reins this way." The horse turned to the right. "If you want the horse to go left, pull this way. Never jerk or pull hard." She paused and let the horse walk a bit to give Tina time to digest everything. Then she continued, "Give just enough pressure with your heels to let the horse know what you want. If you want to stop, you pull back on both reins firmly, but don't pull back fast or he might buck. Keep the reins tight and don't let the horse put its head down and eat the grass. If you do, you'll have a hard time getting him moving again. You have to show who is boss." Tina nodded eagerly.

Turning the horse around to head back to the stables, Cathy gave more instructions. "Now, when you head back, you have to hold the reins tight. See, like this…no slack, but not pulling too hard. If you don't have tight reins, he's going to feel free and run back as fast as he can for his oats and you may get thrown off."

Tina nodded her head up and down. "I'm riding, I'm riding! Can I ride everyday?"

"Sure, when we aren't busy."

Before long Tina rode by herself, but with Cathy beside her. She placed a small child's saddle on the gentle mare and adjusted the stirrups to the length of Tina's short legs. Tina resembled a doll perched so high, but she rode with her back straight and her head held high. She reined well and her tiny boots kicked the horse for more speed, which must have felt like a tap or a fly tickling.

"Look Mama, I'm riding Dixie," she shouted as she passed the lodge. Her face lit up with joy and pride.

"Yes, I see. Just be careful and do what Cathy says." Tina spent most of the day at the stables. She returned home smelling like the horses and happy about it.

Larry and Glenn worked hard all day on cabin preparations. I helped where I could. Everyone was hungry after a full day and suppers always included meat and potatoes. While washing the dishes one evening, I began to wonder about the water supply. "Larry, where does our water come from, a well or the creek?"

He picked up a towel and started drying dishes, which he always did. "Dad found an underground spring up on the hillside behind the trail to American Lake. He adjudicated that spring water. Adjudicate means that he got the legal rights to that water and it's recorded with the State of Colorado. Dad built

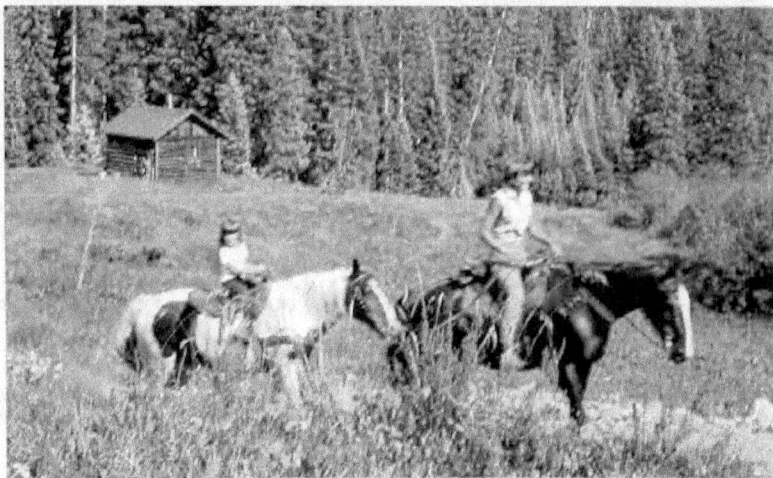

Cathy teaching Tina to ride solo

12

a small reservoir and piped the water down to the lodge and to the outside spigots near the rustic cabins." He put a plate in the cupboard and grabbed another plate from the drainer.

"Dad wanted to get electricity up here too, but we didn't get it until last year when the REA came up valley. The only lighting used to be from kerosene lamps. Then Mom got a good deal on a generator, and the cabins were all wired. The generator ran on gasoline, though, and only lasted for about two hours each night. After that, the guests had to either go to bed or use the lamps."

I grinned. "I'm sure glad electricity came before I got here. I might not have agreed to stay."

He grinned back. "Now the cabins have electricity 24 hours a day. Each has the small fuse box on the outside of the cabin. We keep a good supply of those little round glass-topped fuses to replace the ones that blow out. They blow when someone plugs in an appliance that calls for more juice then it can handle, like a toaster and a coffee maker going at the same time. Then poof… out goes the electricity. I'll show you where the fuses are kept."

So much to learn!

Chapter 2

Dusting off Cobwebs (1965)

A week later, frustration and intimidation took over as I stood by the wood burning stove in the kitchen. "I give up. I can't keep this fire going and get it hot enough to cook on. I'll never be able to master this stove like your mom. I'm not wasting anymore time on it. I need my cup of coffee right away in the morning to get going." I placed the percolator on the gas range burner.

Larry saw my mood and he sure wasn't going to argue. "Okay. That's fine."

"This whole kitchen's a mess. Every so often, the chinking between the logs falls out either in pieces or in piles of dust." The mortar loosened and eventually turned to small fragments and fell to the floor. "This flooring is something else too." I pointed to the thin decades-old linoleum that covered the old wood floor planks. Some of the knotholes in the wood underneath had fallen out and the linoleum wore through, which created small openings to the dark space underneath. The holes were covered with old tin can lids and nailed down. It did not make an attractive floor!

Larry nodded. "I know. Someday, when this place starts turning a profit, we'll see about a new kitchen, but we have to have patience for now."

Not appeased, I muttered, "Well I hope it's soon. What linoleum remains is thin, cracked and the little color left is as drab as a dirty faded washcloth. I hate this floor. It's impossible to keep clean, with everyone grinding in dirt, mud, or horse manure." Larry stayed silent. Breakfast ended and work began.

Later that week, we prepared the store for summer guests. The small one-room building, just a few steps from the lobby, contained shelves on most of the walls except where the cooler and freezer sat. The outside wall next to the parking area held a large topographic map of the area and other notices of interest.

Larry explained, "We stock the store with meat, bread, milk, eggs, canned goods, pancake mix, flour, sugar, ice cream, candy, fishing equipment, lures and bait." Then he pointed to the side of the counter. "Here's the post card rack and some topographical maps of this area. Sometimes we freeze the guests' fish catch to take home. Or, they'll leave it for those who don't catch anything." He told me that we had the store mainly for the benefit of the guests and not for making a profit.

"Who runs the store?"

"We do. It's not that much work, since it's mainly guests…sometimes a tourist."

"How can we keep regular hours for it?"

"We don't. We put up a sign on the door telling people to come to the office for service. Then we come over and take care of them."

Larry walked to the old silver-etched antique cash register sitting royally on the high counter. "We use this for the cash. It's easy to use. After you add up the items and tax, you hit the numbers for the total price, like this." He punched down a couple of keys and numbers popped up in the glassed-in top slot. A bell rang as the cash drawer below slid open.

The lodge as seen from the lower pond

Off to Aspen

After we cleaned the shelves, we made a list of items needed to stock the store. Some case load supplies were ordered from a wholesaler, but not all. I drove to Aspen the next day for the supplies and for us. I enjoyed the 10-mile drive. Spring green and fresh scents invigorated me…as long as I stayed ahead of the dust from the gravel road or another car didn't come from the opposite dusty direction. As I turned the corner onto Main Street, I saw that many of the old mining-day structures had been renovated. Wrought iron fences embraced the Victorian homes boasting well-kept yards with spring flowers blooming in an array of colors.

Further into town, there were some freshly painted false-front stores facing the streets and the tall square fronts hid the roof slopes. The base of the ski runs on Aspen Mountain came right to the edge of town. Snow remained on the ski runs where dips and tree-shaded areas gave protection, but it would soon melt. Some of the newer hotels were designed with a delightful alpine Swiss architecture. The main streets were paved, but a few side streets in the residential areas were still only graveled roads.

I drove on to the newer grocery store. After I filled one cart, I pulled it and pushed another through the aisles. Greg sat in the front cart and Tina tried to help push the other. I had become a bit frazzled with the struggle by the time I got to the checkout counter.

A well-groomed woman behind me seemed to turn up her nose a bit when she asked, "Are you shopping for the month?"

"Oh, I'm buying for only a week, or less, maybe." I didn't have the energy to explain that much of the cart contents would supply our store.

She gasped, "My God!" Everyone stared. After I paid, I pushed and pulled the carts out the door and heard the buzz from the women who were still staring. "Does she belong to a commune?" "I've heard about that kind." Other comments floated in the air as I headed to the car. *Good God! I sure don't belong to a commune!*

Next, I stopped at the post office to pick up our mail and buy stamps. A first class stamp was 5¢. It seemed a high price to send a page or two in the mail, but what could we do? I then picked up the daily newspaper from the Aspen Drug Store. No delivery service came up Castle Creek Valley, but we wanted the daily *Rocky Mountain News*. One section of the drug store wall contained little slots, or boxes, for out-of-town people to collect their newspapers and I collected ours from our designated cubbyhole.

Before leaving Aspen, I noticed the gas gauge was near empty and decided to fill up the car at Conner's gas station. A gallon cost 31¢—a high price, but expected for a resort town on a dead-end highway. Normally, we'd fill the car from our 500-gallon gasoline tank at the lodge because it was less expensive to buy in bulk, but Larry forgot to fill the car and I hadn't paid attention until I got to town. I didn't want to take the chance of running out of gas on the way home, not with two whiney children and a car full of supplies and perishables.

Tourist Season Starts

Back home, we stocked the store. In the next days I helped several customers with food and fishing purchases. I listened to those who came back from hikes or horseback rides with reports of the trails and lakes. I learned about the area from their descriptions.

"You wouldn't believe how many switchbacks and how steep the trail is to American Lake," a tourist exclaimed. "The lake is around 11,300 feet altitude, but I swear the trail is twice as long as they say. It's got to be more than 3 miles and it must mean as the crow flies."

I nodded my head, like I knew the steep trail.

"First you climb through the trees and at certain spots in the beginning you can look back down into the valley. Toward the top there's a rockslide, and the trail is dug out through the stones and boulders along the edge of the mountain. Then when you get to the lake, it's gorgeous with trees next to one edge and open space for camping or fishing. I never saw water so blue, and the reflections were like a picture postcard. Man, you can't beat that."

I visualized the trail and mentally took notes to later tell other hikers. Other tourists told me about the Cathedral Lake trail.

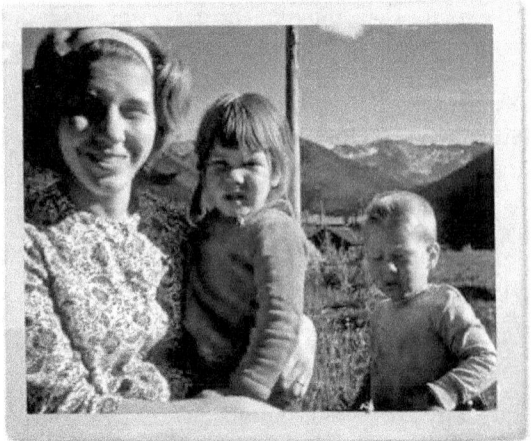

Joanne with Tina and Greg

18

I learned how many switchbacks were on the trails, how long it took to hike and what it was like at the end. The fishermen told me what bait or fly they used and where they caught their prize fish. Then I told other fishermen what worked for some and where others landed their catch. I had never fished, but could tell what worked for others. Fly fishing was preferred for the lakes and either that or worms for the creeks and streams.

After helping a customer at the store one afternoon, I locked up and returned to the lodge. Little Greg was bent over with his hands on his knees looking in corners, under the chairs, table and under the stove. His overall bottom stuck up in the air and his head turned back and forth.

"What are you looking for, Greg?"

"My frog, Mommy. I caught him by the pond. I was carrying him to my room and he jumped out of my hand. Poof—he was gone. Now I can't find him." He raised his head so I could see his worried frown.

"Oh. Well, maybe he found his way back outside. Why don't you go outside and look for him?" I thought, *Good God—that's all I need—a frog in the house. Please let that frog have gotten back outside! I hope it won't be another decaying episode, like the dead mouse I found in Greg's dresser drawer last week. The tomcat must have hidden it there. Now I'll have to watch for a frog!*

Summer breezed on with no more frogs or anything else except constant activity. More than once the Aspen Laundry did not have our cabin linens ready when we went to town to pick them up. It happened again in mid-August. So I washed bed linens and towels and hung them on the clothesline out behind the lodge. An afternoon rain descended on the valley and I raced to unpin the linens from the line and get them inside before the rain came in full force. After the shower progressed on down the valley, I pinned the still-damp linens back up to dry under the sun that had replaced the clouds. Then I still had to iron the sheets and pillowcases.

Goodbye Tourist, Hello Fall

Summer days were full with tourists in and out, the phone, the store, correspondence and keeping the children nearby. Then the season began to fade and disappeared far too fast. Suddenly, Cathy left and Cal picked up the horses to transport them to lower winter pastures. Tina replaced the live horses with her little Breyer plastic play horses.

All the linens, dishes, pans and silverware were packed away until the next spring. Larry and Glenn drained all the water lines except ours so that the pipes wouldn't freeze and split in the bitter cold winter. We closed the store and transferred canned goods to the lodge so they wouldn't freeze.

Fall burst with brilliant gold, bronze and deep yellow colors on the mountainsides and mixed with the pines fading to dormancy. New snow sat on the peaks. Field grass turned a straw color and hinted at cold days to come. It was a perfect season filled with color and tranquility. We took the children for walks across the foot bridge and hiked on the trail alongside Castle Creek. Sometimes we watched the beavers swim and flap their tails. Some evenings we sat on the porch taking in the new snow on the mountains and the sun setting on Star Peak, sparkling like a diamond when the rays hit it. I tired easily now, being eight months along, and was eager to have our baby come.

The fall brought "Flower Children" into the valley. They were a new generation and replaced the ski bums Aspen had seen for many years. One day, a girl in a long peasant skirt and blouse walked in, along with a tall man in jeans and tee-shirt. They smiled and asked where American Lake Trail started. I told them and they thanked me. A few others stopped at the lodge and asked to buy something from the store, but were told it was closed. They flowed with a carefree "whatever" attitude and said, "Have a good day," and gave the peace sign. The flower children didn't seem dirty or discourteous, just easygoing, as if they flowed with the peace of the valley. I thought maybe the hippies I heard about were not so bad after all.

Larry came home from town on a mid-October afternoon with news. "I got a job working with Pitkin County maintaining the roads for the winter. This will give us some income since we aren't renting the cabins in the winter. I begin next Monday cleaning culverts."

"Do you have to work in town?" My panic button began to buzz.

"Yeah, I have to. We just don't have enough money to carry us through the winter. We have to get some money somehow or we can't pay the bills."

"I guess." I felt defeated and still panicky. *God, why did we have to move up here?*

Glenn had his annual winter job at Sardy's Hardware. Tom Sardy owned the hardware store and was also a mortician. The mortuary sat in the back of his home on Main Street. Glenn either worked at the hardware store or hauled bodies to and from various towns and cities.

Phone and Alone (1965)

I didn't like being left all alone while both men were gone all day. I felt isolated, as if I was quarantined in a prison. There were no neighbors to visit; only the children, the dog and the cat to talk to. I kept the radio on all day just to hear adult voices, music and news. Sometimes, I tuned into the Aspen talk show. I listened to the popular songs such as "King of the Road," "Downtown," "It Was a Very Good Year" and "A Hard Day's Night." Because there was no TV in our valley, I couldn't get lost in a soap opera. Days were long, even with all the interruptions of the children. I felt lost, scared, lonely…so lonely…and I was also afraid that I would go into labor and be all alone.

Sometimes the mountains seemed to be closing in on me. About 6 feet of snow covered the valley floor. All that white appeared to be a sea of icy foam, giving no comfort. The dormant pines and grey skeleton aspen trees on the mountainside gave the only contrast. No color brightened the landscape. I wished I could learn to enjoy the winter silence of the mountains. All I ever heard were the rumble of a distant snow slide or a coyote howling down by the creek.

Sometimes, I called Larry to bring home some milk or other staples, or I called a friend in town. One night, when Larry came home I asked him about the phone.

"The valley has one phone line and Mace owns it. A few years ago, the phone company agreed to build one line up the valley from Aspen to be bought and maintained by one owner. Anyone wanting to hook onto the party line

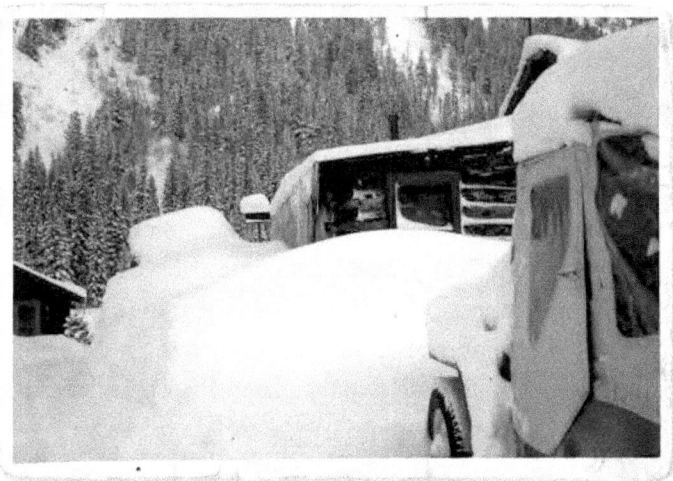

The back of our house as snowed in as I felt

21

had to pay that owner a hookup fee and an annual maintenance fee. We did, so we could have a phone."

"Why didn't your Mom buy the line?"

"She told me that she tried. When Mace told her that he wasn't going to bid on it, she said she made the mistake of telling him what amount she had bid and then he changed his mind and decided to buy it. He put in a bid just a little higher and he won the rights to the line. We paid him the hookup fee and now pay a yearly maintenance fee."

"A party line has about four houses on the same line, right?"

"Yeah. Anyone who wants to use it picks up the receiver and listens to see if someone is on the line. If not, he can call out. If someone is talking, either the person can hang up and wait, or he might be sly and discreetly listen to the conversation."

"Well, sometimes I get a click, click, click instead when I'm on the phone. Is it Mace?"

"Could be, or someone else down the road."

"Has Mace been here forever?"

"He came in 1949, I think. He served in World War II and was in charge of a canine division. After the war, he moved to Aspen and later leased a few acres and built Toklot across the road from Ashcroft. He begins his dog sled trips there and his huskies were used in a 1950s TV series about Sgt. Preston and his adventures in the Yukon. It sure was a popular show."

"Why does he feel he's in charge of everything up here?"

"Well, I guess he thinks he has to protect the whole valley because he doesn't want anyone to abuse Mother Nature. He doesn't like us having horses either and thinks they're ruining the mountains…the same for the cattle that are on open range in the summer. I guess he's determined on keeping nature free of contamination and destruction."

"Well, he hasn't been up here as long as the Brands, even though this is our first winter here. I guess he's just going to have to put up with us."

The next night Larry came home after a day of plowing for the county. I immediately complained, "I hardly ever use the phone, but today I called Mom and wanted to find out about the funeral for my friend's mother. Someone hissed, 'Get off the line' and then kept clicking and clicking. I finally had to give up. I was so mad!"

"Glenn and I are checking with Ma Bell to see if we can get another line up this valley, but it'll take time. We'll talk to MK Mine up the valley and see if we can work together. MK is a big company called Morrison and Knudsen. They're mining iron ore up Cooper Basin."

"I'll tell you, if I have an emergency with one of my kids and need to call an ambulance, or get help, and that person doesn't let me make the call, I'll take a gun and shoot him or her!" We also needed the phone to call the doctor and a babysitter when our baby decided to come.

A week later on a late afternoon, I looked out the window and saw a car drive up ahead of the school bus headed back to town. Both vehicles stopped across the drive to our lodge and a woman got out of her car. She led the young school bus driver through the snow to the telephone pole where the line ran over to our lodge. While standing in the snow, she gestured up and back and forth with one hand and gave him some kind of a tool.

He climbed up on the pole and just as he snipped the line he seemed to lose his balance and jumped down, almost landing on top of the woman. Immediately, he scratched his head and looked up at the pole. The woman said something and used gestures again. Then they both left. I tried our phone and it was dead.

When Larry came home that evening, I told him about the incident. He got his tools and some extra phone line. Then he rewired the line and in no time he had our line hooked back up. I didn't know how the woman could force the school bus driver to do that, but some people have a knack to intimidate, I guess.

Late November, when our baby decided to come into the world, we had the wife of the winter watchman up at the MK Mine road come to stay with Tina and Greg. Larry and I headed to the old Aspen Valley Hospital in Aspen, up on the hill behind the town, and in a very short time our new daughter, Susy, came into the world, healthy and in full voice. A snow slide blocked Castle Creek that night and it was 3 days before Larry could come back down. Then, we brought Susy home and introduced her to her brother and sister. My days and nights were busy with the children.

Holiday Welcome

Thanksgiving came and went and winter continued to roll forth with snowstorms and plowing. On a mid-December Sunday, Larry removed the snowshoes hanging on the pine-paneled wall in the lobby. He strapped them on and began a duck-waddle to the field to locate a suitable tree for our first

Christmas at Elk Mountain Lodge. Soon he dragged home a perfect shaped 7-foot blue spruce pine and placed it in a wood stand that he made. We decorated it with antique ornaments handed down from Larry's family. Fresh pine scent filled the room and I put some boughs around our manger scene on the counter.

On Christmas Eve, we drove down the well-plowed road to midnight Mass at St. Mary's in Aspen. A clear, cold, star-studded night felt perfect and we were bundled up in our warm winter attire. Santa Claus arrived after the children were back home and sound asleep.

Christmas morning, the house filled with screeches long before daylight. Larry and I were jolted awake. We reluctantly rose and drug our weary bodies into the living room for the children to show us what Santa had left. The only thing Larry and I looked for was the coffee and cinnamon rolls I'd quickly heated up. Glenn soon wandered out and joined us. After all the gifts were examined, Larry carried Tina and Greg outside and waded through the snow to the side of the house.

Larry pointed, "Look here. See these tracks? They're from Santa's reindeer."

Larry winked at me when they came back in and the excited children told me. I knew a deer had been enticed by feed or a salt lick.

I fixed a traditional holiday dinner and the tasty aromas filled the house. When we said our usual before-dinner grace, I could almost hear an "Amen" surrounding the room. I smiled and thought maybe it was Elk Mountain Lodge welcoming us because it had spent all the Christmases before alone. It was probably just the wind squeezing through a crack and making a noise, but I liked to think it was a welcoming.

Larry and Glenn had attached the snowplow to the Jeep early in the season, and by December, several large storms had whipped through making plowing our drive a continual process. Both morning and evening plowings were sometimes needed. The storms kept coming and the snow banks kept creeping inward on our driveway. It became a narrow lane and was fast disappearing. If it continued, we would not be able to drive in or out from the county road.

One morning Glenn came in disgruntled. "Dang it! I didn't push the snow back far enough. It's been a record winter so far and there's just too much snow. I can't push it back enough and we're losing the driveway. We'll have to hire a commercial plow to come and make it wide enough for the rest of the winter storms. Next year, we'll remember to push the snow way back in the field."

He headed to the phone and the following day the big plow arrived. The drive became wide once again.

No more road problems occurred and winter moved on with more snowstorms and plowing. We spent New Year's Eve at home with the family. After the children were asleep, Larry and I lounged in front of the fireplace talking of dreams. At midnight, we gave a toast to 1966 and headed to bed.

Sometimes the winter days were scary when the icy wind whined and wailed. All I could see were ice crystals plastered to the single-pane windows. Finally, it all ended with melting and spring's warm arrival, new hope and bright days. As the snow melted, green arrived and soon there were patches of wildflowers on the hillsides. The fields wore bright yellow dandelion blossoms that danced in the breeze. No more snow and colorless scenery. It perked me up and made me smile.

I survived the winter!

Chapter 3

Bear! (1966)

Spring came with preparations for the summer guests. Larry quit his winter job, but Glenn would still work part-time for Sardy. They opened water lines for the modern cabins, the shower house and the outside spigots. Pipes were checked for any leaks in case one held hidden water that froze and split the pipe. Roofs were repaired with new shingles, and every cabin was scrubbed. The walls of most cabins were tongue-and-groove pine paneling, which received a wood preservative after a scrubbing. The three original cabins only needed to be dusted because their walls were logs. I washed, ironed and hung the curtains for all the cabins.

Larry bounced through the door one May morning. His hat tilted forward for shade and his eyes twinkled. "We're going to go get some wood."

I continued to knead my bread dough. "Okay." I blew a strand of hair away from my eye and tilted my head for him to give me a quick kiss. Then he bolted out the door to help Glenn hook up the long-bed trailer to the Jeep and they drove up valley. The Forest Service gave permission to take only the fallen timber for use.

When they returned, I saw them park down in the field. The trailer didn't look full of logs and I wondered if they got tired or didn't find much fallen timber. They walked to the lodge and I poured each a cup of coffee and asked, "How come you came back without a full load?"

Larry grinned and answered, "Well, we wound our way up the mountain-side through the trees and found a good spot for wood. We used our hand saws to remove limbs before loading the timber on the trailer. All of a sudden, we heard a loud deep growl and looked up to see a bear standing on her hind legs about 30 feet from us. Her ripsaw teeth were ready for our meat."

Glenn grinned. "You should have seen her."

"Oh Lord! What did you guys do?"

Larry laughed. "We looked at each other and at the same time whispered, 'Shee…yoot!' We slowly edged toward the Jeep trying not to make any sudden movements that would trigger her. We kept our axes ready and spread our arms out to look bigger. Then I jumped in the Jeep, dropped my ax, and quickly turned the key in the ignition, praying it would start immediately. It did and Glenn jumped in."

Glenn interrupted laughing, "Yeah, and then Larry tore out of there. Tires spit pine needles and dirt when we spun into action and we took off like a scared rabbit. As soon as the engine turned over I saw that bear came down on all fours and started to charge."

I looked for blood on them, but didn't see any. "So, the bear didn't make it to you?"

Larry grinned, "No. I yelled at Glenn, 'Hang on' and jammed my foot down hard on the gas pedal. Then we bounced over a tangle of ridges, timber and rocks and barreled down the hill." He laughed again.

I visualized the logs being thrown upward, hang in the air a second and then slam back into the trailer with the thunder of wood battering wood. I wondered how many logs fell out.

Glenn continued, "I yelled 'Get us out of here' and hung onto the windshield with one hand and the ax in the other. I kept looking back to see where the bear was."

Then Larry took over, "I really had to work at guiding us down the mountain. A high bounce over a fallen tree flew us a foot high and for a minute I thought we were going to fall out, but we landed hard on our behinds. I think the rattling logs scared the bear."

I was sure that the logs had continued to roar, bang and crash. It probably would have scared anything. "Then what?"

"Finally, when we were pretty sure we were safe, I slowed down. It had only taken a few minutes, but felt a heck of a lot longer, especially on my rear end. I told Glenn that we had enough wood for today and he agreed." They both laughed.

I shook my head. "You guys are going to have to be careful. Maybe you should carry a rifle. I don't like the thought of you being mauled or killed by a bear."

"Ah, it isn't going to happen again," Larry said with a grin. "Normally, the bears stay away from humans. Maybe we got too close to her cubs, which we didn't see. Don't worry."

How can I not worry? The mountains are full of dangers!

After coffee, they unloaded the logs next to the big saw, which sat down in the field by the stables. They jacked up the back of the Jeep and hooked up a belt from one Jeep wheel to the saw. The Jeep motor turned the wheel and the saw blade. The smell of cut wood drifted through camp as they cut the logs into foot-long lengths, and afterwards split some of the sections into kindling wood. Next, they stacked the logs in the wood rack on the side of each cabin.

Season Begins and Jeep Tours

The cabins were all ready when Memorial Day weekend arrived with our first summer guests. I registered them when they came and checked them out when they left. I handled phone reservations and most correspondence using a big Olivet typewriter to write the letters. Sometimes, the over-used carbon paper between the sheets didn't print and I had to write the missing letters on our copy. Glenn happily relinquished the bookkeeping over to Larry.

Larry announced, "We're keeping the rates the same. A rustic cabin is $4.00 a night for two people and $7.00 for four. A modern cabin is $6.00 for two and $8.00 for four. A week stay is a 6-day charge." We kept reservations on a large etched Plexiglas calendar, which had months, days and cabin names. Reservations were written with a marker that could easily be erased or changed.

Then Larry told me the plans for Jeep tours. "We'll schedule Jeep tours in between the work. I'll take *Nellie Belle*, and Glenn will take our Land Rover… or, visa-versa. We'll use both, when Glenn isn't working at Sardy's. There's a place in the back of each vehicle to store food, ponchos, or whatever. The half-day trips will be up to the top of Taylor Pass or up to the Montezuma Mine. All day trips will be up to Pearl Pass, or up Taylor and on over the top down to the lake, or from the top back along the ridge and then down Little Annie Road or down Aspen Mountain into town. An overnight trip is up Pearl Pass and over to Crested Butte when the Pass is open, but Glenn can take those."

"What about the lunches?" I had a feeling I knew the answer.

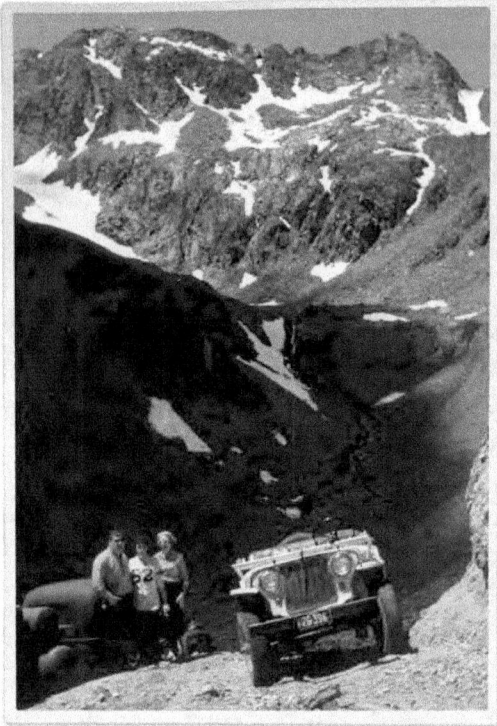

A Jeep tour on Montezuma to Pearl Pass

"How about fixing some ham or chicken sandwiches? Sometimes it could be fried chicken, if you fry extra when we have ours. Better have plenty of potato chips or some potato salad and apples and cookies. I'll take the big thermos full of coffee, cans of soda pop, and I'll strap a big jug of water on the back."

I snapped, "So, I get to fix the lunches, and then I'll have the honor of running the place while you're Jeeping?"

"Yup. Sorry, but we've got to make more money to keep this place going."

Advertising brought many reservations for Jeep tours. I fixed lunches and fried chicken until I had a stove that didn't know it shouldn't be splattered with grease. Because I had to handle the guests, phone, reservations, store and the household, I didn't have time to scrub the stove after each use. I tried to take care of the children in between all the other duties and sometimes I had baby Susy on my hip when I greeted guests or had to take guests to the store.

Larry, the Storyteller (1966)

Our days were filled with work and the evenings were spent visiting with tourists. Larry told stories about the miners at the ghost town of Ashcroft and about the Homestead cabin, and I listened. He usually put some humor in.

His stories were similar each time. "Our family ranch housed the stables for the miners' horses and the extra horses that belonged to the Ashcroft stagecoach line." He didn't know that as fact, but it made a good story. "Ashcroft was a silver mining community. Many miners didn't luck out with their stakes and left with empty pockets, bent backs and a broken spirit. Prospecting was a dirty, hard and dangerous life."

I visualized the miners digging and could almost smell the dirt and sweat. It was a hard life.

"Some miners became grizzled veterans; others couldn't keep up the hard labor and hope while receiving little to live on. Dreams were shattered for many. Some lost their lives when a mineshaft caved in or an ore wagon turned over crushing them.

"Ashcroft was a lively place especially when H. A. Tabor, the famous mine investor, came to town. Tabor bought into the Tam O'Shanter and Montezuma mines. His wife was the famous Baby Doe Tabor and when she came to town, he declared a 24-hour holiday. Drinks were on the house. The miners loved Baby Doe." Everyone laughed.

"There were around 2,500 residents in Ashcroft when it was booming in the late 1800s. It had two newspapers, a school, two sawmills, a post office, at least two hotels, a church and a doctor." He didn't mention brothels.

A tourist always asked, "What happened to Ashcroft?"

"When Aspen got the railroad and the silver veins no longer produced rich ore, mining at Ashcroft died out. The boom ended and the town ceased to live. Many cabins were broken down and moved with the family to a new town. Or,

Cattle grazing in the ghost town of Ashcroft

the family just packed up what personal items they would need for the next town and abandoned the rest. Only a few dilapidated buildings are left now."

We showed them the album on the coffee table with the article on Ashcroft. Most guests hiked up to the ghost town and wandered around the remaining buildings, especially the famous hotel.

Sometimes the cattlemen's herd was also visiting Ashcroft. They were often shooed back down to our lodge. Then we'd shoo them back up.

Summer kept us on the run. I was glad the stables could take care of reservations for the horses. A phone line extension had been buried to the stables. When a call came for horses, I pushed a button and it made a loud buzz in the tack room. The call was handled there.

Free-loading (1966)

Fall swept in before I realized summer's departure. Too soon the summer guests were gone and the camp became quiet.

On a brisk morning, Larry came in to tell me about his discovery. "Guess what? I walked by the Pines cabin and something didn't seem right. I knew it wasn't rented, but it felt wrong. So, I opened the door and saw a hippie couple in sleeping bags sound asleep on the floor. Two more were sleeping on the bed." He usually did not get upset, but I saw his neck muscles were tight.

"I took the lid off the wood stove burner, raised it high, and slammed it back down against the stove and it sure made a loud clang and an echoing shudder. Man! Did that ever rouse those guys. I told them to get out of there fast, if they knew what was good for them." Larry's deep voice always delivered the tone of authority.

"I stood holding the lid in one hand and my hammer in the other. They knew I meant business and they quickly crammed their belongings into their back packs. One asked if they could use the shower house and I told them nope. They'd been trespassing long enough. So, they cleared out fast."

I nodded, "Good. We don't want them here. The cabin must have been unlocked, but from now on we're going to have to remember to lock each cabin every time we leave."

That marked our first experience with hippies. We saw them in the valley and in town, but hadn't encountered any on our land before...that we knew about.

Fall did not bring anymore hippies and we thought maybe we would be hippie-free. Soon, warm days slid away and fall shivered into retirement. Snow began to pile up on the peaks once again and quickly crept down the valley. The golden aspen leaves had all fallen to become fodder and only the barren branches remained. Larry decided not to work for Pitkin County again in the winter, but Glenn would continue to work at Sardy's Hardware.

My love for the mountains grew through the summer and it would help me weather the winter and at least Larry would be with me.

Here Come the Snowmobiles! (1966)

Larry and I talked about the possibility of renting and selling snowmobiles to give us some income for the winter. He headed to town to investigate the possibility and when he came back he said, "I'm thinking of financing 10 snowmobiles. I've already checked with the Ski-Daddler company and they'll give me a financing plan. I can sell and rent the machines."

"We'll buy them on credit and then try to sell them?"

"Yeah, and I can get a trail going up the valley and rent the snowmobiles to tourists. The Forest Service says its okay, and the MK Mine said we could

Larry on one of his new snowmobiles looking down at the lodge

33

use their road, since they aren't open in the winter. The only drawback is that the county won't let us run the snowmobiles on the road. So, I'll have to haul them by trailer up to the turnoff for Taylor Pass and start from there. It's only about a half mile. We'll snowmobile through Ashcroft, then through a field and on up the valley to the unplowed mine road. It goes up to around 12,000 feet and has great views."

By early December, financing had been arranged and Larry sold some snowmobiles to the Aspen Ski Corp and to ranchers who could check their cattle easier or get hay to them. He sold a couple machines to individuals. When each snowmobile sold, we replaced it with a new one. Larry packed the snowmobile trail after each storm and soon rentals began. Tourists came to our lodge and Larry took them to the trailhead in our station wagon. He gave directions and instructions of what to do, or not to do, and then the tourists snowmobiled by themselves. Larry came back to wait for their return, and then he would bring them back to the lodge for payment and their cars. It didn't seem like a problem because they could use the well-packed, defined trail. What could go wrong?

After a couple of weeks, Larry came in disgusted. "These danged green-horns won't listen to instructions. I tell them not to get off the trail because they'll sink in the powder, but they go ahead and do it anyway and immediately get stuck. When they can't get it out, they leave it and ride back with someone else."

I knew the routine by then. "So, you have the fun of bringing it back?"

"Yeah. I have to pack the snow in front of the machine while I'm sunk to my knees or waist. I wiggle the machine back and forth using just enough gas to coax it loose and get some traction. Finally, I'll get it back on the trail. Then I have to tie a rope from it to my machine and haul it down to the trailer. It's one heck of a lot of work."

"I know." I'm not sure if he heard me or not.

He continued to rant. "Then there were the idiots who kill the engine up on the trail. I tell them that all they have to do is take their hand off the throttle and the machine will just sit there purring and not move. But no, they go ahead and turn it off when they stop to take a picture. Then when they try to start it, they can't get it to turn over. So, they keep pumping the throttle and that floods it. Then they leave the machine up there and I have to drag it back. They just don't listen. One is still up there now."

"Like kids…not listening to instructions. I doubt they'll change, Larry."

"I guess I better go and bring back that stuck machine," he said and rose slowly. He zipped up his flannel-lined snowmobile boots, put on his parka, and pulled his knit ski cap over his ears.

When not on the trail, Larry repaired machines in the workshop. One day I told him, "If you're working on a snowmobile, I can keep an eye out for the people when they come back down the trail. I'll see them going through Ashcroft and then I'll let you know. You can drive up and bring them back here to pay."

He liked that plan. "Okay. Then I can go back up and check the snowmobiles thoroughly and call you on the C.B. radio when there is any damage to charge the people. It'll give me more time working on repairs."

Our plan worked well. The tourists usually lingered to sip on coffee, tea, or hot chocolate while warming up. During the day, the temperature could climb to around 20° above zero, but it dropped more drastically with the wind chill factor. The faster the machine went, the colder the wind and the icy blast bit into the driver's face. But cold wasn't the only concern in January.

Joanne Brand

Chapter 4

Unwelcome New Year Greeting! (1967)

On January 11, 1967, we listened to the radio announce a warning from the Forest Service of high avalanche danger for anyone venturing into the back country. Our snowmobile trail went through several slide areas and one large spot in the valley before the trail climbed up Cooper Basin. When a slide broke loose at the top of that spot, the snow surged down the mountainside ripping up any trees in its path. It would swell, gain momentum, and tear down the mountainside. The tremendous velocity gave a force that pushed the angry waves of snow and debris across the valley floor and on over to the other side. The roar would be enough to give anyone the shivers.

Larry investigated the trail that morning. "I don't like the looks of the slide areas. We better cancel snowmobile trips today. I'll work on a machine motor in the work shop. The gasoline truck is coming to fill our tank and I'll come in to pay him when he's done."

The workshop sat right behind our house, only about 15 feet away from the kitchen. Larry began working on the snowmobile motor and turned on the electric heater that sat on the counter. He hauled the machine only halfway in, leaving the rear end sticking out the doorway. The heater warmed his backside while he worked on the motor and listened to the music on the radio.

The 500 gallon gasoline tank sat above ground on a stand and abutted the back wall of the workshop. When the gas truck arrived, the driver climbed up to the top of the tank and put the nozzle in place and locked it open to keep the gas flowing. He climbed down and began kicking the thick ice caked on the tire rims. He didn't pay attention to the gas flow. The nozzle did not have an automatic shut-off trigger, and in time, the tank overflowed and immediately the gas fumes traveled to the workshop.

Larry later told me that in an instant he got an eerie feeling and knew something was wrong. He felt the hair on the back of his neck rise and quickly straightened up attentive to any sound or motion. Then he heard a powerful, deep "whoomph" and he immediately leaped over the snowmobile and out the door, just like a gazelle on the run. There was no hesitation. He just knew he better get out of there fast.

Fumes had traveled to the heater and caused the gas to ignite. The flames climbed out of the tank nozzle opening and furiously reached at least 20 feet high. As soon as the truck driver saw the flames, he stopped the flow and reached for his fire extinguisher, but when he tried to spray, it was dry. Nothing to stop the fire! He drove the truck further down the driveway to get away from the blaze.

As soon as Larry saw what happened, he ran to the lodge. He burst through the door and yelled, "Joanne, get the kids out of here right now! Go to the House on the Hill across the road. The gas tank is on fire and it's going to explode. Get out of here as fast as you can." I had never seen him that panicked.

He immediately called the volunteer fire department in Aspen. I quickly gathered Greg and Susy and put their coats on them. I realized that Tina was in the bathroom and it sat nearest the fire. She had locked the door and didn't want to let me in, but I kept yelling and finally she opened for me. I ran in, yanked her off the stool, and pulled her out with her little panties and jeans dragging around her ankles.

"I don't have my panties on!" With one hand she held on to them and her jeans by the waistband at her knees.

"We'll pull them up later," and I carried her over my hip like a sack of potatoes. When I put her down in the living room, she pulled on her clothing as she ran hobble-like from the house. I carried Greg and Susy to the car and we all climbed in. We took haven in the House on the Hill and watched the fire. I held Susy while Tina and Greg pressed their faces against the window and watched the flames spreading.

The workshop, boiler house and the Montezuma cabin were on fire and the flames threatened the lodge. The thick smoke rose high and seemed to fill the valley.

Tina watched the blaze climb to the sky and so close to our lodge. "Mommy, is our house going to burn up?" A tear had spilled down her cheek.

I tried to sound calm, but I was actually scared to death. "No, Daddy will save our house, if God wants it that way. If God wants us to have a new home, then just think of all the new toys and clothes you'll have. It would be a lot of fun, picking out things that you want, wouldn't it?"

We continued to watch. There didn't seem to be any way to fight the massive fire and no outside faucet to hook up a hose. I prayed silently as I watched in despair and worried if Larry would get hurt. He had gathered important papers and records from the office and placed them in a snowfield far from the fire. Then he began to bring out other items while running back and forth.

Why hasn't the tank blown yet? God, please don't let anything happen to Larry!

Then I saw a four-wheel-drive vehicle pull in at full speed, screech to a halt and a man hopped out and ran inside. Later I learned it was Norm Payne, a new neighbor who had moved into the valley that fall. He saw the flames and smoke a mile away and came quickly. He ran into the laundry room and hooked up a hose to the washer faucet, broke out a kitchen window, and leaned

The House on the Hill where I watched the fire

out to spray water on the roof and backside of our house now hot enough to ignite. He used his thumb on the end of the hose to make a spray. The water sprays peppered his hands and immediately froze, but he paid no attention.

Larry told me later that he ran up to Norm and said to get out of there fast because the tank could blow anytime. Norm shook his head no and said that the tank wouldn't explode because the flames could escape through the uncapped nozzle opening. It would just keep burning until all of the gasoline was gone. He said he had been a fireman back in New Jersey and learned that. So, he continued to spray the water on the outside logs of our kitchen.

I didn't know that the tank wouldn't explode and my fear heightened with each passing minute. It felt like it was hours before the firemen arrived, but in about 30 minutes or so they pulled in. The volunteer firemen had to gather at the station in Aspen after the alarm sounded. Then, they headed up Castle Creek Valley and knew it had to be bad when they saw smoke drifting 5 miles down valley. Because we were out of the fire district, the fire truck could not come, but the firefighters came in their own vehicles and brought a pump. By then, the workshop, the boiler house with the heating furnace and the Montezuma cabin were engulfed in flames and our lodge was in grave danger. The blaze continued to reach for heaven, as if it were hell trying to reach glory.

Glenn had been working at Sardy's Hardware that day. Many firemen knew him and they rushed to tell him the fire was at our lodge. He came in the first pickup along with two firemen. As soon as they stopped by the back pond, Glenn jumped out with an ax in hand and chopped a hole through the 2 feet of ice on the pond almost before the other firemen even got out of the pickup. They set up the pump and began pumping water from the pond onto the fire in hopes of keeping it from spreading. Glenn always had an unrushed manner and I had never seen him move so fast, and I never would again!

Later Claude Conner, a friend of Larry's from childhood, came. Aspen was still small enough for news to travel fast and, Claude heard of our fire. He talked to Larry for awhile and then Claude drove up to the House on the Hill to check on me. I told him I was fine, but I don't know if he believed me. I'm sure I showed the strain. Larry, Claude, his wife and I went to the Elks dances or out to dinner and lounge shows some weekends. We were close friends and all, except me, had known each other for years, but I fit in and loved their stories of their school days.

All the gas in the tank burned until the soaring flames fizzled. The buildings crumbled into ashes and only a couple of charred beams stood in place.

Five hundred gallons of gasoline were devoured along with three buildings. The lodge had been spared, even though flames licked at its backside and roof. Norm Payne's quick thinking had saved it. The walls were seared but did not burn. It was a wonder that the logs had not caught fire, because they were decades-old and dried to a prime condition for igniting. Smoke and water flowed through the broken windows and soot settled throughout the kitchen and filtered into other rooms.

After the firemen left, the children and I came back to the lodge. Smoke smell greeted us when we walked in. Quite shaken, yet thankful my home did not burn, I felt drained of energy. Larry and Norm were already boarding up the windows against the freezing January air, using tools and boards that Norm had handy. Glenn helped bring back inside everything that Larry piled in the snow. He and Larry would go to town later for Glenn's vehicle.

I had a chicken in the kitchen sink thawing when the fire began. After the fire it was completely thawed, warm and covered in a fine ash dust. A pair of Susy's plastic baby pants had been sitting on the edge of the counter by the log wall to dry after I had washed it. Now, only a soft melted plastic glob remained. When I saw it, I remembered that I needed to change Susy.

My God! I was so shook up that I didn't even grab a few diapers when we ran to the House on the Hill!

After changing Susy, I still held her tight and wandered around the kitchen not knowing what to do. Mop up the water? Sweep up the broken window glass? Dust away the ash residue? Scrub the stove, counter and cabinets? What?

Then I saw a four-wheel-drive vehicle roll to a stop in the drive and a stout woman, maybe in her late 50s, came in. "I'm Mickey Payne, Norm's wife. You get your kids and I'll take you up to our cabin while the men finish up here. Let's get you out of this mess." Her white hair shone in the rays of a retiring sun sneaking in from the window. She gave a grandmotherly sweet smile. I thought she could be an angel, a robust angel, but a warm, sweet angel.

I could barely see her through the tears filling my eyes. "Thank you, I'm just going in circles."

Mickey helped bundle up the children. "I have a good hot meal about ready for you and the kids. So, let's get going,"

Mickey, Meatballs and Plans

The Payne's cabin sat on the opposite side of Ashcroft and Toklot. Their drive began just before starting up Taylor Pass road (later they moved half a mile north from us). When we arrived at the cabin, the children saw the box of toys in the corner and began to play. Mickey kept the box for her grandchildren and friends' little ones. The children had not been traumatized by the fire like I had been. Cookies were set out while we waited for the men and the children wasted no time in taking their share. Mickey donned her apron and began stirring the large pot on the wood stove. Homemade spaghetti sauce and meatballs rendered a glorious aroma of Italian spices in the small quarters. The noodles proved to be homemade as well. She took her pan of rolls and placed them in the oven. The warmth from the stove filled the cabin.

The men came after they sealed up the lodge and Larry mopped up the kitchen. My hands still shook, my body had become as taut as a guitar string and my mouth remained drawn tight. Norm looked at me, walked to the cupboard, and got a glass and a bottle. He poured whiskey and handed it to me. "Here, this will help calm you." I didn't refuse. The burning sensation going down wasn't pleasant, but it loosened my tight muscles somewhat.

The men hung their coats on the coat rack by the door. Overall-clad Norm motioned to Larry and Glenn as he sat his round body at the table. "Come on fellas. Sit down. Don't worry about getting any ash residue on these old chairs." His thinning hair looked even grayer now covered with ash.

Larry sank wearily into a chair. "You saved our home. How can we ever repay you?" His face still showed dark smoke smudges and his clothes reeked of smoke. The last couple of hours showed on his face. Glenn also collapsed into a chair.

"Forget it. I just did what came natural, since I'd been a firefighter. You don't owe me a thing."

The men began discussing what needed to be done at the lodge. I sat quietly listening, while Larry took my hand in his and stroked it giving what comfort he could and said, "The first thing is to get a boiler for the hot water baseboard heat."

Glenn added, "Well, a boiler is going to be difficult to get quickly, since it'll have to be shipped in. Aspen plumbers or hardware stores don't carry a boiler that will work for the hot water baseboard heat like we have. I can order one through Sardy's, but it'll still take a few days to get here. I had to order the boiler when I first put the system in and it didn't take long."

Larry let go of my hand and sat forward. "We'll go to town tomorrow to order it. I'll get some lumber and tools so I can begin building a new boiler house for the furnace."

I asked Larry, "But how are we going to keep warm now? We'll freeze."

"We'll be okay. The firemen loaned us a couple of oil heaters."

Glenn added, "And we'll keep the fireplace going too."

Larry rubbed his forehead to ease his developing headache. "A new workshop will have to wait until after the boiler house is built. The Montezuma will have to be forgotten until spring when the debris can be cleared out and a new cabin built. There's a lot of work to be done and none of it planned."

We knew the cost to get a new boiler for the heat and to build the housing for it would put us in a deep hole financially. A claim would be made to the gas company's insurance and hopefully, it would cover the heat and buildings. All we could do would be to find as many receipts as possible for our claim. At least receipts had been kept for many years back and maybe we could find enough. I still had the receipt for the plastic baby pants!

Norm sighed, "My tired hurts." He leaned back into the chair and sagged.

Soon Mickey had supper on the table and we all ate heartily…as if we had released worry and gained hunger.

Later that night, we returned to a smoky home without heat and a bitter cold January night of -20°F. We used the two large oil heaters and the fireplace to keep the house somewhat warm. I didn't sleep well that night and kept checking to make sure the embers didn't flare up, and that the oil heaters and the fireplace remained safe. My fear of fire began to blossom with that frightening blaze.

The next day Glenn went to Sardy's and ordered the furnace. Larry bought equipment and lumber. Every single tool had been burned in the workshop; not even a hammer, nail, or screwdriver remained. Only a big, heavy charred anvil sat in the ashes as a survivor. Larry came home with a supply of lumber, nails and tools that would be needed for the job at hand. Those few items could never replace all that had been accumulated throughout the many years.

By afternoon, Larry had cleared out the debris and began work on the new building. He placed the floor joists on the old cinderblock foundation and nailed down the wood flooring. The job proved not to be easy because the weather remained around freezing during the day. At least the sun gave some warmth. Our snowmobile business had to be cancelled until heat could be restored.

Mickey came to see how we were doing each day. I knew a friendship had been sealed between the Brands and the Paynes. I'd make sure the 32 cup coffeepot would be on and ready for any visit by them. I looked forward to sharing thoughts, miseries and recipes with Mickey.

I just prayed that the rest of winter would be calm and that we wouldn't have another fire.

Chapter 5

Snowmobile Dryer (1967)

In a few of days, the new boiler arrived. Dale Weisbrod, our plumber and family friend, and his partner got it all set up and soon the heat began flowing through the hot water baseboard lines. What a relief! No more bundling up in long johns, turtlenecks and sweaters to stay warm inside our home. How nice to get back to normal!

Snowmobile business started again. The workshop would take longer to replace and snowmobile repairs had to be made in the kitchen. Larry gave strict warnings for no one to touch the parts sitting on the counter. "Don't even put your finger on them."

"Why?" Tina asked.

"Because I have all of them lined up so I know how to put a piece of the motor back together. If a part isn't where it's supposed to be, I can't fix it." Larry hoped that would be enough explanation for her. It was.

On a cloudless, sunny day, a family rented four snowmobiles. When they returned, I collected the rental fee. "Did you have fun?"

The two sons had wide grins. "You bet!"

"Any damages, Mr. Randolph?"

He quickly answered, "Nope," then paid and hurried the family out the door. Just then Larry called me on the C.B. radio and said that a windshield had been broken. The family had not driven away yet. Their car gave only grunts and groans and refused to produce a purr. I immediately donned a jacket and rushed out to the car and knocked on the driver's side window. Mr. Randolph rolled down the window half way and frowned. "What?"

"My husband just radioed that he found a broken windshield on one of the snowmobiles you rented. I was wondering if one of your boys might have broken it."

"Dad did it," the two boys replied in unison from the back seat.

The father's cheeks turned red. "I guess I might have," he muttered.

I stated the price for a new windshield. He pulled out his billfold and unhappily handed me the cash. I smiled and thanked him as he rolled up his window and tried the ignition again. Immediately, the car purred and the family drove off. Maybe he couldn't start the car before because he flooded his engine trying to rush out. Or, maybe the cold air had frozen his car at our high altitude. Or, maybe the snowmobile gods held him back! Whatever, I just grinned as I walked back to the office.

Larry replaced the windshield, but repairs had become commonplace and too many snowmobiles were damaged. Some people broke the hood, some the windshield, some broke the throttle or brake lever, or some ripped the seat by rolling the machine. Larry seemed to always be repairing snowmobiles.

In the mornings, he spent a long time trying to start the machines and move them onto the trailer to haul up to the trailhead. The snowmobiles' ignition switches froze from the nightly blowing snow that sifted into the starters and froze. Larry couldn't insert a key and had to wait until the sun came out to melt the ice. Often, he tried to warm the ignitions with his hands or blow his warm breath on them, but that took time. He asked, "How can I get those ignitions thawed?" I had no answer.

While he had his coffee one day, I noticed him closely watching me dry my hair. He seemed fascinated by my new blow dryer. I held it in one hand and moved it over my curlers and felt each with the other hand to see if it had dried.

Suddenly Larry slapped the table with excitement and his coffee splashed on the table. "I've got it! I can use your blow dryer to thaw out the starters. It'll work great and I can thaw all the ignitions fast."

"What do you mean, use my dryer?" I didn't think I liked what I heard.

"Can I use it in the mornings? I can plug it into the outside outlet with a long extension cord and in no time I'll have the snowmobiles running."

"Well…I guess, but I want it back every morning. You can't keep it. You've got to promise me that you'll bring it back each day."

"Okay," Larry readily agreed.

Every morning, he plugged in my hair dryer, put it on high heat and thawed the ignitions. In a short time, he could insert the keys and start up the machines.

Occasionally, some tourists arrived without proper clothing for snow-mobiling. We kept a supply of snowmobile wear that they could rent such as insulated one-piece suits, separate pants and parkas, gloves, snowmobile mittens and boots, ski caps and goggles, all in various sizes. Without warm attire and goggles, the wind stung like needle pricks, especially with a wind-chill factor at a minimum of 10°F lower than the standing-still temperature.

One day, a man rented a snowmobile for him and his little son, about 8 years old. I advised him to use our children's snowmobile outfit and mittens for his son. The boy had a lightweight parka and thin knit city-type mittens, not the thick-lined ski or snowmobile mittens. The dad said, "Nah. He doesn't need them."

When they returned the little boy cried because his hands hurt from the cold. They were whitish and felt like ice. I held his hands and told the father, "Your son could have frostbite and we need to get his hands warmed now." I quickly got a basin of slightly warm water. Dad waited while I put his son's hands in the water to gradually thaw and warm. I talked to the boy asking him about his school, his friends, his pets and anything that kept him calm and his mind off the pain.

Dad paced back and forth with eagerness to get back to town. I ignored him until the boy's hands seemed thawed and gained color and softness. I felt sorry for the little kid, if his dad would always be that inconsiderate.

Thank goodness we didn't have anymore inconsiderate parents. Business continued and I enjoyed the guests raving about the beauty of the scenery when they returned.

Skiers vs. Snowmobiles

After a fresh snowfall one day, a man drove up and placed several large bundles on the porch. He talked to Larry and then left.

"What's that all about?" I asked Larry when he came in.

"He's with a group that's going to ski up to the Lindley Hut. I agreed to haul their supplies up by snowmobile."

"Where is it and why are they having you haul their stuff up?"

"The Lindley is up Cooper Basin and sits a short distance from our snow-mobile trail. Several ski-touring huts are located in this area. Some look like A-frames and some look like cabins. Cross-country skiers go to one hut, stay overnight or a couple of days and then ski on to the next hut. Or, sometimes they just stay in one the whole time, like this group is planning."

"What are they like inside?"

"They're rustic and maybe with one open room for the living area, kitchen and sleeping. Sometimes there's a loft, but each hut is different. They vary in size, but are large enough to hold 8 to 15 people comfortably. The huts don't have running water or electricity, so they melt snow in pots on the wood stove, or collect water from a stream close by. They use oil lamps or candles for light and the huts are furnished with wood for the stove to cook and for heat. Someday, the huts might have more conveniences. Skiers bring their own food, sleeping bags and personal items."

"These skiers have a lot of stuff." I pointed to the parcels.

"Yeah. Even though they are die-hard cross-country skiers, they don't want the labor of hauling their provisions in backpacks or pulling a sled as they ski uphill. But they still hate snowmobiles."

Larry on snowmobile with sled at Lindley Hut

"I can understand the noise. The motors on the snowmobiles are loud, but lots of tourists want to get into the high country and can't cross-country ski. So, a snowmobile is their only option. When we've snowmobiled on the trail, I'm amazed at the unbelievable beauty." To me, the ice-white peaks sometimes looked like wrinkled meringue with spiked tops, while other peaks looked like blue and white squiggles flowing jaggedly downward. The virgin snow makes the peaks seem closer, and photographers delight in the changes that the sunlight makes as it moves.

Larry got the provisions loaded on the sled attached to his snowmobile and took off for the ski hut. Later, he led a snowmobile group on a tour because just before the fire he had decided to guide all rentals. Guided tours would hopefully stop some of the problems and damages.

After a tour one afternoon, he came in to warm up. "I ran into some of those damned cross-country skiers that refuse to move off our trail to let us by. I'm not about to have the snowmobilers get off into the powder to pass. They'd all get stuck. Finally, after we crept behind for awhile they moved to let us pass. I know they hate snowmobiles, but we could be out of their sight and hearing faster, if they'd just move and let us by"

The Forest Service signs posted at the beginning of the trails were large enough for all to see and showed which trail for the cross-country skiers and which for snowmobiles. Skiers couldn't miss the signs. I asked, "Why don't the skiers stay on their own trail?"

"Because our trail is packed solid and smoother than their ski trail." Larry grabbed a quick cup of coffee to warm his insides. "I've got to get the gas tanks filled before it gets any colder." He bundled up again and left. When he got everything ready for the next day, he finally sat by the fire to warm his bones.

Move Over!

The next Sunday afternoon, we didn't have any reservations, so we took a snowmobile outing and Glenn joined us. Larry hooked the sled to the back of his machine and set Greg and Susy in the back and wrapped them in a quilt. Then he set the food at the opposite end of the sled. Tina rode with me on my snowmobile. A glorious warm, sunny day greeted us with fresh glistening snow. When we arrived near the top of the trail I spread out a picnic lunch. The high altitude increased our hunger and we devoured the food with gusto. The children could not resist the fluffy snow. They sank in the powder and

Susy, Joanne, and Tina checking slide area

flung their arms out to move them back and forth as if swimming to keep from sinking deeper. Soon we all joined in a snowball fight.

On the way home, we came upon a cross-country skier using the snowmobile trail. He was going our way and looked behind when he heard our snowmobiles, but he would not move to the side for us to pass. I had the lead machine and after awhile, I felt my Scottish temper flaring up. Then I edged my snowmobile runners about 3 feet from the backs of his skis. I could see him pushing his poles along to keep his momentum as his legs stretched up and back, making long strides. He'd turn every so often to see if I might run over him. Finally, his frustration must have given in, and

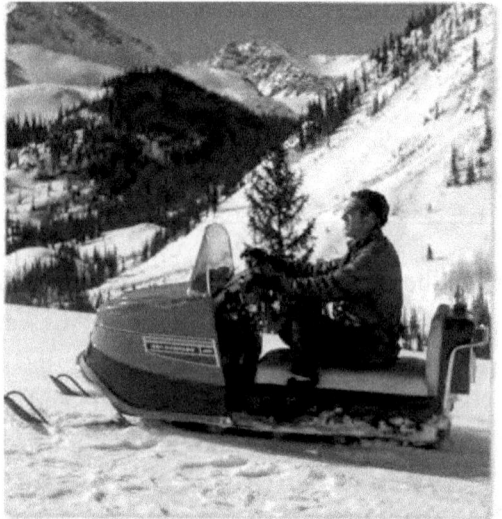

Larry enjoying the scenery

he stepped off the trail to let us pass. I gave him a big smile and a loud "thank you" as I passed. I told Larry later, "That guy is lucky I didn't just run him over."

Larry grinned. "Nah, you wouldn't, but you gave him something to think about."

Finally, winter began to fade…no more big snowstorms and less bone-chilling weather. Spring entered with a month of sleet and rain. The melting snow banks on the side of our drive dribbled onto the drive causing mud and then the cars driving over it caused ruts. Soon, new life began to appear in the valley with baby sprouts and aspen trees beginning to show branches trimmed in newborn life. The pines were refreshed. The warmth of the sun felt wonderful after the freezing months. I wondered what the new spring and summer season for 1967 would yield besides an abundance of wildflowers and dandelions.

On the Frontline (1967)

Driving to town in mid-May, I saw a group camping by Castle Creek. They looked like the long-haired hippies whom I heard were roaming up the valley and I encountered more hippies when I got to town. A few were smoking pot while leaning against a store front and others stood on the sidewalk in front of them talking. In my opinion, they looked dirty and with long stringy hair and torn jeans. It certainly wasn't from hard labor. My nose encountered the strong marijuana smell as I walked by. That odor had become prevalent in Aspen and we became quite familiar with it.

When I got back home I told Larry and Glenn, "I saw hippies camping by the creek and more in town smoking pot right there on the street. They look like they don't care about being decent, let alone being clean."

Larry nodded. "Yeah, there's getting to be too many around here…probably coming from San Francisco and the Haight-Ashbury area. They sure have enough out there."

"To add to that, the woman's liberation is out of control…these girls are burning their bras and they have no morals." I shook my head in dismay. "Don't get me wrong on woman's lib. We need equal rights too, but these girls have gone too far. I'll let a guy change my tire, but I won't give him any favors just for the fun of it!"

Glenn changed the subject, "Well the U.S. has worse problems with the war. I've been reading about it and thousands don't think we should be involved in Vietnam. They want us to get out of there and bring our boys home."

The war ignited a major division, similar to the Civil War between the north and south over slavery, but there was no north or south with this present conflict. It had a mixture of for, or against, in every state. So many families were torn apart because of the war, pitting brother against brother, father against son, and mothers torn between husband, son and their own conscience. Girls followed the draft dodgers to Canada, or volunteered to serve the country as nurses or whatever else they could do.

Larry pointed to the newspaper sitting on the table. "Look at this." The headline in an April 18, 1967 newspaper read, "War Protestors March".

I looked. "Yeah, I saw those pictures of the protests in New York, San Francisco and other cities. The one in New York City is the largest so far with 400,000 demonstrators who marched from Central Park to the U.N. Building on the 15th. Man! That must have been a sight."

Glenn added, "There'll be more protests to come. The polls show that over half the population is unhappy with President Johnson's handling of the war. It sure has upset his efforts for civil rights too."

Larry added, "The protests ought to tell the government something. Thousands of young guys are also rallying and shouting, 'Hell no, we won't go' and they're burning their draft cards." Larry stopped and frowned. "Did burning the draft card come after the gals burned their bras, or the other way around? Or, were they at the same time?"

I rolled my eyes. "Who cares? Both are a disgrace."

"What about the guys who are going to Canada to avoid the draft? I don't think much of them, do you, Glenn?"

"Well, if it was your son called up to serve in a war which he didn't believe in, what would you do if he decided to go to Canada?"

Larry tilted his head. "You've got a point." We both thought of little Greg and hoped that he would never have to go to war or make that choice.

Glenn continued, "These kids are searching for peace, equality and a better political system. They're demanding change in society and politics and an end to the war. I don't know…maybe some day it will come."

We knew that these young men and women and the hippies were the pioneers who would change the lives of all Americans in one way or another. It was the beginning of a new era with a struggle that would be long and bitter. Both sides would fight hard: one side to keep things as they were, the other to change things, but there would have to be compromises for society to adjust. We would have to learn to accept changes. Larry and I had a hard time understanding the hippies, though. We were the typical American family-type: hard working, law abiding, patriotic, paid our taxes, and went to church every Sunday.

Volkswagen vans, or VW bugs and well-worn pickups with a dog in the back began appearing like colorful armies and our valley, as well all of the Aspen Valley, became a favorite site for hippies by May. They camped on Forest Service land or on private property, whichever they wanted. Soon, they were the bane of our valley. I knew that sparks would soon fly between them and feisty me. I expected hippies, or anyone else, to respect us, our property, and accept responsibility for their actions.

We went back to work preparing our cabins for tourists. The red window frames and the door trim had to be repainted on many cabins, as well as the dark brown on the porches. The high altitude sun and the harsh weather wore the paint off fast and we bought cases of paint.

Glenn and Dale Weisbrod often worked on plumbing. Larry repaired roofs where needed, did carpentry repairs, cleaned cabins, and mowed the grass and field. I helped clean some cabins along with washing and ironing curtains and washing blankets. Larry and Glenn gathered the fallen wood in the high country and sawed the logs, chopped sections into kindling wood, and distributed it to the cabins. They did not report any more bear incidents!

This spring came with an additional job. Larry removed all the

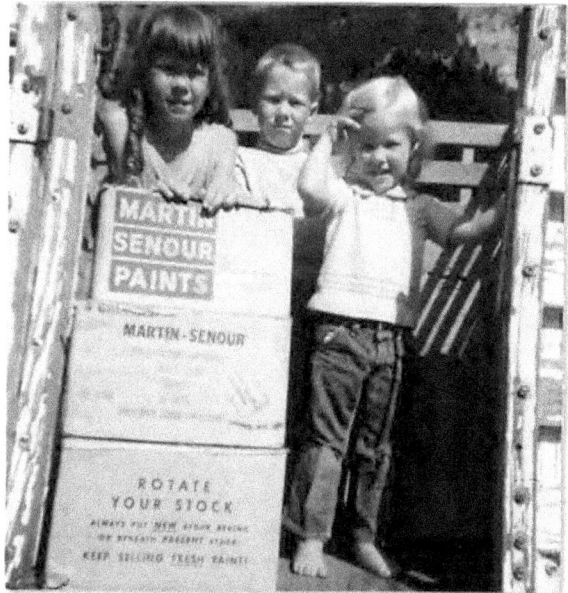

Tina, Greg, and Susy in the back of our stock truck with the painting supplies

53

debris of the burned down Montezuma cabin. He used the same foundation, and began building a new modern cabin with the help of Dale and Glenn. It took all three to hoist the roof joists up. Then, Larry nailed them in place. The new cabin would not be finished until well into June, but they got it done. It would be named the "Montezuma" again.

Chapter 6

Let There Be a Blast! (1967)

Larry came in one morning to tell me, "We have to lay the water line from the new boiler house into the kitchen for the hot water baseboard heat. Since the fire last winter, we've had the line above ground and wrapped with heat tapes so it wouldn't freeze. Now we can bury it since the ground is thawed."

The new boiler house sat about 15 feet from the back of the lodge and was about the size of an outhouse. Larry and Glenn began digging out the trench, but they soon ran into a huge boulder. They dug all around it, but could not dig deep enough to get a winch cable around it and pull it out. They gave up and came in for a coffee break.

Larry told me, "That boulder is huge, so we think we'll just use some dynamite and blast it apart."

"Are you sure you know what you're doing? It's right next to the house."

"No problem. Glenn's done it before. We'll just place the dynamite in strategic points, to break up the boulder. But just to be safe, we'll tack up blankets over the kitchen windows. You and the kids can go to the front of the house when we blow the dynamite up."

They covered the kitchen windows and planned their strategy. They placed the dynamite where they thought it would do the most damage to the boulder. The children and I went to the front porch and waited. Glenn lit the fuse and they ran for cover.

KABOOM! The blast shook the ground and building. Immediately, dirt and debris flew everywhere and the air filled with dust and a burnt sulfur smell. It blew out eight of the small square window panes and tiny shards hit inside the blankets covering the log wall and fell to the floor. Sections of chinking between the logs loosened and the mortar fell in small clouds of dust or tiny clumps.

The boulder remained intact! Larry and Glenn had a good laugh and then started to plan the next move. The children thought it great fun, but I did not.

"You guys act like little kids playing with matches. You're joking and now I've got a mess to clean up."

"Sorry," they said in unison. Still chuckling they soon replaced the window-panes and puttied them in. The trim would be painted later. I swept up the glass shards and chinking while I muttered under my breath. Then I scrubbed the cabinets, counter, table and floor to remove the dust.

The men decided that they better not try dynamite again, so they went back to digging. The boulder had been cracked by the blast and they used a sledgehammer to break it apart. Finally, both sections of the boulder were

Larry enjoying some rare free time with one of our many kittens

dislodged and removed with the help of the Jeep winch. They installed the water line, filled in the trench, and packed it down.

Surprises Big and Small

The dynamite incident brought more tense moments. Susy, now 2 years old, played in the kitchen while I typed letters in the office. I came into the kitchen and found her on top of the refrigerator throwing dynamite blasting caps onto the floor. Larry had put a box of them up there and thought they were safe, but Susy braced herself against the curved logs and shimmied up the side of the refrigerator and onto the top. She sat perched there and looked on with a smile as she dropped the blasting caps one by one.

I immediately grabbed her. "Susy, don't you climb up on the refrigerator again, do you understand? Do not climb up there!"

"I like to climb, Mommy," she replied in her toddler speech with a mischievous smile.

"I know, but you cannot climb on the refrigerator or in the kitchen. Now, you go play with your dolls."

Susy waddled to the bedroom while I carefully picked up the blasting caps. When Larry arrived I scolded him royally. "Why did you put them up there anyway?"

"My God, I didn't think she could climb up there. I'll take them down to the barn and lock them up." He knew the danger of blasting caps…they exploded. It had been a blessing that nothing happened and a special blessing that Susy did not try to bite into one.

- -

One day, I discovered something disconcerting about spring. I poured a glass of water from the faucet ready to take a drink. I stopped immediately because something was floating in the water. I held my glass up and asked, "Larry, what is this stuff in the water?"

He looked at the glass. "Damn it! I'll bet a mouse got in the reservoir."

"What? A mouse?" I almost dropped the glass. I hated mice and pieces of decaying flesh and fur almost turned my stomach.

"The reservoir isn't covered, but there's a screen over the outlet pipe that runs down to the lodge. Sometimes a field mouse falls in and drowns. Eventually, tiny pieces of remains filter through the screen. Then it comes out the first spigots on the water line. Because the cabins aren't rented yet and the lines flushed out, we got it first. Just let the water run for about 5 or 10 minutes and it should be okay."

"My Lord, I'm sure not thirsty anymore!" Needless to say, I dumped out the water.

Larry headed to the door. "I'll hike up to the reservoir and remove what's left of the varmint. Then, I'll open all the spigots and let them run full force to clear the lines. I think I'll put some Clorox disinfectant in too for sanitation. Just let the water run for awhile and it'll be okay."

I left the water running in the kitchen for over an hour. From then on, I knew I would check for debris in my glass before taking one little sip.

Then spring flew by and summer came with all the guest ranch activity. The water remained clear of anymore "debris."

Summer brought another worry and it concerned toddler Susy again. It was hard to keep track of her because guests were often in the lobby wanting my attention. She could open the kitchen screen door and waddle off in search of the other children. When I talked to guests one afternoon, a young boy carried Susy into the lobby. Both were dripping wet.

"Susy came out to play with Greg, but they had a fight and he pushed her into the pond. She couldn't get out. So I jumped in and pulled her out. I saved her." His chest puffed out in pride.

"Thank you so much." I quickly picked up Susy and pushed the wet curls from her face. I told the guests, "Sorry. I have to take care of my Susy. I'll be back in a bit."

"No problem. You take care of her." They understood and left.

"Okay, Sweetie, let's get you cleaned up." I bathed and dried Susy and dressed her in dry clothes. Soon she played with her dolls in the bedroom. Then I found Greg and told him, "Go apologize to your little sister."

I realized I needed to do something to keep Susy safe so I bought a child's halter. It had a long strap, which I tied to the back door handle and put the halter on Susy. Sometimes she played on the back porch while in her halter; other times she played inside without it, but I checked her often. Some might call Susy's halter child abuse, but I considered it child safety instead.

A Jumpstart for the Day? (1967)

A severe rainstorm swept through the valley early one June morning. Lightning hit the reservoir and electricity traveled into the water line. I was at the kitchen sink when all of a sudden the copper water pipe suddenly burst open in minute cracks and sprays of water went every which way. Thankfully, Glenn was there and quickly shut the water off. He mended the pipe and I mopped up.

Pretty soon, a guest came to the office. "I got a good shock a few minutes ago when I showered and turned the faucet to get more hot water. It sure made me jump. Can you have someone check it? I don't want my kids to take a shower until I know that it's fixed."

"Oh good heavens, I'll have Larry check as soon as he comes in. I'm sure it isn't anything to worry about."

Soon, another guest came to complain, then another. I paced back and forth looking for Larry. Finally, he returned and I related the problem.

"It must be from the lightning. I'll flush the line out." He quickly drank his coffee and went to remedy the problem. All was fine again…no more shocks, so we thought.

The next day, a man came to the office and said, "I just got a jolt from the pop machine. I don't know what happened, but when I deposited the coins I got a good shock. You better check it." The soda pop machine sat against an outside wall of the store and sat on the ground.

Later, when another guest came to complain I decided to put up an "OUT OF ORDER" sign until it could be checked. While doing that, I stepped in the puddle and got a good jolt when I touched the machine to tape the sign on. I swore under my breath while rubbing my arms, but at least I got the sign up.

Larry and Glenn came in and heard my complaint and went to check it out and I followed them to make sure they remedied the situation. Larry pulled the fuse for the electricity. Then Glenn pointed. "Okay, here's the real problem…it's this frayed wire. When the machine sits in the puddle, anyone who touches it will get a shock. I'll re-wire this, and it'll be as good as new. We'll put it on a platform too and keep it out of the water." By day's end, all had been fixed and no more shocks reported. Thank God!

Blast on the 4th

When July 4th came, the traditional celebrations at Elk Mountain Lodge had Larry and Glenn planning their strategy. Glenn purchased fireworks weeks before and they retrieved a huge supply of fireworks stored in the barn. Then they set them up next to the front pond.

Larry told me, "We're setting it up by the pond so we can go along the side and light each fuse quickly. As soon as the first round of fireworks is lit, we'll start on the next round. We've got it all figured out. It's sure going to be a good one."

"Are you staying at the pond to guard all the fireworks until night?"

"Nah, nobody's going to bother with it. All the camp knows what's going on and they want to watch the fun tonight. They'll keep their kids away."

I fixed the American July 4th traditional fried chicken for supper and apple pie for dessert. Larry and Glenn ate with the excitement of young boys. When dusk arrived in the valley, our guests congregated on their cabin porches. Some came to the lodge porch to watch with me. All the children were given sparklers to wave.

When darkness crept into the valley, Larry and Glenn headed to the pond and started the display. Rockets and Roman candles propelled high above the pond with a shrill hissing sound. The fireworks exploded into sprays of red, blue, green and white sparkles and then cascaded downward. The spectacle was nonstop for almost a half hour and delighted everyone. Many "oohs" and "aahs" could be heard along with applause. Of course, the dogs hid under the porches and whimpered.

At the end of the display, Larry and Glenn had a surprise for the guests. They set off a couple of sticks of dynamite for the occasion. When they lit the fuse, they ran for cover. The powerful blast not only echoed loudly through the valley, but it shook the cabins, the ground and the pond. Clapping and hoorahs came from everyone.

Later that night, I told Larry, "The trout in the pond will probably be traumatized for days after that blast."

"They'll survive, but may be a little deaf," Larry snickered, stretched his long legs under the table, leaned back, and raised his arms over his head. "It sure was fun. I can't wait 'til next year."

Not Horse Fun! (1967)

A pounding on our door disrupted us one early August dawn and I quickly grabbed my robe. "Larry, wake up. Someone's at the door."

He raised his head and tried to rub the sleep out of his eyes. "Well, go find out who it is while I get dressed."

I opened the office door and saw a man standing there. I didn't see his vehicle, and wondered why.

"Hi. I work up at the mine. Sorry to bother you so early, but one of your horses is caught in the cattle guard down the road. She's in bad shape and shied away from me when I tried to get her out. She's mighty scared…probably tried to cross the grate last night looking for greener pastures."

I knew the cattle guard lay across Castle Creek Road about a half mile away and it had several metal bars placed horizontal over the ditch. Each bar was spaced just far enough apart that an animal could not cross without a leg, or legs falling in between the bars and down into the ditch. Cattle and horses shy away from cattle guards and it keeps them in a certain area without a gate.

"I think a crane is the only way you're going to get her out. How about I call up to the mine and they bring down a crane?"

"Okay, sounds fine. Come on in. The phone's on the desk." I pointed to it and stepped aside to let him enter.

By then, Larry came and yawned while I told him the situation. He agreed the crane would help. He attached the horse trailer to the truck and the miner hitched a ride to the cattle guard because his pickup remained on the other side. I could only wait for Larry to return and tell me what happened.

When he came, Larry sat at the table and ate his oatmeal. In between bites, he told me what they did. More miners were stopped on the other side of the cattle guard and tried to calm the mare, but she shied, causing more injury. The crane arrived and was unloaded from the trailer.

"We tried to calm the horse while they got the straps around her belly and attached them to the crane. Then, it slowly and carefully lifted her until she had no leverage to fight. We guided her wounded limbs up and out of the grate. Her legs are a bloody mess and she sure was limping when I walked her to the trailer."

He had already unloaded the mare at the stables and called the vet. Meanwhile, the wrangler gathered antiseptic and bandages and tried to stop the bleeding.

The sun was pushing down on the valley floor when the veterinarian arrived. He sewed the wounds and bandaged the horse's legs where the flesh had been ripped clear to the bone from the struggle. "This poor horse is never going to be a riding horse again," he told us.

Larry called the owner, Cal Bennett, and he came that afternoon to take the horse back to his ranch. Then Larry walked the fence line to find the break. It wasn't long and he was back. "I found it easy and got the wire restrung. Hope it holds."

After that, we had calmness for a few days, but it didn't last. The wrangler rounded up the horses in the morning and after their oats they were saddled for the day and ready for business. By mid-morning one day, the only horse not out on a trail, Blaze, remained tied to the hitching post. Then, out of nowhere, something spooked him. Perhaps it had been a small snake slithering by, but no one saw a thing. Blaze bolted with bulging eyes and shinnied to the left with his head jerking high. He reared, then in mid-air shifted right, then left, and quickly wrenched the post loose, but the reins remained tied to it. Blaze took off at a full gallop and the post bounced off him with every stride, which

Horses taking it easy in the pasture

caused more panic. He ran, zigzagged, reared and raced hard again to get away from what kept jabbing into his legs, belly and rump.

The frenzied horse barreled through a barbed wire fence and a section ripped away and tangled up with the post. The razor-sharp barbed wire made him spook more as it bashed and ripped into Blaze's side, rump and legs. In a deep panicked state, he raced around the cabins to try to get away from the attacker, but his actions made it worse. Guests came out of their cabins to see what all the commotion was about. They made sure their children were on the porch and out of danger. There was nothing they could do but watch and they didn't dare get in the way.

Finally, Blaze became exhausted, slowed down, and eventually came to a defeated stop. His wild eyes still bulged; he panted excessively and his sweat and blood showered the ground. He trembled in fright totally spent, but we knew he would be ready to run and evade the post again, if it moved. Cautiously, the wrangler approached, talking softly and gently to Blaze. He grabbed the reins and held him steady while Larry cut the post and wire loose. Blaze limped and bled back to the stables, and we again called the veterinarian.

When the vet arrived, he examined Blaze. "Half of the hoof and fetlock are torn away, and I can only try to save what is left. The other limb is badly damaged and his flank, back and abdomen have gashes. I can doctor the wounds, but he'll no longer be able to walk properly."

As he finished doctoring Blaze, I looked up and saw the colt in the corral. "Oh my God, look at the colt," I yelled. The colt stood perfectly still just staring at us, but bled from a long gash all the way across his neck. He didn't wobble or collapse, but just stood and watched all the commotion and almost seemed in shock.

The vet looked up. "Okay, I'm done here. I'll check it." He quickly went to the colt and upon closer examination said, "Its okay. It's a long, deep gash, but none of the main arteries are severed. I'll sew her up and she should be fine." We all gave a sigh of relief. "Blaze must have gotten too close and the barbed wire probably swung out and sliced straight across the colt's neck like a scalpel. I'm surprised there isn't more damage." He quickly numbed the neck area and sewed up the long curving wound while the wrangler held her neck area and someone else held her front legs. When he finished, he loaded his bag into his truck. "The colt sure gave me some worry at first. Just keep the wound clean and call me, if you need."

Cal came that evening and loaded Blaze into his trailer. Before the trailer gate latched Tina tearfully gave her goodbye to Blaze with a kiss on its white blazed nose.

In the next few days, the colt received a great deal of attention and affection from Tina. After a couple of weeks, he seemed fine and by the next month it became hard to see the scar.

Thankfully, we didn't have anymore horse disasters that season.

Chapter 7

TV and War

The summer of 1967, Larry and Glenn declared we were going to somehow get TV in our valley. The only media communication at Elk Mountain Lodge was radio. No TV broadcasting signals could transmit into our valley through the high mountain walls.

"Larry, how are we going to get TV?"

"We'll do it on our own. We'll buy a booster station and transformer so we can rebroadcast into the valley, but we'll only be able to get ABC. We have to get a license for our booster and it will have to be installed up on top of the mountain in order to transfer the signal down to us."

Glenn chimed in, "We'll have to convert the booster so it'll work on propane gas tanks because there's no electricity on the mountain. The propane will run a generator for the electricity. We'll set the gas tanks up on a tandem basis, so when one tank runs out of gas, it will automatically transfer to the next one and keep the juice flowing. I'll apply for the license."

They got everything ready and then they had to wait for the equipment, license and approval. Both Glenn and Larry were eager to try this system, but it took time before the license was approved and the arrival of the equipment.

When fall approached, everything was ready. They loaded up the Jeep with the propane gas tanks and headed up the Little Annie four-wheel drive road to the top of Richmond Hill. Larry told me that they would turn off the trail and head to the ridge towering above the lodge. From there, they would see the

Sawtooth Range and all the surrounding peaks. Looking down into the valley, Elk Mountain Lodge cabins looked like tiny squares dotted here and there.

When they got set up, Glenn called me on the C.B. and told me they had the booster ready. He said Larry climbed a tree and perched there holding the antenna and pointing it down into the valley toward our lodge. He asked me to tell them what reception I got on the TV. The citizen band radios were our only means of communication at that time. I had been waiting for my signal and yelled back on my C.B. that the picture was full of snow and I had no sound. He told me Larry would slowly move the antenna around and for me to yell when I got a good picture. I kept saying, "No…no…no" until there didn't seem to be another way for him to turn. We were getting discouraged, but he inched another twist.

Then I yelled, "Stop, stop! Okay, that's it. The picture is coming in good and so is the sound. Just don't move." My eyes were fixed on the small screen.

"Great." Glenn shouted for Larry to hold that position. He told me, "We're going to anchor the antenna and then you tell us if it still comes in clear."

It worked and the reception came in perfect at the lodge, or as perfect as a small black and white 14-inch TV screen could be. Then, Larry anchored the antenna and climbed down with a grin.

As soon as they came home, Larry told me, "Remember the TV will only work while the propane gas is available. It ought to last until the end of March and when the tandem of gas tanks run dry, the signal will die. Then, there'll be no more TV until the snow disappears. We'll have to go back with a new supply of tanks when the Jeep can make it back up the trail.

We were excited to finally have a view of the "outside world" through TV, but we didn't watch that much, maybe sports, a couple of programs and always the news. The children tuned on one or two programs and the rest of the time they played. On Saturday mornings, they got up early to watch cartoons. Many evenings, our family played board games instead of watching TV.

The 1967 news was full of reports on the Vietnam War. None seemed good and too many lives were being lost. Servicemen were listed as missing in action (MIAs). Others were prisoners of war and they were listed as POWs. It became popular for people to wear a bracelet with the name of an MIA or POW so that no one would forget that person. News gave no hope for the war ending soon.

Norm and Mickey Payne came for a visit one evening. We all sat at the table drinking coffee and discussing the events.

"Here we are, still in Vietnam and the war still raging." I remarked. "The body bags arrive in the States at a steady pace. I don't care if you are for or against the war, you have to have compassion for those who are losing their loved ones. How horrible."

Mickey agreed. "We have lost so many boys. And the MIAs are increasing along with the POWs. When is it going to end?" She asked and raised her eyes to heaven.

Larry chimed in, "The media is full of propaganda from the government. They tell us about all the victories of our forces and that the casualties are a necessity for winning. With victory, there are so many losses, and it is bitter-sweet. Right, Norm?"

"You bet." He remembered his days in the service. He didn't elaborate and was the same as most veterans…burying those memories in the far reaches of the mind.

Visiting ended, but another kind of war began to brew at Elk Mountain Lodge.

Critter Evictions (1967)

Our war did not threaten lives, but it did sabotage our home and noses…a skunk invasion. The cute-faced little critters dug beneath the lodge foundation and made a cozy home underneath. The crawl space under the original lodge had barely a foot between the ground and the floor, but the new bedrooms had a deep crawl space and both provided plenty of room for skunk rendezvous. When they got excited, they released their perfume and it permeated the whole building. It quickly became too much to tolerate.

There were many discussions on ways to get rid of the varmints. Larry and Glenn continually filled in the holes where the skunks dug under the foundation, but the openings kept reappearing.

"Glenn said he heard that skunks don't like mothballs. We'll try it. I'll get some when I go to town," Larry told me.

Later, he opened the bedroom trap door to the crawl space and scattered a dozen boxes of mothballs all over the crawl space. At least, the mothball aroma became more pleasant than the alternative and I hoped it would do the job. The skunks, however, ignored the mothballs and continued releasing their perfume. Their pungent odor overtook the mothball aroma.

"Well, I heard that skunks don't like light. So, let's get some spotlights and put them underneath the floor," Larry suggested to Glenn.

They rounded up four floodlights and anchored each light to a floor beam. They positioned them so the entire crawl space area was lit. After a few days, we knew that this method did not work either. It was seldom that the lodge had any freedom of the unbearable odor. I used incense, but it didn't completely cover it up and I could only apologize to guests.

Larry came in with hope one day. "Someone said that if skunks cut their feet on broken glass, they don't return. So, we can put the glass shards in the hole they dig to enter and cover it just slightly. Then, when they come out, they'll scratch and cut their paws. Maybe that'll do it."

He had glass panes on hand to replace broken windows. Pieces were chopped into smaller fragments and placed where the skunks dug under the foundation. It did not stop them either and brought our discouragement to a new low.

"Get rid of those damned skunks!" I demanded. I had become frustrated with the continuous odor. It permeated the building and I hated it more and more with each passing, obnoxious, smelly day. "Our clothes are beginning to smell like skunk."

"Okay. Okay. I'm trying." Larry, utterly discouraged, frowned in thought. He consulted Glenn again. I knew the two would decide to try another hare-brained idea thinking it surely would work.

"We're going to try noise and see if that'll work." Larry and Glenn removed the can lids over the holes in the old kitchen flooring, lit firecrackers, and threw them through the holes to the crawl space. They hoped it would teach the intruders that it would not be a safe place to abide. The firecrackers exploded and shook the floor boards. Puffs of dust billowed up and were followed by a phosphorous smell.

I angrily cleaned up the dust. At least the skunks did not retaliate with their perfume right after the firecrackers, but it did not get rid of them either. Soon, the pests let loose once more and their odor sifted through the house again.

"Well, I guess the only answer is to trap and shoot the danged things," Larry finally decided. He didn't like to shoot an animal, but he got desperate and knew either the skunks were gone, or I would move to town.

Larry and Glenn set traps at the entrance holes while the skunks were under the house. The critters unwittingly vacated the crawlspace by the same hole and right into the trap. Every day one was caught. Larry dragged the traps down to the field over the rough ground and bumps. As long as it dragged and bounced along, the skunk couldn't get footing to spray. When Larry stopped pulling the trap, Glenn immediately took aim, but even with its dying breath the critter released its spray.

I think after killing about eight of the pests, the invasion stopped. At last, the house became free of the god-awful odor and we had peace once again between nature and man's nose.

More Critters (1967)

Our wars weren't done yet and a new invasion came: gophers in the field where Larry tried to make a play area yard for guests and our family. He erected a swing in the mowed field grass area. There was also room for a game of volleyball.

Larry came in one afternoon and spouted, "Those danged gophers are at it again. The field is a playground for them instead of the kids. Those varmints tunnel all over and come to the surface to pop their heads out and investigate their surroundings. I swear they're sneering at me."

I smiled and had seen the gophers from the lodge. They were cute, but they picked the wrong field. The tunnels made humps and the holes made elevated dirt mounds. I knew Larry would do everything in his power to clear the field.

"I've got to find a way to get rid of them. I don't want those pesky pests ruining my yard. I want it smooth so the kids can play without falling into a gopher hole and breaking a leg…or a horse falling and breaking a leg."

Glenn said, "How about we try hooking up a hose to the spigot and begin filling the tunnels with water? Maybe we can drown the little devils."

"Good idea. Let's go try it now."

Off they went like two excited little boys on a new venture. Soon, they had the hoses hooked to an outside spigot and began to flood the holes. The gophers poked their heads out at an opening where the water hadn't yet reached and scampered off. The next day they were back, sitting up on the mounds with their front paws up and their noses high, as if taunting Larry.

"Okay. Now they've really made me mad. Glenn, how about if we hook a hose to the Jeep exhaust pipe, then we insert it down the hole and try to asphyxiate them?"

One nod from Glenn and they were off again. They hooked up the hose and gunned the engine. It took time and they felt they were successful, but within a half hour the gophers were poking their heads out again. This time they seemed even more defiant, and their little noses were higher, as if grinning in victory while they sat with their front paws in front of their puffed out chests so proud.

Larry's shoulders sagged in defeat. "They enjoy tormenting me and ruining my field."

There appeared no way to rid the field of the gophers, so Larry decided to live with it. He was out in the field every evening filling holes and smoothing down the mounds with a steel beam dragging behind the Jeep.

Finally, after all the harassment, the field seemed to be clear of the pests. For a country field yard, it seemed fairly smooth. Larry beamed, "I did it! I got rid of those damned gophers."

Of course, they just moved and ended up in other areas. Because they were part of country living, Larry decided to let them reside in other fields, but not his grassy play field.

Too soon, summer retreated and fall courted in cold winds. Gradually, the golden aspen leaves fell and coated the earth with its colors while the pastures and fields turned a straw color. Then, winter arrived and the mountains became clothed in a virgin white garment. I no longer felt isolated with the winter seclusion.

Wide–Not So Good

Thanksgiving and Christmas passed with no excitement, and 1968 blew in with snowstorms. It brought deep drifts and more snowmobile tours as the popularity grew.

Larry packed the trail on a bright sunny day after a night snowstorm. Later, I saw him hobbling, but he kept the tours going all day.

When he came in to check reservations, I asked, "Are you okay?"

"Yeah. I didn't pay attention when I packed the trail and I drug my right foot along the side in the snow to help widen the trail. All of a sudden, I hit a bump and my foot twisted inward and tangled with the moving track. I released the throttle right away and stopped. So, it didn't get twisted too badly. I kept my foot on the running board after that, but it's a little sore that's all."

He worked until all tours were completed and the snowmobiles parked back at the lodge. He limped in, sat in the kitchen, and carefully removed his boot.

"Shee-yooot! No wonder my ankle hurts so much. Look at how bad it's swollen." He could hardly stand on it and black and blue blotches were vivid. The swelling intensified as soon as he took off his boot.

"We have to have a doctor check that. I'll drive you to emergency. Mickey can watch the kids." I quickly went to the phone.

An Aspen Valley Hospital nurse examined Larry's foot and said there were no broken bones, just bruising. She gave him some pain pills and said to go home and keep his foot elevated for a couple of days.

Larry felt better after taking one of the painkillers. Back home, he sat in the easy chair with his foot propped up on the footstool. Snowmobile tours were cancelled for the next few days. A loss of income for us.

If the children or I got too close, Larry bellowed, "Get away from my foot! Keep 2 feet away from me." He didn't want anyone to accidentally touch his painful foot and ankle. I felt like I had to care for another child…and a temperamental one at that!

Finally, *finally,* he recovered. He became the normal easy-going Larry again. Thank God, because his yelling had worn heavy on me. I was ready to yell at him!

Joanne and Susy on another winter outing

White to Color at Last

Soon, winter faded and the spring season bloomed with tall grass, wild flowers, dandelions and fresh life on the mountainsides. The sun warmed the valley and parkas were shed. The snowmobiles were lined up behind the stables, and put to bed until the next winter. Ahh! The joy of warmth and new life.

Spring gave new energy. All the usual cleaning, repairs, painting, woodcutting and stocking the store had to be accomplished. Gradually, mud turned to dirt and dust.

Larry and Glenn decided to build a new modern cabin by the front pond. They knew it would bring more income and a modern cabin would help to keep up with the demand for a country atmosphere, but with conveniences. Larry used his engineering skills to draft the plans and calculated the lumber needed. After they got the outside walls up, both men decided that the large window facing the pond and the peaks should be on the other side of the porch door. So, they tore that wall out and turned it around. Then, everything seemed to go according to plans. The cabin contained a Ben Franklin stove instead of a fireplace in the living room. When they finished, we decided to just call it the #14 cabin. We never did come up with a name.

Assassinations (1968)

Spring brought more news and politics seemed to dominate. We began to replace our coffee conversations from hippies to the political scene. Senator Robert F. Kennedy declared his candidacy on March 16th for the Democratic presidential nomination. Then, President Johnson surprised the nation on March 31st and dropped out of the race, which gave Kennedy a big advantage.

Glenn commented, "Maybe a new president can change things. Kennedy is a name that everyone knows and it would be something if another Kennedy became President, wouldn't it?"

Larry nodded. "He may make it, but Richard Nixon swears he'll end the war. There's something, though, that I don't like about Nixon. I'd bet ol' Tricky Dickey doesn't play fair."

I added, "Well, I guess we'll just have to see what happens. Politics….it seems to bring out the worst in people." They agreed. Coffee ended and it was back to work.

Then one evening, Larry yelled, "Listen to the news! Martin Luther King was assassinated at a Memphis hotel." I heard an announcer on TV saying, "It is a sad day this April 8th …the country has lost a man who believed in change by peace…." He continued with all the tragic events and told of the accomplishments of King.

We had heard and read about Martin Luther King since 1964 when he had received the Nobel Peace Prize for his constant effort for peaceful means to equality. Our subscription to the *Time* magazine displayed King on the cover in 1964 and then several times later. We, and Aspen, had little connection with the Negroes at the time and only read or heard about their struggles.

When I grew up in South Dakota, I saw the prejudice against the Indians and felt it may have been similar to the Negroes. I recalled that whites did not hire Indians for anything except menial labor, if at all. Indians could be shot without provocation and Negroes were hanged without provocation. They were kept on the "other side of the track" and were looked down upon. I remember when I went to see a Harlem Globetrotters game in the 1950s, the Indians were seated in a separate section and not allowed to mingle with the whites. I thought the Indian and Negro situations were probably similar, but who knew which was worse?

Larry lowered his head and shook it back and forth. "King's dream of change by peaceful means ends in violence, but I don't think that people will go against his dream. He was so adamant about change through peace."

Days went by with reports on the assassination and the funeral. Some sang "We Shall Overcome." It began as a gospel song and changed from "We *Will* Overcome" to "We *Shall* Overcome" when it was adopted as a civil rights song.

I hoped the assassination would not be the end of a peaceful means toward equality. It couldn't, if the people really believed in Martin Luther King's message. He had been a strong leader and tens of thousands followed him. Time would tell.

It wasn't long and history changed again. TV showed Senator Robert F. Kennedy's speech after he had won the Democratic presidential nomination in Los Angeles on June 5th. A little later the announcement came that Kennedy was shot by a young man. Immediately, they rushed Kennedy to a hospital, but the next day the news announced his death.

Larry said, "That sure has dashed the hopes of seeing another Kennedy in office."

I groaned, "My God, that's two assassinations in a couple of months. What's happening to the country?" There could be no answer.

As always, the current news eventually faded. We wondered what would be next in our country in such terrible turmoil. Killings in Vietnam took enough tolls, and we didn't need more in the United States.

Guests Unite as a Family for Susy (1968)

By late June, there were no more assassinations reported on news. Cabins were full and the camp buzzed with children and adults. Susy, now 3 years old, became friends with 3-year old Sarah, a guest's daughter. We parents let the two little girls play outside near the cabins.

Sarah's mother came to the office one day. "Are Sarah and Susy inside playing?"

"No, I thought they were at your cabin." My heart began to beat faster and my mind thought of the creek right away.

"Oh God, where are they? I looked all over and didn't see them!"

"I'll get Larry and we can begin searching, and I'll call the wranglers to check around. They have to be here somewhere." I ran to tell Larry and held my tears back. Larry reassured me that the two would be found safe in a few minutes. I'm not sure he felt that way inside, but he remained calm as always in a crisis.

We began searching and when the cabin guests heard, they came in force to help. Echoes of yells for Susy and Sarah filled the camp. It was just the way the guests were…help one another, especially with children. Many had been coming for years and were almost like family.

Larry and Glenn walked along the creek looking for clues and yelling, but found nothing. Their serious frowns told their worry. I walked the grounds and checked with other cabins, but didn't find the little tots. Twenty minutes passed and I got a sickening feeling in my stomach. I decided to go back to the lodge to check in case the little girls somehow showed up and no one saw them. The others continued looking and all were beginning to expect the worst. Larry walked the creek again and went further downstream and Glenn stayed behind him double checking. The water wasn't at the spring-high level, but it had some swift sections that could easily pull in two little tots. When I opened the office door, the phone rang and I rushed to answer.

"Hi, Joanne. Its Mickey. I've been trying to call you. Susy and her little friend are down here. They must have walked down through the field. Did you know they were coming?"

"No, we've been searching high and low for them. Are they okay?" I wiped my tear-filled eyes.

"Sure, just a little tired and dirty. They needed some cookies and milk to replenish their little bodies. I can bring them up, but I have to wait until my bread comes out of the oven."

"That's alright. I'll come down and get them. See you in a few minutes. Thanks." I gave a big sigh and shed a few more tears of thanks to God.

Then, I ran outside and rang the dinner bell, which stood anchored to a pole in the ground. We had arranged to use it as the signal when someone found the girls or had news. The loud clangs of the bell quickly brought the searchers on the run. They expected bad news when they didn't see the little ones. When I told them where the tots were, a chorus of hoorays rang out. I saw tears trickle down the cheeks of some of our long-time women guests.

Then, I quickly drove down to pick the little girls up. When I got to Mickey's, I asked Susy why she had gone so far.

Susy, safe at home on the front porch

"We were picking flowers for you an...an...her mommy." She pointed to Sarah.

"Oh, that was very nice. But you know, Susy, you aren't suppose to go anywhere without telling Mommy or Daddy. Next time, you must remember to tell us where you are going, and you must never go in the pastures without a grownup." Susy nodded in agreement.

As soon as I pulled in our drive, Betty ran to Sarah and grabbed her up tight in tears. Larry picked up Susy, kissed her curly top, and asked her what she did along the way. Then he told her next time he wanted to go too and to be sure and let him know.

There was a difference of people with the summer guests and the hippies that seemed to be invading the area. Summer people cared and helped like family. The hippies seemed to be more selfish and disrespectful. I can't help but compare!

Chapter 8

Homemade Ice Cream (1968)

The next week our family friend, Dale Weisbrod, came to visit. Sometimes, he and Glenn took a Jeep trip with other friends and sometimes he helped with a chore. Occasionally, he brought his ice cream maker and we all knew that meant homemade ice cream, and there is nothing better!

He brought all the ingredients and we sat on the porch and took turns grinding until the ice cream was ready to eat. Visiting made for a good time to catch up on the latest local news or discuss other events. When Dale's brother, Neal, visited from Missouri, he joined us. When the ice cream was ready, everyone gathered for the homemade treat. Delicious!

Dale became almost a part of the family and spent several holidays with us. His sense of humor could keep us laughing when he told stories from town. Many included encounters of the old-timers with the hippies. Because he was a plumber, it often meant a job for a landlord to unplug a drain. He told us about a home that was rented to hippies and they vacated leaving disaster. He had to unplug the toilet while trying not to gag. Then he had to unplug the kitchen sink drain, which had a mass of greasy substance. He made sure it did not land on him when he removed the P trap. On top of that, cockroaches scampered everywhere. When he got home he said he had to almost scrub himself raw in order to feel clean.

I imagine some of our experiences were relayed to others in town when he returned. For years, Dale had hunted in our area during the season and downed some of the largest deer and elk. The meat never went to waste and was shared with friends. Some hunters rented our cabins, but most didn't like the high altitude. They couldn't breathe when they hiked up a mountainside.

Dippy Hippies and Bad Choices! (1968)

Fall brought the worry of how to make money for the winter. Snowmobile rentals were not quite enough. Glenn kept his annual job working at Sardy's Hardware and some-times using Larry's and my station wagon to haul caskets to or from another city for Sardy's Mortuary. No ghosts remained with our car after the bodies were delivered. Anyway,

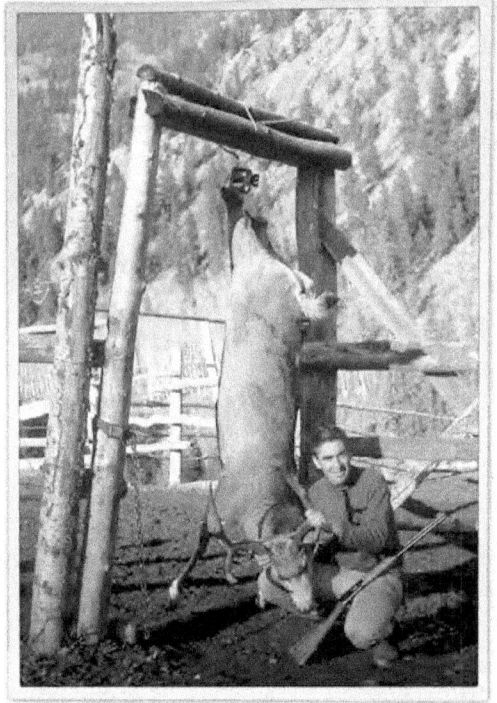

Dale Weisbrod shows off his huge buck

we never felt or saw any ghosts...probably because they had been too scared to remain with our car after the way Glenn drove!

We decided, after much discussion, to rent the cabins long-term for the winter to the young people who worked in town. Soon an application, lease and rules were printed.

Winter forced the young people to leave their tents or tepees in the high country. Many sought shelter in town and some at Elk Mountain Lodge after they saw our ad in the paper. I wouldn't trust them, though, because I felt if they had loose morals, it might include a lapse of responsibility. Stories abounded about the hippies who damaged properties. We had also heard of too many landlords who lost rent because a tenant would just up and move out owing a month or two of rent. Wild parties and drugs were another story that circulated.

If we rented to any of the hippies, they would be under my watchful eye and I wouldn't let them break rules. We really didn't think, though, that they would be too difficult as renters...or so we thought.

Hippie vans and bugs displayed the new hip art in psychedelic colors of bright yellow, orange, green, blue and red, which surely was inspired by drug use. Some females wore long flowing skirts and peasant blouses, but most of the young women in the Rockies preferred to wear jeans and a tee shirt…with no bra underneath. Braless became the fashion highlight of the day among those girls. I knew the men liked it, but my cheeks burned red when I saw the girls bouncing along. Both men and women let their hair grow long and it flowed down their backs. Some had it braided, or in a ponytail, or some had a band around their foreheads in Indian fashion to hold their loose locks away from their faces.

"One rule we will insist upon is no unmarried couples allowed," I told Larry. It didn't take long for us to realize that they always said they were married. "I ought to ask to see their marriage license."

He laughed. "Don't bother, or we'll have empty cabins."

I began to wonder how we could tell if an applicant would be any good. Most had no past rental history. We soon realized referrals were almost nonexistent and only the present employer could be checked for reliability. No other work history could be found. A person may have only been working a week or a month. All we could do was to use our instinct and give them the benefit of the doubt. Larry's judgment seemed better than mine. In time, we learned if our instincts were right…a short time.

We also had a clause in the lease that each additional person in a cabin would be charged $3.00 per day, which would be the responsibility of the tenant who signed the lease. Short stays of guests were not considered an abuse of the rule, but limited in number, such as one or two guests. Three dollars seemed like a lot to charge, but we wanted to make sure that the tenants didn't load up a cabin with many friends, which we had heard about.

I kept vigil with binoculars and I would have no rule-breakers in my camp. If they had to be treated like children, I would do it.

One morning, I counted 12 extra people coming out of a cabin. The next morning I saw the same 12 again getting ready for a ski day on the slopes. I walked over to the cabin and surprised the long-term tenants with a bill for the extra people.

"I expect immediate payment and they cannot stay here any longer."

The tenant argued that the friends only stayed one night and that the lease said they could have overnight guests. A marijuana aroma filtered through the door and assaulted my nose.

I made it clear that the extras stayed two nights and I had counted them both mornings. He then argued that it had been only 6 extras.

"Listen, I counted 12 each day and you will pay for 12 now, or I'll have the sheriff evict you immediately." They didn't know that I gave an empty threat, because we could not legally evict on the spot. "The rules are clear and your friends will need to leave today."

The tenant sighed then decided to give up and pay. Within an hour the friends had packed and left.

We knew the only way to keep from having a tenant pile in the extra people would be to crack down and not give an inch. I became vigilant and two more cabins were fined for extra people in the next few weeks.

It's a wonder I don't end up with permanent raccoon circles around my eyes from binocularitis.

Winter continued, and on Christmas Day, Larry decided we would keep our snowmobile business open for the day. "It's a big play day for tourists."

I knew it would be busy enough for me without business, but his mind was made up. He had no idea how much work I normally put into preparing the big holiday meal from scratch. It took time and attention. The children would also want us to play with them and teach them their new games.

So, by late-morning tours began. I remained busy the rest of the day with the tourists in and out, renting gear, collecting money, taking phone calls, preparing coffee and visiting. The children wanted my attention and became very naughty. They got into things, fought, screamed and kept interrupting me while I tried to take care of customers. They were attention-starved hellions and by the end of the last tour late that afternoon, I was frazzled and exhausted.

Dinner was expected to be served when Larry and Glenn came in. I quickly put together a slap-stick meal. At least there were plenty of Christmas sweets for dessert, because I had baked poteca, cookies, fruitcake and breads in the preceding weeks. I planned to have wine with the dinner, but while preparing the hurried meal, I grabbed a beer in frustration. It didn't take long for me to down it even though beer was never my favorite.

After unloading the snowmobiles, Larry came in whistling. "That sure was a good day. We made good money, didn't we?" Glenn walked in behind him.

I greeted them with a set jaw and snapping eyes and placed my hands on my hips. "From now on if you want to have snowmobile business on Christmas Day, you are going to do it alone. I will *not* take care of the business or reservations. I have had a terrible day with the kids and they need attention. So don't expect me to help you on Christmas Day from now on." My eyes glistened.

Larry lost his smile. "I'm sorry. I didn't think about that. Here, let me help you set the table." After that, he poured a cup of coffee, sat at the table and stretched his long legs underneath. Glenn had already sneaked into the living room. I smoldered over the stove.

"Daddy, Daddy. Come help us play this game. Come on, Daddy," Tina and Greg both chimed in while trying to pull him out of the chair.

"I'll play with you later. I'm going to sit and have a cup of coffee."

"But Daddy, we want you to play with us. Mommy wouldn't all day," Tina complained and pouted. Her eyes pleaded.

Now he could see the picture better and decided to play with the children. He did not tell me that there would be no snowmobile business on future Christmas Days, but he accepted my verdict. We did not discuss it further.

Six-Foot Thaw and Not an Edible Carrot

On a bitter, cold January morning the tenant in the Montezuma cabin reported frozen water pipes. "What are you going to do?" I asked Larry.

"We have to dig down through the frozen ground to get to the pipe: about 6 feet down. It's probably frozen under the parking spot where there isn't much snow for insulation. We have to build a fire over it to thaw the ground enough to shovel it out. The fire usually thaws about a foot each time and we'll repeat the process until we get down to the pipe. Then we can thaw it." Frozen water pipes were common in mountain life.

Larry and Glenn got logs and built a fire and then dug out the soil. They repeated until they finally reached the frozen pipe and thawed the ice in the line with a torch. Afterward, the hole was filled with the frozen earth and tamped down with the Jeep and then topped off with some snow to give some insulation.

They still had to check and see if there were any split water pipes inside the cabin wall. Frozen ice could travel and cause breaks in the line. If a pipe burst inside the wall, it had to be torn out and the pipe repaired. Then the mess had to dry out before the wall could be replaced. They lucked out and no pipes burst inside the Montezuma.

Two more cabins froze with the bitter cold winter, but Larry and Glenn didn't have to build a fire and dig. They shoveled snow away from the foundations and one crawled under the cabin and used the torch to thaw the pipes. Some pipes were wrapped with heat tapes to prevent freezing. If the snow had not piled high and thick around the cabin, a pipe underneath could freeze. If not frozen pipes, occasionally a gas wall heater in a modern cabin went out and then Larry, Glenn, or I relit it as soon as the tenant let us know.

February brought another surprise. One of the men's toilets in the shower house plugged up. Larry couldn't plunge it enough to clear whatever was clogging the stool. Then, Glenn tried to use a snake, but with no luck. So, they removed the stool and found a large carrot blocked the drain! When it was dislodged, the stool flowed fine once again.

"Who the devil would put a carrot down a stool?" I asked when they told me.

"Some idiot was probably drunk or high and dropped it when he was trying to take a bite in front of the stool," Larry said.

"Yuck!"

Welcome Spring!

Finally, winter began to fade. No more frozen pipes needed to be thawed, no more fines for extra guests and no more toilets plugged. The spring season of 1968 began to bloom and the sun warmed the valley. Parkas were shed, but snow still carpeted the north side of the cabins, and mud replaced the snow-packed drive. Too much mud appeared on my old kitchen floor, which still hadn't been replaced 3 years after the initial promise of a new floor.

We began the usual cleaning, repairs, painting, woodcutting and stocking the store. Because most of the long-term tenants didn't bother to clean bathrooms, kitchens, or even mop floors, we had extra scrubbing. Some tenants had thrown pans, dishes and silverware out in the snow when they were dirty. We found the items peeking out as the snow melted. What a wakeup for us! I vowed, "Next winter I will not allow the long-term tenants to have our pots, pans, dishes, silverware or anything else. They will have to furnish their own. It's a good thing that we didn't furnish linens or blankets because they probably would have never come clean or been rid of the marijuana odor and accumulated filth."

By the end of May, all cabins were clean and summer guests soon arrived. They were certainly welcome after we endured the winter tenants.

Some first-time guests stated that they knew how to build a fire in a wood stove when they registered and did not need instructions. Others listened as one of us explained how to use the stove. I could instruct them, even though I never got the hang of keeping the fire going myself. I just didn't tell the tourists about that. The truth always came out about guest's true abilities when smoke flowed out of the cabin door or windows and not up the chimney.

One day, I looked over at the Buckskin cabin that had just been rented. Smoke billowed out the door. I knew what had happened and walked over. I knocked on the screen door and tried to sound concerned. "I saw smoke coming out and wondered if you have a problem?"

He opened the screen door for me to enter. "I built the fire in here and the smoke won't go out the chimney. It must be clogged."

"Well, that's the oven. The wood is supposed to go in this little firebox on the left topside. Then the smoke will vent out the chimney." I pointed to the correct location. "You'll have to put the fire out in the oven and then build it in here."

"Oh…it's not like the one I remember," he declared with embarrassment.

I left with a smile. Some new guests built the fire in the oven and some built it in the ashbin. But this season, we only had the Buckskin guest who didn't need instructions and learned the hard way.

- -

Summer seemed to just vanish. Maybe it went so fast because we stayed busy every day. Fall surprised us with a quick entry and then we braced ourselves for the troubles to come with long-term-tenants again. I would be ready with my binoculars and fine those that did not obey the rules.

Snowmobile business began by Thanksgiving week and the tours had become more and more popular each season. Skiers were flocking to Aspen and some took a day off to snowmobile and some local Aspenites came for tours. Larry kept the trail packed and constantly watched the snow slide areas. He had many snowmobile repairs or adjustments to make when not guiding.

The long-term tenants were pretty quiet this winter. We weren't sure if the word had spread that we would not put up with troublemakers, or if we had just picked decent tenants. I would still remain the mean witch, if needed, while Larry and Glenn were the good guys. They didn't like to argue, but it didn't bother me to tell the tenants right from wrong. I could be tough, but I could also be fair. A mistake was accepted, but outright disrespect or rule-breaking was not allowed in my book. I also was concerned about any damage to our property and cost of repair. I kept the binoculars handy, but hadn't had a problem the first couple of months.

Elvis and Those Dang Hippies! (1969)

Larry got a nice surprise on January 28, 1969. He agreed to rent five snowmobiles for about a week to Elvis Presley...the ELVIS PRESLEY. He became our first winter celebrity, but others followed later. Elvis had rented a home in Snowmass Village, a ski resort near Aspen. Larry and Glenn delivered the machines to him. I had to stay at the lodge for business and did not get to meet the famous music star.

When the men picked up the snowmobiles, Elvis Presley wrote a check. We deposited the check, the money being more important at that time than keeping it for the star's autograph. The release form that Elvis also signed on delivery was somehow thrown away later. What a shame!

After our excitement with Elvis, things were pretty normal with regular snowmobile business. The tenants seemed to spread the word that we would not put up with any trouble. But they still seemed to lack common sense.

On a February morning, I saw the men's shower house door standing open. I checked and found no pipes frozen, but the stools were not flushed. I put up a sign to close the door when leaving. Every day for about a week, I checked and eventually found the door closed, but the stools were not flushed. I made another sign asking the tenants to flush the stools after use. That didn't work and so I changed the sign and made it larger. It read:

**IF YOU DON'T KNOW HOW TO FLUSH A TOILET,
PLEASE COME TO THE OFFICE AND I WILL SHOW YOU.**

Apparently, the males had their mommies, or maids, at home who cleaned up after them, including flushing the stools for them. The women's side had no problems with flushing. Maybe they were just pickier. At least I finally got through to the guys and the toilets were flushed.

We got to know the tenants pretty well. They had to earn our respect by showing us that they were reliable with paying rent and abided by the rules. A few we liked, even if we did not approve of their lifestyle. Personalities made the difference. A disrespectful tenant was given a strong ultimatum, but a tenant with a good personality, respect, or humor, may have received just a warning. I could be a nice witch at times!

Finally, spring appeared on the horizon and offered a sigh of relief and winter melted with the warm days. The long-termers moved out and many began camping in the mountains for the summer. Frustration came with the cleaning and repairing after the tenants departed.

We were beginning to see more and more examples of how the hippie's attitudes were so different from ours. These young people proved their lack of respect for people or private property. They seemed to think that they could do what they wanted and camp where they wanted. The Aspen area had become one of their favorite places to express their freedom. Many of the older residents, including us, became disgusted with their attitude. We ran some hippies off our land and I ran off a couple who camped by our reservoir who I suspected would contaminate our water if they took a bath or put their feet in our water supply. To me, that would be as bad as a mouse in the water!

On a warm spring day, I saw two people wander into our camp. It was hard to tell if they were male or female with the long hair, jeans and baggy tee-shirts. One was taller than the other. The shorter one walked with more of a sashay and was probably the female.

Both peeked into the Pines cabin window and tried to open the door. Then I saw Glenn walk up to them and talk for a bit. Later, he told us that he asked what they thought they were doing and the guy casually answered that they were just looking and that the cabins looked neat. Then they both peered into the window again.

Glenn said, "I told them that this was private property and the guy answered, 'So?' and jiggled the door handle again. I said, 'So, get the hell out of here.' I figured I didn't need to be nice about it. The guy answered, 'Okay, man. Don't have a fit. We weren't doing anything, just looking and we thought we could camp here for a night.' Well, I told them no and said again to get the hell out of here. So, they shrugged and walked away and headed toward

Ashcroft." That was the only time I knew of Glenn standing up to the hippies. He usually stayed clear of any confrontation with them.

One day, I quickly got my binoculars and watched four people waltzing out of the shower house with long hair glistening in the sunlight. Two came from the men's side and two from the women's side. I assumed that they probably had camped either on Forest Service land or on our land. I knew they hadn't rented a cabin and I marched down to meet them.

"Okay, you guys. I saw you coming out of the shower house. You owe me $3.00 each for the use of the shower house and I want to be paid now."

One of the guys answered. "Hey, we just wanted to take a shower. We didn't do any harm. You can't charge us $3.00."

"Oh yes I can. You're trespassing on private property and I'll call the sheriff if you don't pay"

"Aw, come on lady. We just used a little water."

"You used our facilities. All our guests pay for it and you will too." I didn't want the word to get out that a free shower could be had at Elk Mountain Lodge, or we'd have every hippie camper in the county at our place. "You want me to call the sheriff?"

"Okay. Okay, lady. We don't want any trouble." He turned to his companions, "You guys got any money? I'm broke." The others dug in their pockets and paid reluctantly.

"Now, you're still on private property, so I want you out of here. Plus, if I catch you again, the next time it will be double the price." I stood with my hands on my hips and watched them walk to the road. *At least they are clean.*

Larry experienced another sample of hippie disrespect while he worked on the pasture fence near the House on the Hill across the road. He used a big mattock, like a pickax, to loosen dirt and make it easier for the posthole digger to be rammed down and dig out the earth to plant a fence post. Then he would tamp around it with the blunt end of the mattock to hold the post tight and secure. While he worked, Rick, one of the remaining long-term tenants, walked up.

I had been cleaning the House on the Hill and walked out on the back porch to shake my mop. I listened to the conversation.

Rick told Larry, "Hey, man, I need you to give me a jump-start. I can't get my van going." He was not one of the more likeable tenants and always seemed demanding.

"I'll do it after I'm finished planting this post." Larry straightened up, wiped the sweat from his brow on his shirtsleeve and held the mattock in his other gloved hand.

"You can do that later, man. I'm supposed to meet some friends in town, and I'm late." He stepped a little closer and was eye-level with Larry. "So, you've gotta do it right now. Come on, man, it'll only take a minute. You can come back and finish this later."

"I'll help you when I get this post planted. Got it?" Larry lifted the tool up from his side and purposely rested it in both hands across his waist. I knew that he didn't appreciate anyone demanding a favor, and I saw his muscles tighten under his sweaty shirt.

Rick backed away. "Okay, okay. Get the post in and come as soon as you get done." He turned and stomped back to his van and I could almost see him tapping his foot counting the minutes.

When Larry finished, he walked down to his Jeep and pulled up next to the van. He hooked up the jumper cables and pushed down on his gas pedal for the jump. Rick turned his ignition and the van quickly began to purr and Larry unhooked the jumper cables. Later he told me. "Rick didn't bother to say thank you. I mumbled a few choice words under my breath. I'm glad that the Dippy Hippie Season is about over."

I laughed and agreed. Good riddance. Welcome summer guests.

Another gorgeous day at the lodge

Chapter 9

Panniers and Switchbacks (1969)

Spring moved forward and the new wranglers arrived in late May. Duke, his wife Doris and his brother Jud all began the '69 summer season.

In June, they scheduled an overnight pack trip to Cathedral Lake for a family. Duke located the canvas panniers, racks, tents and other equipment in the tack room. The panniers were square-type bags that fit over a saddle rack and rested on each side of the horse. Strap bindings held the panniers tight. Duke packed the gear and food in the two panniers. One tent was tied on the back of the packsaddle and another behind his saddle. Doris led when they rode out of camp and Duke took up the rear leading the packhorse and Jud stayed behind at the stables to take care of the other rides scheduled for the day.

Mid-afternoon, Duke rode back into camp leading the packhorse with just the saddle rack and no panniers. His cowboy hat tipped forward half-hiding his eyes and his shoulders drooped forward. His boots didn't stir up much dust as he slowly dismounted and came to the lodge.

"Uh, Larry, the panniers fell off the packhorse and the tent too. I don't know how it happened. I left them on the side of the trail and went back for them after we got the camp set up, but when I got back there, everything was gone. I can't believe someone would steal our stuff."

Larry's square jaw tightened and then he said, "You don't leave pack gear lying on the side of the trail, especially the panniers full of food, or the tent. You didn't pack right or they wouldn't have slipped off."

I listened and gave a sigh. "I'll get some steaks, potatoes, eggs, bacon, pancake mix and the rest of the foodstuff together. You take care of the packing, Larry." I headed to the store while Larry stomped down to the stables with Duke.

I hauled the food down to the stables and saw Duke had another tent and Larry had another set of panniers. I watched Larry demonstrate how to pack the food in the panniers and keep them even in weight for balance. Then he hooked the pannier straps over the rack crossbars on each side and cinched the bindings securely around the belly. He showed the proper way to tie the tent on the back of the rack. Larry had a great deal of knowledge on packing because he worked for the Forest Service out on the trails during school breaks in the summers. He had used a mule to pack in the supplies for a week or two out on the trail at a time.

"Okay, thanks," Duke said. Then he mounted his horse, took the reins of the packhorse, and headed back up the trail.

"He'd better return with the second set of tack." While we walked to the lodge, Larry said, "We're going to have Duke take us on an overnight pack trip up to Cathedral Lake. We'll act like tourists and see if he packs right, and how he sets up camp."

"Sounds good to me. I've never been up there. Mickey Payne can stay here with Susy and handle the guests. Glenn will be here to help too." Excitement filled me as I eagerly waited to see this high country that everyone exclaimed about. I had only hiked up to American Lake once and had never been to Cathedral Lake.

On the planned afternoon, Tina, Greg and I rode out of camp with Doris leading and Duke in the rear with the packhorse. Larry preferred to hike along behind us. We used the trail beside the creek up to and through Ashcroft, then through a field full of wildflowers. We turned up the trailhead to the lake. Eight year old Tina rode like a pro while Greg sat perched on his mare like a reluctant puppy. Soon, we started to climb the mountainside.

The trail began to weave back and forth on switchbacks as we ascended higher and higher. I had never ridden a horse on a narrow trail and became frightened when I looked down the steep side of the mountain. I clenched my teeth while holding tight to the reins. Then the trail widened again and began to wind among the pine and aspen. I gave a sigh. We arrived at the campsite among the trees a few yards below the lake.

On the trail to Cathedral Lake

Larry gave some quiet comments to Duke on the setup of the tents. He fought his eagerness to help and show how it could be done better.

We hiked to the lake and the children tossed rocks and played in the water. I took a deep breath of the pure mountain air, which had a hint of pine sweetness and the newly melted snow which dribbled over the rocks and dirt, giving an aroma of moisture mixed with earth. Cathedral Peak loomed above and still held much of the winter snow in its crevices.

Later, Doris grilled the dinner steaks ,and she certainly knew how to cook over an open fire. I watched fascinated. This was my first cookout meal and camp trip. How fun!

We kept shooing the camp robbers away from our dinner while eating. Camp robbers are the unofficial name for the Rocky Mountain Jays who are unscrupulous beggars for scraps of food. If not given food, they try to quickly snatch a piece and dash away. When we finished eating, they moved elsewhere. During the evening, we heard the coyotes singing down the mountainside. A porcupine wandered nearby, a marmot sat on the rocks warily spying on us ,and the deer and elk ventured nearby in the trees. An eagle flew high above in its search for food. I basked in God's glorious nature.

Night came quickly with a temperature drop to around freezing. Everyone retired to their toasty sleeping bags. My family shared one tent and the wranglers another. The high altitude had worn us out and we quickly fell asleep.

Early the next morning, we woke to the brisk clean air. The aroma of coffee, eggs, bacon and camp toast seduced our senses and we eagerly consumed breakfast.

Larry and I watched the children play by the lake while the wranglers packed up. I told him, "There's something fascinating about the mountains."

"You bet. When I was a kid I used to love to camp out with my buddies. Our kids will enjoy the experience many times, just like I did growing up."

The trip back home went smoothly and I would keep that memory. It was my only pack trip.

OK Corral? (1969)

Stable business thrived and the corral seldom contained any unused horses waiting for riders. Another use was needed for the wranglers that season.

Three old-timer residents of Aspen, Bob Sinclair, Delbert Copley and Jens Christiansen, held a Forest Service permit to pasture their cattle up Castle Creek in the summer. All the public land was considered open range and if a landowner didn't want the cattle on his land, he needed to fence off his property. The three men were collectively called "The Cattlemen" and they also owned land in the valley and elsewhere around Aspen. Ashcroft was not fenced and the cattle munched on the tall grass around the remaining buildings until someone shooed the cattle back down toward our property. They could meander into our camp because there was no gate at our drive. We would then shoo the cattle back up the valley.

Bob Sinclair rode into camp on his horse one mid-afternoon. His small stature sat proudly in the saddle. He reminded me of an old-fashioned cowboy straight out of the movies with his Stetson shading his face and his pistol strapped at his side, but hidden by his jacket. When he dismounted he said, "I checked on our cattle and I found three tents pitched by the creek on my land down in the canyon. I told the hippies that they were on private property, but they just laughed and said they wouldn't leave. They were pretty nasty and told me they were staying put. So I told 'em I'd be back."

Larry knew Bob's small appearance made them believe that he could be intimidated. "Hippies are camping all over anymore and they don't care if its on public or private land."

Bob nodded. "I'd sure appreciate it, if you and the wranglers would go down with me to help get them out of there. I think there are at least 12 of them…male and female."

Larry not only got Duke and Jud, but he also enlisted the aid of Norm Payne, and Mickey's son, Bill, who happened to be visiting that day. Larry gave a mischievous grin. "The more the merrier. We can run those guys off. Bill is young and big with hard muscles from his ranch work. He won't take any nonsense from anyone."

The men gathered at the lodge and soon drove caravan-style in pickups and Jeeps to face the trespassers. Larry returned smiling and seemed satisfied. "We met at the site and the hippies saw us walking toward them. The six guys lined up opposite us and belligerence set in on both sides. It must have looked like the OK Corral in living color." He laughed.

"What did you guys do?" I couldn't see any bruises.

"The group elected me as our spokesman and so I told those hippies that they were on private land and had to pack up and get out of there right then. Their leader told us that they didn't have to because the land belongs to everyone and Mother Nature is to be shared by all. So, they were going to stay. His buddies all agreed with a nod and 'Yeah man.' I thought we would have a fight, but I wanted to try again."

Larry was enjoying the story. "Well, what happened?" I asked eagerly.

"I told them that the land they were on is private land and they couldn't stay. I said they were to pack up and leave immediately on their own. Or, we would tear down their tents, and pack up for them, and it wouldn't be a pretty job. I added that they better get started because we'd only give them 10 minutes."

"Okay. So, you guys didn't have to fight did you?"

"No, Bob moved his jacket so that his holstered pistol showed and he gave a sly grin to the group. None of the rest of us carried a weapon, but Bob always had one while out on the range. He didn't want to run into a wild animal and not have some protection."

"Did the hippies have any guns?"

"No, and when they saw Bob's, it was the clincher. They looked at each other and reluctantly nodded their heads and one said 'no sweat' that they would leave. Then they began scurrying like ants in a disturbed nest, packing up as fast as they could. They threw everything in their three vans painted in psychedelic colors. A large peace sign decorated the back end of each. In no time, they were driving toward town and our group shook hands and came home." He definitely had a satisfied look.

"Well, maybe that will teach them that they can't just camp wherever they want."

That night a friend from town called and told Larry that a group went to the sheriff and said 20 men with guns ran them off. Larry roared with laughter.

It seemed that the word began to spread about Castle Creek valley and it would not put up with freeloading on private land. By the end of summer, we hoped there would be fewer hippie squatters in the valley…especially if the word continued to spread.

Moon Walk (1969)

No more trespassers were found and summer pushed onward. Then news came about the landing on the moon that would take place July 20, 1969. It created national excitement.

Larry told me, "We'll invite all the guests up here to watch since the cabins don't have TV. I'm sure a lot of them will want to see it."

"I'll spread the word. It's going to be quite a sight. Who would have thought we would ever see someone walking on the moon?" I certainly couldn't believe it.

On that eventful day, the lodge held 33 guests, plus us, all crammed into the lobby. Some sat on chairs or on the sofa and some sat on the floor with arms wrapped around knees. All eyes were on the small TV. The rabbit ears were adjusted to give the best picture possible. It was grainy, but no one noticed. Many leaned forward, not wanting to miss a thing. Tension filled the air, afraid something would go wrong.

The first communication from the moon was Armstrong's "Houston, Tranquility Base here. The Eagle has landed." The Apollo 11 landing was perfect. The hatch opened and Neil Armstrong slowly descended. As he stepped onto the moon surface, he radioed back to NASA and the world, "That's one small step for man, one giant leap for mankind."

Our group applauded and yelled "hooray!" We had just watched a glorious piece of history. I knew that space adventures had begun earlier, but not with man setting foot on a satellite. The United States and its archenemy, the Soviet Union, were vying to gain power in astronautics. The Apollo walk put the United States ahead in the space race.

I served coffee from our 32-cup percolator. Some made a toast with the cups; others made a toast with their beers. National pride helped in this time of discord in the country.

The next day the *Rocky Mountain News* had a big headline: "YANK WALKS ON MOON." The article stated that Neil A. Armstrong and Edwin E. Aldrin, Jr. landed the Eagle at 240,000 miles from Earth. It described Armstrong in his bulky space suit with the bubble on his head, slowly climbing out of the spaceship and down the ladder. Michael Collins remained in the mother ship 69 miles above, which continued to girdle the moon as it waited for the return of the two men 22 hours later. The cost of the expedition was said to be $24 billion.

The government knew this historic event would give people a sense of hope and renew their faith in the United States. But I wondered if it would really change anything.

Drowning (1969)

The children were more interested in the two Shetland ponies than the moon landing. The stables had leased the ponies, Scotty and Irish, for the summer. Tina, Greg and Susy were at the stables every day and rode them around the grounds. It became an attraction for the tourists' children and the rental of the Shetlands brought in more income. Parents sat their tots on the ponies and lead them around the camp. The small children loved it. On a warm sunny day, the ponies were tied up to a bush near the back pond by the stables, so they could graze on the tall grass. The Shetlands munched with abandon.

Soon a young woman who rented the Trout cabin, closest to the pond, ran to the office and yelled, "Help, Mrs. Brand, get help!"

"What is it?" My eyes widen, ready for bad news.

"Scotty got tangled up in the rope and fell in the pond. He panicked and couldn't get out. My husband jumped in and pulled him out, but he doesn't look good."

By the time I got to the water-dripping pony, the wranglers were already leading Scotty toward the stables and we called the vet. They dried, cleaned and talked lovingly to help him relax, but he couldn't breathe. Water had gotten into Scotty's lungs.

The vet came, but could do nothing. There was no way to clear the lungs. When he left, everyone had long, sad faces. After an all day fight to breathe, Scotty gave up and died…death by drowning, but on land.

The men dragged the pony down into the pasture. It took almost an hour to dig a large enough cavity. Then they buried Scotty. The children gathered wild flowers and put them on the grave. A child prayed, "God is good, God is great. May Scotty be in heaven and have lots to eat." That was it and the children went on to play. Soon, the trauma headed to the forgotten land.

The horses never failed to bring problems and worry. Some problems were caused by the city dudes who didn't understand the equestrian behavior. A few riders could not, or would not, control their horses when heading back to the stables. If not reined in, occasionally a horse raced back through camp to the hitching post for its oats upon arrival. The rider always bounced uncontrollably and screamed for mercy while holding tight to the saddle horn and legs straight out, stiff, as if trying to brake. When the horse reached the hitching post, he would stop abruptly and the rider would loose momentum and almost fly over the horse's head.

On a hot summer day, one of the horses began racing back. I heard the screams and knew what was happening. I looked out the kitchen window and saw the screeching rider hanging onto the saddle horn and her horse galloping toward the stables. Then I froze when I saw Susy playing in the road leading to the stables. "Oh God!" The horse galloped straight toward Susy. I bolted out the door and just knew I would find my daughter trampled to death.

When the horse approached Susy, he jumped over her in one swift, graceful movement as if he were a show horse vying for a ribbon. She looked up when the horse jumped over her, but was not frightened and continued to play. When I reached her, I picked her up and checked every inch of her body. Not even a tiny scratch could be found. I walked back to the lodge holding her tight.

"Susy, you cannot play in the road. Do you understand me? Do not let me catch you playing in the road again." I tried to keep close tabs on Susy, but the lobby buzzer, or the phone, usually kept me busy.

Car Scrape (1969)

The tranquil summer days flew by and Susy did not play in the road again. My mother arrived in August for about a month's visit. Grandma became a big help with cooking, laundry, and the children. She was short like me, but her curls were streaked with a delightful gray and white. Her temperament was the opposite of mine and she was always a proper lady. She loved to read to Tina, Greg and Susy. Years of teaching had taught her how to handle children and she had handled me…until I grew up.

On a sunny day, we two women drove to Aspen for groceries, mail and the newspaper. When I neared an intersection, a VW van stopped in front of us. A lanky young guy on the opposite side of the street, sauntered over to the driver's side, bent down, and leaned into the open driver's window. His thin dark hair fell forward as he began visiting.

I waited for the van to move again, but it didn't. So, I walked up and asked, "Would you please drive across the intersection and pull into that parking spot right over there so I can get by?" I pointed to the open spot across the street. "I don't want to go around you, because it's too close to the intersection and I can't see. I could hit an oncoming car at the cross section. Will you please move?"

The hippie straightened up and sneered, "No. He's not moving. I'm talking to him. If you don't like it, go around, lady." He leaned back into the van window and continued to chat. His feet were over a foot away from the van, and his backside stuck out about even with his feet.

"Okay, Mr. Smarty Pants," I hissed. I gritted my teeth and stomped back to the car, stepped on the gas and swerved around, getting as close to him as possible. As I passed him, the side of my car scraped the rear pockets of his jeans. He immediately straightened up, moved close to the van, swore at me, and used hand gestures. By then, I had made it safely through the intersection and went on. I didn't wait to hear what he yelled and gestured, but had a pretty good idea.

"Joanne, what on earth were you thinking? Don't get so mad." My mother clasped her hands tightly in her lap around her purse.

"Oh, these danged hippies think they own the world and I'm not about to let them bully me. I didn't hurt him."

"Well, just remember that tempers can fly both ways."

We continued on our way, and did not run into anymore hippie problems. Grandma was thankful.

Labor Day weekend came with a full camp and the last big outdoor hurrah for the families before school. Snow arrived that Sunday. We received only about 4 inches, but a few guests from the South were worried they might get snowed in and left early. By the next day, the sun came out and the snow melted. After the weekend, business died down and only a couple of cabins were rented to tourists.

Then we prepared the cabins for the long-term tenants. Ahh! Let the battles begin!

I often walked down by the Homestead cabin to sit on my boulder and watch the season move forward. The surrounding mountains were ablaze with orange and gold mixed with the deep hibernating pine greens. The peaks were accumulating snow and Star Peak was brilliant with white. Fall was my favorite season because of all the glorious hues and the virgin snow beginning to build on the mountains.

Life continued from season to season and the Vietnam War continued from year to year. We saw on TV and in newspapers thousands of Americans demonstrate against the war. The country cried for a stop to the killing.

So many servicemen have to weather the storm of hate in the United States and still try to hold their heads up high. How many will instead retreat within and suffer mentally in silence. This won't be the last war. History always seems to repeat itself. Will peace ever come?

Chapter 10

Pay and Private Line! (1969)

Peace was not to be, but at least we could have a little at our lodge from the phone harassment. Larry tore down the old front porch in the fall. A cinderblock foundation replaced the stone base and he erected a new lobby in front of our living room that had been the lobby for years. I admired Larry's ability to apply his college engineering and drafting skills, plus his common sense when building…or on any other problem.

Now the reception counter sat in front of the entrance to our home. There were plenty of chairs for guests. Only friends would be allowed to go behind the counter now to visit in our living room. The best change of all really thrilled me—the pay phone in our new lobby and our private line! We no longer had to share the phone line.

I exclaimed, "How about that? We finally have our own private phone line and a pay phone too, Larry. No more harassment since we don't have to share a line."

"Yeah. MK Mine sure helped us. They paid more of the cost than we did."

Larry finished the new lobby just as the fall season died and winter galloped in on the wicked winds of a fierce snowstorm. Snow swept onto the drive filling it with waves of white just like sand sweeping over a desert. Plowing was a constant rumble of the blade sliding over ruts and then the loud whop when it hit the snow bank hard. By now, I found the mountains beautiful in the winter and no longer felt the season gave no color or loneliness. The snow glistened with white purity as a tribute to the joy of a new season.

The payphone was in earshot of our office and brought additional insight into the new era. I heard two different sides and found some good tenants and some that floored me with their disrespect and foul language.

I worked on correspondence one afternoon and overheard one of our non-favorite tenants on the pay phone. "Mom, I didn't get my check today. I've got to have it and you sure as hell better send it fast or I'm coming home for it."

Silence came for a minute while he listened. Then, "You tell Dad to get it in the mail tomorrow. No messin' around." He slipped in several expletives. "I need it for gas and my ski ticket." Another pause…then, "Quit your crying, Mom." He paused. "Okay, okay. Just get the damned check here to General Delivery fast." He slammed the receiver down, cussed some more and left.

I told Larry what I'd heard. "No way would I put up with that. I'd set my kids straight and they'd be on their own."

"We wouldn't send any money, that's for sure. Don't these kids have any pride in themselves?" Larry shook his head back and forth.

That tenant was often seen sitting on his porch with friends smoking a joint. We saw a few others smoking pot on their porches also. Upon seeing it, my comment remained the same each time, "What a waste of their minds." I hoped my children listened.

Two brothers came to use the payphone one afternoon. They called their folks every so often, but I never heard any yelling for money or any swearing. They seemed to have a normal conversation about the happenings since the last call. Donny and Kenny rented a rustic cabin and worked in town. They were nice enough boys, just out for adventure, and they always paid rent on time. We knew they were afraid that they would be drafted into the service and sent to Vietnam. Like all young men, they had to register with the U. S. Government for the draft as soon as they turned 18 years of age. These two told Larry they had received their "greetings" and went home for their physicals. They were awaiting the results. I overheard them discussing the draft after a call home and no results had been received yet.

Donny said, "If I pass and have to go in the Army, I'm going to Canada instead. I'd rather do that than go to Vietnam to kill or be killed." He appeared to be the younger brother and of slight build. I often saw him on his porch reading rather than smoking pot. I thought he had to be a gentle, friendly young man.

"Well if I pass, I guess I'll go. I just pray that I won't end up in Vietnam, or be killed." Kenny said. Taller and more physically fit than his brother.

100

I imagined he may have been captain of his football team. He also seemed friendly, but more outgoing than Donny. They were only about a year's difference in age, from what I could tell.

I heard Donny say, "I hope we hear soon. This waiting is the worst part of the whole thing."

A few days later, I worked on correspondence again. Donny and Kenny called their parents to see if the mail contained the results of their physicals. I heard the conversation, without even trying to listen, because they spoke loudly over the long distance line. Kenny began the call and talked to his Dad. The results had been received. Soon, he jumped up in the air and let out a high, loud whoop. "Yahoo! Hallelujah! Hot damn! I didn't pass the physical. I won't have to go."

Then he listened again for the results of Donny's physical. The tenseness in the air seemed to freeze time. Suddenly, Kenny jumped and yelled, "Hallelujah again! Donny, you didn't pass either." He looked upward and said, "God Almighty, thank you, Lord."

Soon, they told their parents that they loved them and hung up. They left the lobby with arms around each other's shoulders, almost dancing back to their cabin, as they whooped and yelled. Their free arms flew up to the sky and their feet bounced to the beat of their cheers.

I had never heard more elated yelps of joy and relief. I had to smile and these two boys proved to me that there were still some decent kids after all.

I told Larry the news. He said, "I heard that Kenny had a hernia, and Donny has some eye problems, I guess. I figured they would be deferred."

One-Eyed Vet (1969)

Another tenant, George Donovan, had already spent his time in Vietnam. He rented the rustic Paintbrush near the lodge. Tall, lean 20-some years old, he had dark hair that accentuated one deep hazel eye and it gave a hint of mischief. The other eye was covered with a patch. His disability did not tarnish his personality, which shined with his smile.

George told us the reason for the eye patch. "Before my tour of duty ended, my buddy stepped on a land mine." He paused and swallowed hard. "That's how I lost the sight in my right eye. Shrapnel hit me all over, and I've still got one piece next to my spine. The doctors said it was too risky to remove or I'd be paralyzed. I have to watch it. If I hit it wrong, that's all for me and I'll be using a wheel chair. I got an honorable discharge from the Marines last year."

Larry asked, "I know you like to ski, but is that good for your back? You need to be careful."

"I don't think skiing will hurt my back. It hasn't so far and it's my favorite thing to do. Shooting down the mountain feels like all the freedom in the world. I can go as fast as I want and swoop back and forth and around and over each mound." He paused for a second as if he was picturing the scene. "It's like being in Freedom Heaven with no nightmares or pain." He had a carefree optimism and why not? He'd spent his fear in Vietnam and paid his price.

On a clear, frigid winter night, George had a party in his cabin. His many friends crowded in and loud music blared. Liquor bottles clanked, and laughter carried through camp along with the music. I always seemed to think the worst and I just knew that some drugs were being used…at least Mary Janes. Marijuana always seemed to be present.

I looked out the window about 11:00 p.m. and saw some boys rush out to get something from the back of a van. It looked like a 4'x8' board. I quickly got our binoculars to check. Another backed up the van as close to the cabin as he could and someone swung open the back doors. Then they carefully moved someone, who had been lying on the ground, onto the slab as if it were a stretcher. I couldn't make out who in the dim porch light. Two of them slid the "stretcher" into the back of the van and climbed in. Two more hopped in the front and they drove off. That ended the party and the others left. The camp fell silent.

I told Larry, "I don't know what happened, but I'll bet it was an overdose and that they're heading to the hospital."

"Could be. At least the party has ended and all is quiet. I'm going to bed. You might as well too. You can't sit there all night peeking out with the binoculars and waiting for someone to come back. They haven't broken any rules."

I knew he was right, but I had a hard time falling asleep with all sorts of images going through my mind. What is an overdose like? Who was it? What happened?

The next day, I walked to the shower house to clean and came upon a tenant. She had been at the party the night before. "How about that party last night? Why did it break up early? What was all the excitement about?" I tried to appear nonchalant, but probably didn't succeed.

"Well, George went outside to get more stove wood from the rack and he slipped and fell. He thought he'd become paralyzed if he moved…the shrapnel from Vietnam, you know. So he yelled for help." She stopped to see if I nodded, which I did. "So, anyway, some of the guys put him on a board and rushed him down to the hospital. The doctor took X-rays and said that he was okay, but would be sore for a few days. So, they brought him back here. We sure were scared."

"Well, I'm glad he's not seriously hurt. That would have been horrible."

Later I scolded myself. I had been so sure it was drug-related. *My motto seems to be guilty until proven innocent. I have to learn to give the benefit of doubt. Larry keeps trying to get that through my head. I guess I can't trust these kids because of all the things I consider wrong in their behavior. Yet, do I have the right to judge them?*

Long-Term Capers (1969)

"Jeff the Jerk," as Larry called him, seemed the opposite of George. A large, muscled young man, he had pale blue eyes that seemed cold with anger. He rented the Homestead in October and always seemed to grumble about something. He got 2 months behind on rent by December and kept promising payment, but no money came. We gave up on the promises and had an attorney draw up an eviction notice.

Jeff came to the lodge after he was served with the pay or vacate notice. His blonde hair fell forward as he leaned on the counter and one hand scratched his thick beard. "What happens next?"

"You'll just have to wait and find out." I wasn't sure myself what was next.

The next day Jeff came again and asked what would happen. I could see he fidgeted nervously and my answer remained the same, "Just wait and find out." By the third time I said it with a smirk. He got more nervous with each passing day and would not leave his cabin. He told me he possessed several guns and didn't want the sheriff to come and confiscate them. I didn't like the idea of him having guns because he seemed so angry about everything. It couldn't be good. *Would he get mad and use them on us?*

When I told Larry, he said not to worry, but I did. Later a tenant told us that Jeff was afraid that if he went to town, we would change the lock and he wouldn't be able to get his belongings, especially his guns.

He did not vacate and a court date was set, but he did not appear in court on the appointed day of the eviction hearing and the judge ruled in favor of Elk Mountain Lodge. A sheriff's deputy delivered a written notice to Jeff. He was told if he didn't vacate by the next day, he and all his belongings would be thrown out.

The next morning, Larry didn't see Jeff's van so he went to check. He knocked, but got no answer and tried to open the door with his key, but it wouldn't budge. Peeking through a window he saw that Jeff had left, but barred the door from the inside. He checked the windows and all were locked. One side window had been nailed shut from the outside, apparently after Jeff climbed out. Larry had to use his hammer to pry the nails out of the window frame so I could climb in and remove the bar holding the door tight.

"Look at this mess!" I told Larry when he walked in.

"It doesn't surprise me."

"Well, I'd like to give him a piece of my mind," I thought about all the hours of cleaning and removing all the trash.

A tenant from another cabin came over and peeked in. "I heard Jeff leave last night. He piled his stuff in his van and raced out of here."

Larry replied, "I don't know why he thought he could stay without paying."

We weren't through with trouble, though, and more long-term problems soon arrived. We rented the Buckskin to Cole, known by Larry as "Cagey Cole." He had long arms and legs and reminded me of a sneaky spider. When he didn't pay his rent, I told him to move out. "No problem," he said. "I'll move into Kent's cabin and stay with him." Kent rented the Columbine.

When Cole moved out of the Buckskin, he left a damaged and filthy cabin. He had pounded large nails into the pine paneling to hang up blankets and a wooden chair had been used to chop his wood, which broke the chair seat and one leg. He nailed a stained dirty rug to the wood flooring and to top it off, he removed the doorknob leaving a gaping hole. The door could not stay latched or locked. There seemed no reason for him to take the knob. My temper flared and I wrote a list of the damages and the total due. Then, I marched down to Kent's cabin with my bill.

"Cole, you ruined the floor and walls with those big nails. You broke the chair chopping wood on it and you even took the doorknob. Plus, you left us to clean up your filth. Here's the list of damages. You owe more than your deposit and I want it paid now."

He grinned, stooped over, and rummaged through his duffle bag. "Well, if you want the doorknob, here it is." He pulled it out and handed it to me. "I'll try to get some money to you next month. There's no reason to get so shook up over this."

I angrily shook the doorknob at him. "You owe rent, damaged the cabin, took the doorknob, and now you don't know why I'm upset? You have to accept responsibility for your actions, Cole. But since you won't, you just move out of here. I don't want any more of your irresponsibility. I want to see you gone by tomorrow."

He saw my anger and looked like he expected to be hit with the doorknob. "Okay, okay. I'll leave. Don't have a heart attack, Mrs. B." His hands rose on each side of his shoulders.

I walked briskly back to the lodge swinging the doorknob. I hated to see these tenants not accept responsibility. I considered Cole old enough to know better.

Glenn put the doorknob back on, but changed the lock and key because he learned locksmithing. By the next morning, Cole had moved into town. I wondered if he would ever become a responsible citizen.

This became the winter of all discontent. It seemed these young long-term tenants were getting the best of us.

Another rustic cabin had been rented to "Dippy Danny" who seemed to be high on drugs too often. He had a cat, acceptable under conditions in the lease. One Saturday, he drove out of camp in his VW van. In a few days his cat could be heard inside his cabin meowing pitifully and Danny had not returned.

Another few days passed and no Danny. I told Larry, "He has been gone for a week and that cat must be starving. We're not supposed to enter a unit that's rented, but this is getting to be an emergency. We don't want the cat to die and we have no idea where Danny is, plus he's past due on rent. Maybe he just packed up and left. I checked with the other tenants and no one knows where he went."

"Well, I think this is an emergency and we can't just let the cat die. We have to go in."

When we entered the cabin, the litter box odor almost gagged us and the cat begged for attention. We found some cat food sealed in a large canister and I filled one bowl with food and another with water from the spigot outside. I put more kitty litter in the box. It would be left for Danny to clean out, if he came back.

Larry noticed that the mattress for the bed was gone. "He can't just take our mattress. I'm taking something for collateral just in case he returns. He may come back and try to move out in the middle of the night. I know it isn't legal, but I'm taking something anyway."

"I'll put a note on the door in case he returns. It'll say to pay or vacate and to return the mattress in good condition or pay for a new one." I looked around, "What on earth is good enough for collateral in this mess?"

"All I see is this old banjo, which can't be worth anything, but it's something." We took it back with us and in a few days, we fed the cat again and got more water for it.

Five days later, "Dippy Danny" returned. He immediately stomped up to the lodge taking long, quick strides and his shoulder-length coal black hair bounced with each step. When he entered, I could feel the anger before he uttered a word.

He yelled a tirade of obscenities, and pounded on the counter as his dark eyes squinted in hateful slits. In between the swear words he yelled, "I want my banjo back now. It's my dad's. I put your damned mattress in my van to sleep on and there's nothing wrong with it. You have no right to get upset and I'll come up with the rent later. Give me my banjo." His bobbing head kept time with each obscene word interjected.

I never used foul language with the tenants because I would not lower myself to their level; however, I was tempted this time. I just kept repeating, "When you pay your rent, you'll get your banjo." I stood firm as Danny called me more foul names than I even knew existed.

Larry walked in the back door and Danny's bellowing obscenities hit him like a lead pipe. He burst around the corner and into the lobby and faced "Dippy Danny" as if he were a 250-pound Irish fighter towering over a weakling. His fists were clinched on the counter, muscles bulging in his shirt sleeves and his eyes showed a threatening rage.

"Don't you ever talk to my wife that way, got it? We didn't know if you had moved out or what. You left your cat to starve, you owe rent, and you took our mattress. Now, when you pay rent you'll get your stinking banjo back. And if you don't get out of here right now, I'll beat the hell out of you." I had never seen Larry that angry.

That silenced Danny. He knew he came close to excruciating pain and he backed away. He looked from Larry to me, turned and stomped out in a huff slamming the door. I wanted to make him come back and close the door properly, the same as I would my children when they were mad, but I decided I better let well enough alone.

In a couple of days, Danny stomped up to the office. "Here's your rent. Now give me my banjo." He threw the cash on the counter and glared at me.

"Okay. Let me write a receipt and then I'll get it." I took my time. "Here you are. Thank you." I handed him both the receipt and his banjo. I did feel bad that he almost lost his dad's banjo, but maybe he'd be more responsible after this.

He grabbed the instrument, stomped out the door slamming it hard. I let it go again.

The winter hadn't died yet. A young couple rented a rustic cabin and they had a little boy about 4 years old. Both Blake and Maggie were college graduates, and Maggie majored in child psychology. They were taking the winter off to ski.

"We want to be free and do our own thing," Blake told me proudly.

Several days later, I saw the little boy playing outside in the snow without a coat or mittens. Later, little Johnny became sick with a terrible cold. After a few days of coughing, a runny nose and fever, he got worse. Maggie came to the office and told me, "Johnny has had a fever of 103°F to 104°F for 3 days. Now, he's incoherent and really burning up. I guess it's time to call the hospital to see if I should take him in."

I stared at her. "Yes, it is. Your little boy needs help right away from the sounds of it."

Maggie answered all the questions posed by the nurse over the phone and then listened. When she hung up she said, "The hospital says to bring him in immediately."

Soon, the couple left for town. In a few hours, the hospital called the lodge asking me to have Blake and Maggie come back because little Johnny kept crying and couldn't be quieted. She said the parents left as soon as their son had been placed in a room. She also said that the child probably would not have survived the night, if he had not been brought in. He had pneumonia and was in serious condition.

I hadn't seen Blake and Maggie drive in, but just to be sure I walked over to their cabin and knocked. I got no answer and their truck was nowhere to be seen. I had no way to get hold of them, so I kept watch. They came home after 2 hours of my pacing the floor waiting for them and worrying about little Johnny. I immediately bundled up and hurried over to their cabin.

"The hospital called about 2 hours ago and they need you back there right away. Your little boy is crying, scared, and won't quiet down."

Maggie gave a sigh. "He was fine when we left the hospital, so we went to a friend's for tea and a visit. Damn! Now I won't get a good night's sleep."

I looked at her in astonishment. If one of my children was in the hospital and almost died, I wouldn't have left and gone for tea and a visit. How could they?

The 1969 winter season turned out not being a good winter, but it taught us more about the hippie free-thinkers. The tenants came up with something new each year and usually not good. What next?

Chapter 11

We're In Pictures…Kinda (1970)

Later that winter, when the back pond had at least 2 feet of ice, Larry decided to plow the snow off so we could ice skate. He slowly eased the Jeep onto the ice, inched a little farther and again a little farther. If he broke through the ice, the Jeep and plow would sink into the muck and icy water. Then, he'd have to wade out and hook the winch to the truck in order to pull the Jeep out. He lucked out and the ice held and it didn't crack, break into pieces, or even moan. Larry gave a sigh of relief. It did not take long to clear the pond. Then he hooked up a hose and covered the pond with a thin layer of water to freeze and leave a smooth surface. By the next day, the ice glistened in the sun as if diamonds were clustered into one immense crystal on a bed of polished blue-white. On crisp sunny days we ice-skated between snowmobile tours or in the early evenings. Tina and Greg raced from one end to the other. Susy preferred to glide, make circles, and try to skate backwards. After each snowfall, Larry plowed the pond and re-glazed. We enjoyed ice skating, but the long-term tenants didn't seem interested.

When we came back from town, rounded the bend and saw the glistening pond, it could have been on a postcard. We weren't the only ones that noticed that picturesque scene. A New York advertising agency scouted the mountains for a perfect setting to make a commercial for Enco Gas Company. When they drove by Elk Mountain Lodge and saw our ice skating pond, they stopped in. The director asked for permission to use the pond for a segment in their TV commercial. The fee offered seemed quite generous and Larry readily agreed.

The director seemed to be a man charged with energy. His hair bounced wild in the dry air and his eyes bounced from here to there, never settling. "We're going to hire kids from the skating club in town for the ice skating segment."

"Okay, as long as you are responsible for the kids. I'll get the pond as smooth as I can." Larry asked how soon they wanted to film.

"Tomorrow, okay? We'll hire a professional ice-sculptor from town to build a snowman. We think it will look good on that slope over to the side." He pointed between the lodge and the road.

"I can have the pond ready by tomorrow. My kids can build pretty good snowmen. How about using them to make it?"

"Sorry, man, but we've got to make this a top-notch snowman for the commercial." Off he went to instruct the crew. His arms flew this way and that as he directed the crew on where to check camera angles and use the sunlight. Soon they left to make more arrangements in town.

The next day, a larger crew arrived plus the skaters and the snow sculptor and we watched all the action. Larry said, "This film crew sure is a crazy bunch. They're hyper and flitting around like cats on catnip. I don't understand half

The picturesque Chipmunk cabin all covered in snow

of what the director is saying when he gives instructions to the crew and it's not just the fast talk, but also the lingo or expressions."

I chuckled. "Yeah, and they're full of adrenaline or something that's keeping them high and happy. Of course, it could just be this high mountain air."

"When they need something for a shoot, they dole out the cash like its just paper or candy. They gave me a twenty just to plow a pile of snow where they wanted it. I'll move a lot more snow, if they keep giving out twenties."

Mickey Payne helped me prepare a lunch for the crew and skaters of about 30 people. A beautiful warm, sunny day sure made me thankful we could serve it outside. We set it up buffet-style out in the drive on a couple of long tables with paneling placed on saw horses and covered with white sheets for tablecloths. We put out a variety of cold cuts and cheeses for sandwiches, several salads, relishes, condiments, soda, coffee and homemade cakes and cookies for dessert. Everyone devoured the food.

It took the full day of shooting to satisfy the director. Then they loaded up their equipment and finally left. After they were gone, we gave a sigh of relief, but it had been fun to see how commercials were made. Life for us would get back to normal, if there could be such a thing.

The rest of the 1970 winter passed with no more advertising agencies, no snowmobile accidents and no more hippie problems. Ahh, how peaceful it became!

Spring arrived late, but finally the intense sun began to melt the snow and ice on the pond. Then we were in the mud season with the children, dog and cat making dirty tracks throughout the house. Larry and Glenn did not want my wrath and took their boots off when they came in. Training the children was as bad as training hippies! Spring sun dried the mud and soon the road turned to dirt and dust.

Kent State War Protest

The whole world was changing, not just the season. We followed everything through TV, newspaper and radio. Larry looked at the paper when he came from town with the latest edition the last week of May. "Joanne, did you hear about the protest at Kent State University, in Ohio?"

"Some. What does the paper say?" I poured us each a cup of coffee and sat at the table.

"Well, in a nut shell, the ROTC building burned to the ground, four students were killed and nine wounded."

"Lord! I heard that the kids were protesting because President Nixon sent troops into Cambodia." We had heard before that the Mayor of Kent called the Governor for help. Rumors said there were radical revolutionaries on the campus ready to destroy the buildings. The Ohio National Guard arrived that night.

Larry added, "The protestors set the ROTC building on fire and 1,000 demonstrators blocked the firemen and cheered while it burned to the ground. Tear gas finally dispersed the crowd." I shivered at the word "fire."

He continued, "The report says that the next day 1,000 Ohio Guardsmen were on campus and ready for action. By noon on the 4th, about 3,000 protestors came and the National Guard was ordered to disperse the crowd or use teargas. The Guardsmen got trapped and the protestors began to yell and throw rocks at them. The Guard finally made it back up a hill and then at the top 28 turned and fired. It says some shot up in the air or into the ground and some shot into the crowd." Larry paused and his voice lowered. "It ended with four students being killed and nine wounded. That ended the protest, but look at this photograph."

I leaned over him to see. "How horrible!" It showed a young girl kneeling over the body of a male student. Her arms were held up over him in anguish. "You can almost hear her cries, and look at her expression of terror and horror. I can't imagine the chaos and anger the shooting must have created. What a pity."

"When you think of it, though, the Guards were probably scared and wanted to end the situation. Maybe they didn't think they would make it out safe. Or, maybe they thought they had been ordered to fire. Who knows?"

"But, how sad that it came to this. We have enough killing with the war."

When will all this hate and violence stop? Isn't there some way that the country can become one nation again and heal?

Bush Cash (1970)

Before the summer rush began, Larry and I decided to again take our annual vacation. Every spring, when it was quiet, we headed to cities and excitement to get away by ourselves and see a different world far from country life. We needed that relaxation after the winter's stress. Glenn usually took his vacation at a different time. Mickey Payne always agreed to take care of the children. Larry and I headed for the bright lights of Las Vegas and the West Coast.

We went to many shows when in Las Vegas and also enjoyed the lounge shows. While on the West Coast, we toured the tourist places and spent evenings on the beach. When we returned home, everything had remained under control. The children were clean and well fed, the house was clean, the laundry done and all as it should be.

Although everything went smoothly, Mickey couldn't wait to tell us about the "Passion Pit" treasure. The small cabin got its name because it had been used for storage in the past and the ranch cats had made it their home. Many kittens were born there...thus, the name, "Passion Pit." It had since been cleaned and remodeled into a rustic abode.

Mickey eagerly told us, "I walked toward the creek with little Susy in hand. When I got near the Passion Pit, I looked at it and the bush, still not budded, had green on it. I stared and then walked over. There were one-dollar bills sitting on the branches. I couldn't believe it! Despite the weather recently, all these bills were in good condition. I picked them up, and counted them... there were 20 bills...all $1 bills."

"My God, we've got a money tree." Larry laughed as his head tilted upward and his hands rose to the sky. We all joked about the money bush, and hoped it would "bloom" again.

Mickey asked, "I wonder whose money it is. How did it get there?"

"It probably belonged to one of the hippies who rented the cabin. Maybe they had an envelope of cash that they stashed away and forgot." Larry laughed again.

I thought about it for a moment. "Could be. Or, maybe it's from some drug exchange and they might have been afraid to come back for it when they remembered. Or, maybe they were high, hid the cash and then didn't remember where. I sure don't know how it came out of hiding, though."

Larry said, "Since no one has come to claim it and the cabin is vacant, it doesn't belong to anyone. So Mickey, you get to keep the money, but if the bush blooms again, I get it."

We all laughed, but didn't wait for another cash blossoming. No such luck!

Not for Horses! (1970)

By the end of May, the summer tourist season began in full force. It also brought new wranglers: Tim and his wife. The horse business had grown considerably and another cowboy, Fran, had also been hired to help the wranglers and we hired his wife, Lynn, as our maid.

In July, a couple rented two packhorses for several days of camping at Cathedral Lake. They had their own Arabian horses to ride, which were much more impressive looking than our stable's plain dude horses. The packhorses were loaded and the couple left leading them, saying they didn't need a guide. The well-marked trail wouldn't be any trouble without a guide: however, we knew our horses were suited for the mountains, but we weren't sure about their Arabians.

Late that afternoon, the husband raced back to the stables, on his wife's horse. "I need help," he squeaked, out of breath.

After Tim found out what happened, he came up to the lodge and told us, "The guy said they got to the lake and decided to go on over Electric Pass since they still had plenty of daylight." He stopped for a minute to make sure it registered...Electric Pass!

That pass is a difficult, dangerous hiking trail above Cathedral Lake. The trail reaches the top at 13,500 feet and there is no definable trail back down the other side. It was, and is, strictly a hiking trail. It is recommended that Electric Pass hiking begin early in the morning after a night at Cathedral Lake because there can be an early afternoon storm and lightning hits are a common occurrence.

Tim continued, "He said the trail got real narrow and turned to mostly loose shale. They came to a point where his Arabian and the packhorse behind started to slip and the shale crumbled away. Both scrambled to get their footing, but panicked." He stopped to inhale deeply. Then he continued, "The guy jumped off and slid a ways, but dug his heels in and caught himself, but both horses rolled down the mountainside."

I could almost hear the wretched, sickening sound of horseflesh, saddle and panniers crashing against rock and sliding on the shale. It would be a horrible, sickening sound.

"I told him that Electric Pass is not for horses. Didn't they see it marked on the map...only for hikers?" Tim took his hat off and wiped his sweaty brow and pushed his hair back as he replaced his hat.

"What about the horses?" Larry asked.

"They landed on their feet on a small out-cropping about 500 feet down. He said they looked dazed and frozen."

"So, they are alive and probably okay?"

"Yeah, I guess so. He didn't know what to do and figured the best thing was to come back here for help. His wife had been a ways behind and stopped before her horse slid. They backed her mare and the other packhorse down to a wider spot where they could turn around and get back to the lake."

"Well, ignorance wins no favor with me." Larry seemed almost as angry as Tim.

"I agree. The guy said the pass didn't look that bad and that sometimes maps are wrong. I sure hope he has learned his lesson." Tim took a deep breath. "Everyone is out on rides, so will you go up with me, Larry? I told the guy to give his horse some water and walk him for a while to cool him off and I'd check with you."

Larry agreed to go and it wasn't long before they began climbing the trail, hoping to beat the dusk. I anxiously awaited their return, but knew it would be hours…and it was. They arrived back at the lodge about 10:00 p.m., dog-tired and hungry. Tim drug himself back to his quarters. Larry unwound with a beer and sandwiches while telling me about the rescue.

"When we arrived at the site, Tim and I scooted down the steep drop-off to the ledge where the horses stood. Neither horse had any injuries except for a few scrapes and bruises. The panniers were still intact on the packhorse. The fancy leather saddle had some scrapes and sat askew."

"How were the horses when you got there?"

"Well, both were terrified, trembled like crazy and were paralyzed on the ledge. Only their bulging eyes moved, following us. Their nostrils flared in and out in short rapid breaths. Tim and I kept saying 'It's okay fella. It's okay.' We tried to calm them and gently massaged their necks. Then we removed the panniers from the packhorse, but decided that the saddle would be fine on the Arabian." He took a long sip of his beer and stretched his legs out.

"We tried to coax them to head up to the trail, but they wouldn't budge. They were shaking statues. We coaxed and begged, but they seemed as strong as tanks in stubbornness. We finally knew coaxing wouldn't work and we'd have to dig out a trail all the way back up."

He told me that Tim had brought a small folding pack shovel and began digging the shale. Larry used his gloved hands to widen the trail and pack it down with his feet.

The makeshift path finally became wide enough for horses to walk single file. Tim took hold of the Arabian's reins and patted her nose and talked sweetly while he gently pulled the reins to urge the horse to move. Patience is a virtue and Tim proved that. Finally, the horse took a cautious step, then another and began to show her trust in Tim as she began to climb the new path. Larry said he took Tim's lead and softly coaxed and coaxed and soon the packhorse began to step forward again and again. It was slow going, but they made it back to the main trail and then down to safe ground below the pass. Tim and Larry scooted back down to haul up the panniers and fought the oncoming night. They finally made it back up before darkness crept over the pass. What a blessing that a lightning storm never materialized.

When the horses were secured, the couple decided to camp at the lake that night. Larry and Tim left and he told them, "I don't think we have to warn you about the pass."

The next day, the couple returned the packhorses. They were more humble and said they'd decided to cut short their camping trip.

Maroon Bells Rescue/Recovery (1970)

August 15, 1970, brought more news of disaster on the peaks. A group of four attempted to climb the North Maroon Bells. They were experienced climbers and wanted the challenge of the difficult and dangerous 14,000 foot peak. The only woman in the group wanted to climb all the Fourteeners in Colorado before her 40th birthday and this was her second to last climb. The famous Maroon Bells, which are in the next valley over from Castle Creek, are also known as the "Deadly Bells" because it seems too often someone may die trying to climb them.

Glenn was called on the mission and when he returned he told the story. About 11:00 a.m. the morning of the 15th, the two climbers above were clearing a rope to prepare to belay up the two below. A falling rock struck the man below and he lost his balance and fell. He, or the rock, knocked the woman behind him off and both fell about 1,000 feet to their deaths. I could envision the head of the one climber hitting the first outcropping and then becoming a rag doll bouncing off outcroppings until his fall was broken on a

*The deceptively beautiful Maroon Bells
(Aka Deadly Bells)*

level spot below. His motionless body would have ended at a crooked angle. The woman, right behind him, must have also hit, bounced and smashed into the boulders. The two survivors probably froze for a second and then quickly regained their senses and carefully rappelled their way down to go for help. It was late afternoon by the time they were down and able to call the sheriff.

Aspen Mountain Rescue had been formed with the guidance of Fred Braun and became one of the oldest and most skilled, well-trained rescue groups in Colorado. It was, and is, an all-volunteer organization, first incorporated in 1965. The volunteers spend hours and days training and in education before they become full-fledged rescuers. They become well-seasoned and are an invaluable arm of the Pitkin County Sheriff. Glenn was one of the rescuers and had spent a great deal of time in training. He had been on many rescues by this time.

An Army helicopter from Fort Carson happened to be in Aspen on maneuvers and helped by following the climbers' route and they located the bodies by late afternoon. By then, the sheriff determined it too late for the Aspen Mountain Rescue to ascend that evening and plans were made for the next morning to begin the recovery. Glenn had been called for the recovery and he immediately gathered his gear and left early the next morning.

A couple of days later, Glenn returned and told us what had happened. "The family members of the two killed requested the bodies remain there on the peak as their graves. They didn't want more lives in danger and more sorrow for others, but we had to retrieve them."

The Mountain Rescue men worked as a team with thorough preparation, knowledge and training. Each gathered their ropes, pitons, anchors, pulleys and everything else needed for a recovery. The Army helicopter flew the team to the west side of the mountain and then they climbed to the east side. It was a long and difficult assent, as the climbing became more and more demanding. The herculean strength required and the slow, calculated process of the climbers was needed for this mission…as so many.

Glenn told us, "A team member lost his footing and began to fall. We held his rope tight and immediately took up all slack. We broke his fall and he grabbed a rock to get his footing again. It was a close call and we all continued very cautiously." He stopped to stretch his legs under the table as he sat down. "We finally reached the bodies Sunday evening, but too late to descend safely since darkness was approaching fast. So, we knew we'd have to wait until morning to continue."

The late rain made the boulders slippery and night blackness surrounded the team on the mountain. Glenn continued, "We hunched over for protection against the weather, trying to catch some sleep. Each of us had our poncho, but it didn't give much warmth. It got danged cold up there." By mid-August, the nights may reach around freezing at that altitude.

They had no choice but to endure the black, wet, bitter cold night with no comfort. They had no room to build a campfire and no wood to start it anyway. Sometimes, they would be able to get to a base camp where hot food would be prepared, but not this time.

"What did you do for food then?" I always thought of food!

"We carried our bottled water and energy bars or nuts in our backpacks and ate what we had. When daylight arrived we were cold, tired and hungry. I got stiff too. At least the rain had stopped and the sun was promising a warm day. We got warmed by mid-morning.

"We packaged the bodies and carefully began the descent. We came to an open area where the helicopter hovered above and lowered its litter basket so we could place one body in and signal it to be lifted up and into the chopper. We repeated with the second body. Then the chopper headed to town."

I knew that the pilot had to be a professional and calculated just how close he could fly to the side of the mountain without risking his rotor blades hitting. He also had to do his best to not let the litter spin and sway too much from both the downwash of the rotor and the wind on the peaks.

The rescuers descended back down the peak, hiked to the waiting vehicles and headed home for food, warmth and rest. It had been about a 36-hour ordeal. Each man came back exhausted and lost at least 20 pounds from the strain on his body. I could see the weight loss on Glenn of over 20 pounds and the energy drained from him. Those men had risked their lives, and when I heard about the recovery, I knew rescuers were special people.

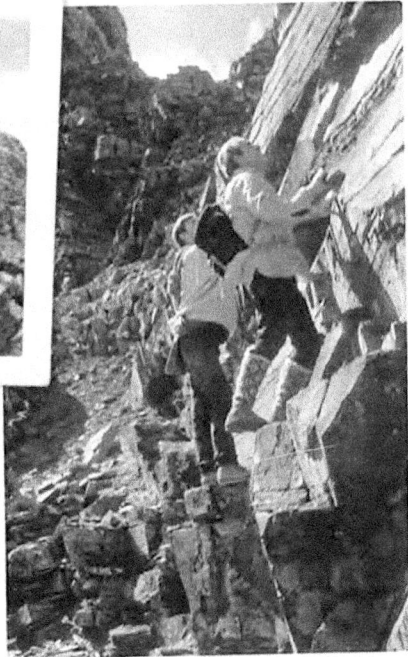

Glenn's climbing buddies and members of Aspen Mountain Rescue demonstrating their climbing technique

Chapter 12

Breaks and Greed (1970)

August continued and Glenn didn't go on another rescue that season. The horses, however, brought more headaches. On a cool morning, Tim came up to the lodge and said, "That danged Ginger broke her leg in the pasture; probably last night. She didn't come in and I went lookin' for her. She stepped into a gopher hole and is standin' on her three good legs. The other has her bone sticking out the side. It doesn't look good."

"What do you think? Call the vet, or put her down, Tim?"

"I think the break's too severe to be fixed and she won't walk right or be any good. I say she oughta be put down."

Larry called the owner and he agreed. No sense paying a vet for a horse that couldn't earn its keep. That was just the way a dude horse's life worked. Everything had to balance out.

Tim didn't want to shoot Ginger and Larry didn't like to kill animals, especially when they looked at him with such soulful, trusting eyes. So, Larry called Norm Payne and he agreed to come and do the deed. I heard later that Norm aimed between Ginger's big brown eyes and pulled the trigger. Immediately he closed his eyes, even before lowering the rifle and said it sure wasn't the same as shooting an elk or deer. He dug a grave in the field with a small rental backhoe.

Horse problems weren't done yet. Several days later, two young men rented horses to take a half-day ride up Taylor Lake Jeep road. They took a roan gelding, Marlow, and Dolly, a sweet filly. In about an hour, Marlow came trotting back to the stables with the two men on his back. They jumped down when they got to the stables and wiped dust from their jeans as they walked toward the wrangler.

One told Tim, "Dolly fell off the side of the Taylor Pass road, and I think she's broken a leg."

Larry and I happened to be at the stables right at that time. "How'd he fall?" Larry asked. We knew that the road, wide enough for four-wheel drives was not like the narrow trails.

We waited for the answer and Tim pushed his cowboy hat back and hooked his thumbs in his back pockets. I knew that thumbs in his pockets meant he tried to hold back his anger.

"I might have pushed Dolly a little too close to the edge to look up the side of the mountain, but I didn't think so. I jumped off when the horse started to lose footing and then Dolly rolled down the side of the mountain." He rolled his hand demonstrating the fall while almost grinning. He told us they looked down where Dolly landed and said there wasn't anything they could do. So, they came back on Marlow.

"How far up Taylor?" Larry asked, ready to put his thumbs in his back pocket also.

"Not far, maybe a mile or two. We're not sure."

"I'll take the Jeep and check the situation. You stay here and handle business, Tim. I know it's busy." Larry went for his rifle, feeling pretty sure he'd use it.

I don't remember what was decided on the price the young man owed, but we might have decided it would be the price of another dude horse. It probably amounted to around $50.00 or $75.00 at the time.

I waited to hear the news when Larry returned, which wasn't very long. He told me it didn't take long to find the spot and saw Dolly down among the trees. "I skidded down the hillside with my body leaning into the slope and my boots digging in on the upside. Her left hind limb bone protruded out at an ugly angle and there was a deep long gash on her shoulder. A puddle of blood had settled beneath Dolly while she stood on three legs. Boy! Did her eyes show her misery and pain."

I poured him a cup of coffee as he sat at the kitchen table. After a couple of sips, he continued. "I knew that she had to be put down and this time I would have to do it. I loosened the cinch and removed the saddle and blanket and set them aside. Then, I took the bridle off and apologized to Dolly and had a sickening feeling in the pit of my stomach."

"Just a minute, let me refill your coffee." I took my time so Larry could take a deep breath. Then I sat back down to listen.

He continued, "I swore at the rider, pointed the gun between Dolly's eyes and pulled the trigger. I knew I did the right thing, but still hated it. I just stood there for a few minutes and then I picked up the saddle, blanket and bridle and came back."

The horse's final resting place became amongst the pines, aspen and brush down on the mountainside. Nature would take its course with Dolly, the same as it did with dead wild animals.

I said, "Well, summer isn't over yet. I wonder what will be next." We found out in another few days.

Burlap, a large horse named for his color, became a troublemaker. He looked as old as he was and just as cantankerous as any old man. He didn't like to just eat the pasture grass. Often, he reared up and placed his front legs over the fence and pressed down with his chest. The barbed wire didn't seem to bother him. He must have known just how much pressure to exert so the barbs did not poke him too deep, or maybe he just considered it no worse than a horsefly bite. Then he stretched his neck as far as he could and ate the grass on the other side. When he finished grazing, he reared up onto his hind legs and backed onto the fenced pasture side. He seemed to always be the first to head for the corral to get his oats in the morning. I thought "Greedy" would have been a better name for him.

Dawn just began to break on a Monday and loud knocking on the door woke me. I put on my robe and went to answer. An MK miner stood at the door. "I'm heading to work, but saw one of your horses straddling the fence. I think he's stuck and needs help."

I sleepily told the Good Samaritan, "Burlap's fine. He does that all the time. He just raises his front legs and backs into the pasture when he's finished eating."

"Okay, if you're sure. Sorry to bother you." He tipped his cap and left.

I didn't try to go back to bed. I dressed and got the coffee perking for breakfast.

Several different miners woke me on the following mornings. Finally, they recognized Burlap and knew there wasn't a problem, but by then I wanted to shoot greedy Burlap myself.

Summer moved on and Burlap continued to move where the grass was taller on the other side of the fence. At least there were no more dawn knocks on our door.

Doctors' Beverage (1970)

Dandelions painted the fields creating patches of yellow gold mixed with the tall green grass. All the yellow blossoms inspired Larry and Glenn in July to make dandelion wine. They found an old recipe and wanted to give it a try. No insecticide or fertilizer had been used on the field, so the dandelions grew free of any chemicals.

Instructions were given to pick the dandelion flowers. The children and I took buckets and headed to the field. Soon, our buckets were full of fluffy yellow heads. Larry and Glenn placed the blossoms in large 5-gallon crocks, along with water, sugar and yeast. The crocks sat on the kitchen counter, covered with cheesecloth and began to emit a sweet aroma of yeast as the process of fermentation began. After awhile, the contents were tested daily to see when the wine would be ready.

Much later, excitement filled the air when I heard Glenn say, "The wine is ready to be bottled!" We washed bottles and the corks were set out. Larry and Glenn tasted the mixture.

Larry's lips puckered. "Ooo-wee! This buttery-white wine is powerful, and it's really sweet."

"Let's see what it says." Glenn had bought a tester to determine the alcohol content.

"Wow!" Larry's eyes widened. "It says 30 percent. Liquor store wine, is only around 12 to 16 percent. We've got some pretty strong stuff, I'd say." They bottled and corked it.

I thought that the dandelions in our fields must be pretty potent weeds. I wondered how come the hippies never tried that kind of a high!

The next week, Dr. Vincent Price…yes, Doctor, not the movie star… arrived. Three other doctors registered for their two weeks at the lodge. They came for the pathology conference in Aspen, but wanted to be out in the mountains as much as possible.

The 50-ish balding and smiling Dr. Price stood only a few inches taller than me. His spindly white legs apparently never saw the sun, except at the lodge, where he wore his Bermuda shorts. He happily tramped around the valley, hiked the trails, or strolled on the rutted dirt road from his cabin up to the lobby for a chat. When not at the conference, he enjoyed the outdoors.

While chatting one day, Dr. Price discovered that we made dandelion wine. The word spread and soon all four of the pathologists marched up to the lobby.

"Larry, we have to try your dandelion wine. We've never tasted wine made with dandelions and we must taste it." The other doctors nodded.

"You don't want that stuff. It's just dandelions and it's too sweet."

"We insist on trying it," said one.

"We've got to find out what this wine is like," said another.

"Please Larry. Just let us taste it." Dr. Price tilted his head to the side innocently and looked up into Larry's eyes begging. The group of pathologists acted like little kids waiting to taste homemade ice cream, fidgeting and looking at Larry with soulful, pleading eyes.

Larry finally gave in and brought out some bottles and glasses. The doctors cautiously sipped, then licked their lips and smiled.

Dr. Price licked his lips. "It's great! It's so sweet. I like it."

Dr. Sullivan agreed. "I've got to get that recipe."

"Mmmmm, so smooth." Dr. Kerry smacked his lips and took another sip.

The wine had a sweet, smooth taste. Larry warned them of the alcohol content, but they paid no attention. After all, they said, it's only dandelions. They emptied several bottles and discussed Aspen restaurants, wines, food and adventures while sipping. They became more relaxed and open than at any other time we had seen. A few slurred words were ignored. They sipped, talked, bragged, and soon got a bit giggly. After emptying another bottle, Larry held up his hands. "Enough. No more."

The doctors reluctantly left after they drained their glasses, and no refills were forthcoming, even with more begging.

"Seems they're swaying a little walking down to their cabins, right Joanne?"

"Yeah, but they're sure happy. At least they had fun, and it's interesting to see them without their doctor faces on."

Time passed too quickly for the pathologists and they were forced to head back to reality, busy schedules and city traffic. Dr. Price gave Larry a vigorous handshake and me a gentle hug. "We will be back next year. Keep that wine for us."

Our Elk Mountain Lodge delighted many people, including doctors, lawyers, oil executives, artists, authors and the rich and famous. One poet, Mrs. Jarvis Thurston, professional name of Mona Van Duyn, was the first female appointed U.S. Poet Laureate and the recipient of the Pulitzer Prize. Her husband, a respected lawyer, also wrote two novels and one was about a Jewish lawyer. They loved our valley. The last name of another author was Lebowitz, but I can't remember the first name! I am not sure, but maybe it was Fran Lebowitz. I just don't remember and my notes didn't give the information, but her picture looks familiar.

Tops on! (1970)

Summer went by far too fast. Hunting season came and went and the cabins were rented once more to the long-term tenants with additional rules in the lease. It seemed that every year more rules had to be added to the lease, yet we seemed to always overlook something. We had to remind the tenants about common sense. I had my binoculars at the ready and I'd set the tenants straight, if needed. Larry left that job to me. He was too much of a softy and would give in to the tenants' arguments. Glenn was worse…he shunned any confrontation and referred me to any problems.

We braced ourselves for the long-termers. We weren't far into the season when I had to set the rules straight.

Two young girls, Peggy and Amber, rented the Paintbrush by the road. On a warm sunny day, I looked out the window and saw the girls on their porch sunbathing with only short shorts and no tops. A car drove by and honked several times and two men leaned out the windows and whistled. This sent me flying over to the cabin.

"Get your shirts on right now and stay dressed! You can't do that here." My clinched hands rested on my hips.

"We have a right to sunbathe without our tops if we want." Peggy's long brown hair hung loosely around her face.

"No you don't, not on my property and if you don't put a top on immediately, you'll be moving out. Get dressed now or leave." I thought about their mothers who would probably react the same way.

The two gave up the fight and I stood there until they reluctantly put on their shirts. I warned them not to try it again, stomped back to the lodge and told Larry about the girls.

"Had to wait until they were covered before telling me, huh? I miss all the good stuff," he teased. I gave him an easy slap on the rear and a quick smirk. He always tried to get me to lighten up.

Gonzo in Power...No Way!

Soon, our attention changed from long-term tenants to a possible long-term disaster. We became especially interested in all the news about Hunter S. Thompson running for Sheriff of Pitkin County this year. He lived near Aspen and wrote in the style he called Gonzo Journalism. I would call it a rambling of sarcasm, hate, humor, maybe truth mixed with exaggeration and profanity. He enjoyed drugs while writing about whatever he wanted. His articles appeared in the *Rolling Stone* magazine.

Thompson ran on the "Freak Power" ticket, and we considered that appropriate for this man and we sure didn't want him to win. His journalism had become well known, but seemed bizarre to us. Thompson's platform included the decriminalization of drugs for personal use and he apparently was a big user of drugs. One of his slogans said, "It never gets weird enough for me" and it reflected his writings. His platform also included tearing up all the streets and turning them into grassy pedestrian malls, and he wanted to ban any building so tall that it obstructed the view of the mountains—not a bad idea. He also wanted to rename Aspen "Fat City" to deter investors who wanted to capitalize on the name of Aspen—"Fat City" not a good idea. The famous "Gonzo fist" symbol used by Thompson showed two-thumbs crossed over a hand palm with four fingers raised and in the palm sat an image of a peyote button, the bud of a cactus plant used for hallucinogenic purposes. He used this symbol on his posters for sheriff.

The actions and boisterous claims by Thompson, who had to be half out of his mind in my view, appalled me. Maybe some ideas weren't that bad, but I absolutely could not vote for what I considered a "druggie nut."

Hippies started to pour into Aspen and Pitkin County and registered to vote before the deadline ended. We were being invaded by hippies! The Democrats and Republicans each wanted their own candidate and that made it a three-way race...the third party being the "Freak Power" ticket for Thompson. A few days before the election, the Republican candidate agreed to withdraw. That made it a two-way race and gave hope.

Then Election Day came. The international media covered this story, as well as the local media. It was big news around the world. All were eager to find out how the election would come out. Aspen became as popular as Height-Ashbury for the hippie movement. Our friends and old-time Aspenites made sure we all got to the polls to vote. After Larry and I voted, we encountered the BBC trying to get comments from people and they interviewed Larry. I do not remember what Larry said, but it would have been reasonable comments for being against the "Freak Power." I stayed in the background. I don't think my opinion of Hunter Thompson would have been allowed on air!

At the end of the day it seemed everyone in Pitkin County must have voted. The town of Aspen appeared to have voted him in, but all residents in Pitkin County did not. Hunter Thompson was defeated, but only by 500 votes out of 3,000. I think it had been a record number of voters for Pitkin County at the time.

We gave a sigh of relief and were glad that there were still people with values who cared about our county. Maybe some of Hunter Thompson's thoughts weren't all bad, but we were not ready for that yet. Many of the hippies that registered to vote didn't stay and we were happy they left our area.

Gunshots!

Winter pushed forward with plenty of snowstorms. Soon everything turned to a mass of white and covered the fields and mountains. Fran and Lynn came in the fall to see about work for the winter.

We hired Fran to help guide the snowmobile tours and that way Larry could work on repairs easier. We hired his wife, Lynn, to help me take care of the people in the office. The wrangler's quarters would be part of their pay. Fran stood as tall as Larry but not as seasoned. Lynn was taller and thinner than me and both had likeable personalities.

Later Larry told me, "I checked at the bank to see about a loan for our new snowmobiles and the interest rate has gone up to 20 percent. That's sure going to hurt." By now he had switched from Ski-Daddlers to the Scorpions or Polaris snowmobiles. I don't remember which was next.

Larry's reputation spread as an honest businessman who kept his word. He demonstrated the snowmobiles to the ski areas and sold several to them. A few private sales were made to families, and more were sold to ranchers who would use them to check their livestock. Larry was available whenever the Ski Corp or an owner down valley needed a snowmobile part or repair.

We had several feet of snow by mid-November. Another foot was added on Thanksgiving Day. The drive had to be plowed that morning and again in the evening. In between, we had our traditional turkey dinner and pumpkin pie. Then December and Christmas swept by. Both holidays were uneventful and full of smiles. No snowmobile tour income those days!

Fran guided a tour on December 29th. He had a story to tell when he returned sooner than expected. He told us that the group stopped to take pictures and one man turned off his machine. When he tried to start it again, he flooded it. Fran tried to get it started while the rest of the group went ahead. The trail, well marked, should not have been a problem. When the machine purred once again, Fran and the errant driver headed up the trail to catch up with the others. Before they caught up, two machines raced back down the trail.

Fran told us that he couldn't get them to say what the problem was, only that they had some sort of trouble and wanted to go back. He turned around and came back to the lodge with them. When they walked into the lobby, Larry got the man to tell us what happened.

"The other machines raced way ahead of us and we lost them. I drove with my son on my machine and my wife and daughter on the other snowmobile were following. I somehow must have accidentally turned onto the wrong trail. The sun must have blinded me, I guess." He stopped and gave his wife an apologetic look. She had tears rolling down her cheeks.

"We were going up the trail and all of a sudden someone started shooting at us! I know it was gunfire because I saw the snow splatter when the bullets hit the snow close to me. And I heard the crack of a gun. Then I saw a man by the trees on the hillside with what looked like a rifle. I waved my arms up in the air and yelled to stop and we'd get out of there. The shots stopped and somehow I got the machines turned around and we headed back." He seemed scared, yet angry.

Larry stepped closer to the counter and leaned forward, "You need to file a complaint with the sheriff, Mr. Fender. A man with a mean disposition rents a cabin near the Cathedral trail. He keeps people off the cross-country ski trail and the dogsled trail. I'll bet it was him. He can't get away with that."

"Hey, we aren't getting involved. I don't want my wife and kids to go through anymore. This scared the hell out of us. We just want to get away from here and forget it." He raised both hands up by his shoulders and his wife stood by him with an arm around each child. Fear lingered in their eyes.

"I sure wish you would file a complaint. We don't want others to have the same thing happen. And this man needs to know he can't go shooting at people."

"Nope, we won't do it. We aren't getting involved and that's final." He quickly turned and waved for his family to follow. They piled in their car and drove away.

"I wish they had filed a complaint. Damn it. I'm pretty sure that the shooter did not aim to kill, but just scare. That doesn't make it right, though. We still need to call the sheriff and tell him so it's on the record." Larry headed to the phone and Fran went back up the trail to find the others and hoped he wouldn't find more trouble. He didn't, but we knew the snowmobile haters would come up with something else.

1971 arrived with icy wind. The temperature in the morning was -37°F on January 6th and the high was only about zero. Two cabins had frozen pipes and had to be thawed. By mid-January the temperature changed drastically and it climbed into the 40s during the day. That worried us and the ski industry, but it didn't take long before cold and new snow came again. The brief warmth bolstered us for the rest of the winter.

Then snowmobile haters were at it again. Larry came back after packing the trail one day discouraged and mad. "I found lead pipes with jagged edges barely sticking out of the snow on our trail. The pipes must have been put in last night after we were done with the tours. If I hadn't seen them, they would have ripped up the track on my machine. That would have been an expensive repair."

"Honest to God, how much more can someone think of? We are not going to stop snowmobile tours or be run out of the valley. So, why can't those idiots grow up and act like decent adults?" I asked. My eyes flashed with anger.

Lost Skiers, Found Skiers (1971)

On a beautiful sunny day, a group of three cross-country skiers from town ventured off from the Sundeck on top of Aspen Mountain and planned to ski the backcountry to the top of Taylor Pass and down Express Creek to Ashcroft. They planned only for the day's venture, but it would be around 10 to 15 miles and not on flat terrain or all downhill.

When they failed to return to the hotel by late afternoon, their friends got worried and called the sheriff. A rescue party was sent out. Mountain Rescue called us and Larry answered the phone. "Can you and Glenn take your snowmobiles up Taylor Pass and see if they got that far?"

"Sure. If we see them, we'll let you know."

When they returned, Larry told me how he and Glenn snowmobiled up to the top of the pass, turned off their machines, and yelled. They received no answer, only the sound of the cold wind whipping icy snow. Turning in all directions they called several times, but got no reply, so they drove back toward Aspen a ways and tried again, but had no luck. Finally, they headed back home.

Somehow, they missed one of the skiers who made it to Mace's Toklot at 7:00 p.m. He said the other two were up Taylor and one had twisted his ankle. Rescuers came at 8:30 p.m. and used our snowmobiles to go up Express Creek and to the top of Taylor Pass again. Glenn led the group. They didn't find the skiers and came back to the lodge at 11:00 p.m. Then they took a Snowcat up Little Annie Hill and back south to about right above Elk Mountain Lodge, but farther East, to the Barnard Hut on Richmond Ridge. It was one of the cross-country ski huts. They searched all night, but radioed that they didn't find the lost skiers.

Bright and early the next morning, Larry and Glenn went back up Taylor, but had no success. Again, they missed the skiers. The injured man had also walked into Toklot. The other came about an hour and half later. The rescuers who used the Barnard Hut as their headquarters overnight were radioed that all lost skiers had been found. They boarded the Snowcat and headed back

Larry at the top of Taylor Pass

down to Aspen. I am sure a few words were used about unprepared skiers. It seems that people never think about "what if," or seem to be prepared for the worst in the mountains…summer or winter.

The next day, snowmobile business boomed and Larry kept busy all day helping Fran. While filling the snowmobile gas tanks that morning, Larry was approached by the tenant in the Homestead cabin. He said his car slid when he parked and now couldn't get traction to back out. He demanded that Larry stop and pull him out of the snow bank right then. No please or sweetness came from the tenant's lips, just "get me out now."

Larry looked up and said, "I can't help until I get some time later. We have to get these machines ready for the tours."

The tenant slammed his fist on a snowmobile hood. "No, damn it, I need a pull now. It'll only take a few minutes." He painted the air blue with filthy names to Larry.

"After all that, you expect me to help you? No damned way. In fact, you can move out if you don't like it. We don't want your kind here." The tenant swore again and stomped back to his cabin.

In a few minutes, the roommate came to ask and she used the same language when told to wait. Larry tried to explain that business came first, but she kept cussing him out. That sealed it. When Larry finished with snowmobile business he came into the office. "Joanne, write a notice to the Homestead to move out. Those damned hippies can go elsewhere and I told them I wasn't about to pull them out after that."

I did, and walked down to the cabin and handed the notice to the woman when she opened the door. She grabbed it and bellowed curses while her partner read the notice. I turned and walked away while they both yelled every filthy word that their small minds knew. In a few days, they packed up and left, but we found the usual cleaning. At least we were rid of them.

Avalanche Search

It seemed that every winter we had a tenant, or a few, that would not turn out to be decent or mature. Sometimes, it warped our memories and we forgot the good tenants. Many of the long-term tenants were okay, just not up to my moral standards, but tolerable otherwise.

Winter paraded onward with icy winds that swept down the valley and left drifts. We had plenty of snow, but kept the drives open, the water running and the heat going. Sometimes the snow banks reached almost to the roof edge and icicles hung deep from the eaves.

March brought more snow and avalanche warnings. On the 16th, another rescue took place about 1 ½ miles southeast of the Sundeck on the steep slopes of Independence Bowl. It is a very dangerous avalanche area.

That afternoon, Glenn got a call for a rescue. The report said a Snowcat took a group of skiers on the backside of the Sundeck. Tom Simpson, a guide for the party, saw ski tracks that led into an avalanche area. Because he couldn't see if the tracks came out the other side of the bowl, he left the group to investigate. The ski party went on and later returned to find that a series of avalanches had occurred and no Tom in sight. The sheriff was notified.

On Glenn's return that night, he told us, "We figured that Tom traversed along the steep slope following the tracks he had seen. Right in the middle of the slide path, the crest probably broke loose and the avalanche caught him. One man said that the slide must have triggered another massive slide on the other side and they joined together. It's one of the largest slides ever seen in that area."

I could envision the snow thundering down with wicked force, billowing out, flying high and increasing in speed and sound as it cascaded down. Tom would have been caught as the savage force crashed down on him and then in a few minutes the roar would have stopped and all would be silent. Not even a moan would have been heard.

Glenn continued, "When we got to the site, we immediately began probing in our usual pattern, but found nothing except his ski poles. We found one near the top and the other near the bottom. It's a huge area to probe. We had to quit about 10:00 p.m." Glenn sagged in his chair and took a bite of the sandwich I fixed him.

The next day, the search became a recovery mission, but was forced to give up about 4:00 p.m. due to blizzard conditions. For a couple of days, 120 people probed the mountainside, but the body could not be found. A small group of friends continued to search on their own. Everyone wanted to give Tom Simpson a proper burial, not just a snow bed.

Winter continued and then spring finally brought a sigh of relief with warm breezes and the snow began to melt. By late-May, some hikers stumbled onto a body. It was Tom Simpson. In a few days, his friends and family gathered to give their final respects and say goodbye to him. Glenn had learned that the sad part was that the ski tracks Tom saw had actually gone on past the slide area, but were not visible to him.

I often worried that Larry would be caught in an avalanche while snow-mobiling and my worry grew every time Glenn went on a rescue caused by a slide. There were several areas on our snowmobile trail that often had slides… the worst being above the valley floor before the trail climbed. Something always seemed to hold the slides until the snowmobilers passed.

Chapter 13

Our Pasture Tenant (1971)

The end of winter finally arrived and brought new life. Spring became alive with trees full of infant green and the fields painted in yellow blotches of dandelions and tall grass. The elegant pinks and lavender of columbine and the berry red of paintbrush sprinkled the hillsides. The muddy drive made ruts, which Larry smoothed down by attaching a heavy metal beam on the back of the Jeep and dragging it on the drive. He slowly went back and forth until the ruts were demolished.

On a warm afternoon in May, I watched a woman ride up to the lodge on her mountain bicycle. I saw a water bottle hooked onto the handlebars and a roll tied on back of the seat containing a sleeping bag and a small pup tent. Apparently, her backpack held some personal gear. She parked her bike by the Ranch Store and walked slightly bent over from the waist. Her Bermuda shorts accentuated her bowed legs and wrinkled tan, the same as her bare arms. Brownish hair had a touch of gray, especially around the temples and it peeked out from a knit band around her forehead. Her face looked like a corrugated tan field of ridges, but accentuating smile furrows around her mouth. I frowned and wondered who she was…certainly not one of the hippies! I went to the counter when she entered the lobby.

"Hello. My name is Georgie Leighton." She squinted and displayed deep sun-baked reddish grooves around her eyes and around her smiling lips. "I would like permission to camp in your pasture this summer." Her French accent did not seem too strong and I had no problem understanding her.

Foreign accents were common around Aspen, but well-covered with English. "I can pay by cleaning cabins, helping with the horses, with the children, or whatever you want. I just wish to be out in the mountain air, surrounded by Mother Nature and the animals. I promise I won't cause you any trouble." Her dry cracked lips gave a pleasant smile. Her age showed hard times, but her friendliness was genuine and sincere.

"Where are you from?"

"I live in town in the winter, but in the summer I just camp out. I have bicycled up Castle Creek Road many times and you have such a beautiful place. I would love to stay the summer."

"But where are you from originally? You have an accent."

"Oh, I came to the United States from France after World War II."

She didn't elaborate, but I felt she was friendly and I liked her smile. I would wait to learn more about her. "Well, it's a pleasure to know you. I don't see a problem with you camping in the field, but I have to check with my husband."

"Of course. I'll walk down to the stables and see the horses while you talk to him." Her pleasant smile came again. Only now, I saw that her eyes also carried sadness and possibly some pain. The war must have taken a terrible toll on her, apparently not only physically, but imbedded in her heart.

I talked to Larry and soon introduced Georgie to him. We agreed that she could pitch her tent in the pasture. She gratefully thanked us and then set up her pup tent in the pasture near the stables. After a few days of visiting with our unusual guest, she revealed some of her past.

"I fought in the French underground against Hitler. We were a well-organized group of warriors. Toward the end of the war, though, my family and I were put in a detention camp. Conditions were beyond description." She swallowed hard and paused. "We were malnourished, maltreated, had diseases, and we had the fear of other inmates who could have been spies for the Nazis."

She told me that she came from a wealthy family, but lost everything. Her father was in the hotel business and the family spent half their time in Nice and the other half in Lausanne. The Nazis took their homes, classic books, pianos and violins, original paintings, the family jewelry, photographs, savings and everything. After the war when France was liberated, Georgie tried to get work and a place to live, but didn't have much luck.

I asked, "So, what did you do?" I had not heard much about the conditions after the war.

"Well, a university friend had immigrated to the United States just before the war, and I finally contacted her. She helped me immigrate to the U. S. in the 1950s, and she found a family to sponsor me. I speak English, French, Italian and German, which helped me acquire an excellent job and it paid high wages. I was thankful to be in America and for my good job, but I could not endure the city and felt claustrophobic. After several years, I decided to become a wanderer. I bicycled all over the country, from state to state, and in Canada. I worked my way from place to place, if I needed, and I've bicycled around 80,000 miles, I guess. The United States fascinates me." Her eyes sparkled again and the sadness seemed to retreat in her mind when she talked about biking.

"Is that how you ended up in Colorado?"

"Yes. When I came back to Aspen in 1964, I decided to stay. I love the mountains, the small town and the people. It reminds me of my home years ago. I've worked as a maid, dishwasher, a clerk at City Market and a proofreader at the *Aspen Times*. I save my money so I can enjoy my loves in the summer, which are hiking and camping. I go skiing in the winter on my days off work."

Georgie didn't talk much about her underground work and I wondered if she might have lost her lover during the war. He probably had been another underground warrior and no one else ever captured her heart. She must have found peace in Mother Nature. On many days, Georgie could be seen hiking up a trail, leaning forward in eagerness, with her sun-baked bowed legs pumping in short strides ready for a new adventure.

The children liked Georgie and were often at her campsite to listen to her stories about animals or the environment. She willingly cleaned the shower house, helped clean some cabins and helped with the horses. Her personality blended with the spirit of the lodge. She lived the free life, but respected other people and their property and she wanted to pay for everything that she received. I decided that she represented the epitome of what a true hippie should be.

The horses learned that Georgie was not a risk and knew how to beg for treats from her. She usually had a sugar cube, an apple or a carrot. They sauntered up and "talked" with her and then received a nibble while she patted their noses and kissed them. She thought all creatures pretty or cute, including skunks and mice. Horses were her favorites and she believed that no animal should be exterminated, not even a field mouse.

The summer guests met Georgie and enjoyed hearing about her travels. We all found her to be very intelligent and up to date on many issues. She scoured the newspaper every day and held it close, almost touching her nose, while she squinted to read. When in town, she stopped at the library to read the Washington, D.C. newspaper, magazines, or anything else about politics, national and international news. She looked for articles about the environment, or animal abuse and became an avid animal rights advocate. Often she joined us for dinner or tourists invited her for meals with them. She always brought interesting stories or information. Sometimes tourists gave her their fish catch. She loved trout, regardless if it was a Rainbow, Cut Throat, or Brown. She helped the wranglers every day with the feeding, grooming and saddling. It didn't take long before she fell in love with one particular roan horse named Doc. I don't know how he got his name. Maybe it was because he was so loving and healed human hearts.

In mid-June, she came up to the lodge all excited and told me her plans. "I'm going to rent Doc for a week. He's the most beautiful horse! We'll go up Taylor Pass and maybe I'll go along the rim, or down the other side." On the scheduled day she started up the pass with visions of camping high in the Rockies with Doc as her companion. Her excitement gave me a smile.

The next day we heard her tale. "At the end of yesterday's trek, I removed Doc's saddle and bridle, but I did not want to hobble him. I set up my camp close to Express Creek among the pines and aspen. I told Doc that he could roam free to graze and after cooking my meal, I read a book for awhile."

I envisioned her squinting, holding the book close to her nose and adjusting to get the campfire light right to see. She needed glasses, but would not give in.

"Then I crawled into my sleeping bag and promptly fell asleep. The next morning I woke to discover Doc gone! I searched and searched, calling to him while shaking my can of oats, but he did not come. I had been so good to him and he didn't stay by me." She didn't sound angry, only disappointed. "I knew I had to go back and tell the wranglers and I dreaded it. I hid my bedroll and the saddle in the brush, and hiked back down here. Every so often I'd stop and call for Doc."

I knew the rest of the story. Sure enough, when she walked to the stables, there stood Doc looking at her with a smirk on his face. He had his breakfast at the stables.

The wrangler said Georgie got so excited to see Doc and she cooed and rubbed noses with him. Later, she took off again leading him by the reins as they walked up the trail. At the hiding place, she gathered up her gear, saddled

Doc and took off for the top of Taylor Pass. She hobbled Doc every night for the rest of the trip even though she hated to do it. When she returned to the lodge after five days, she had happy tales of her adventures. She was a good storyteller.

Family Affair

Summer sped by and in late August my sister and her family came for their annual weeklong visit. Gail and Vince had seven children, so it was a full house and pandemonium reined with 10 children from ages 6 to 18 years old and six adults, which included my mother and Glenn.

When they first arrived, I scrambled to figure out the sleeping arrangements. "Okay, Gail, we're going to have you stay in the Homestead and some of the kids can stay here with my kids in sleeping bags. Mom, will stay in the Chipmunk cabin."

"Sounds fine. Okay, you kids listen up. Lynn and Anna, you take your suitcases and sleeping bags into the kids' bedroom. Then Mike and Kevin, you come help me unload at the Homestead along with Pat. You girls keep Tim and Shawn out of the way." Gail became the drill sergeant with small troopers to keep in line. Being only 5 feet 2 inches made no difference. She was in control and the children knew it. They unloaded the van quickly and put things in order. Then, children flew every which way enjoying alpine freedom and fun.

Vince, shorter and fuller than Larry, tagged along on a couple of Jeep trips and Larry was always happy to show the beauty of the high country. Vince also helped load the wood rack at each cabin. When time came to pick up trash from the cabins, the children rode in the back of the old 1938 pickup when

My sister's family on one of their visits with Grandma

Larry or Glenn drove it to each cabin. The pickup had long ago lost any luster of color; it was scratched, dented, and the shocks were non-existent. The children sat on the tailgate and bed walls, loving the bumps as it rattled from cabin to cabin. The older ones hiked the trails, fished and rode horses.

Mom, Gail and I cooked the meals...an endless job. We prepared pot roasts, hamburger casseroles, chicken and, of course, trout caught by the boys. Plenty of potatoes and gravy, vegetables and fresh baked bread accompanied the meat or fish. Pies, cakes, cookies and bread were constantly being baked. The oven only rested at night! The men and children devoured everything placed on the table.

One day, I made rice pudding in a 5-gallon pot. It looked like enough to feed an army and I jokingly said, "I hope it's enough to feed everyone." I laughed.

Gail looked at it and said, "Well, I'm not sure it's enough for everyone... seriously." She was not joking and I sagged in defeat. Our army ate every last scrap of the rice pudding.

Toward the end of their stay, I became frazzled. It was always fun to have the relatives, but I also would feel relieved upon their departure when there

Back pond and new snow on peaks

would be some peace and quiet again. We were not used to having that many people under foot all the time. Tourists were easier. Larry and Glenn escaped with the Jeep trips, or hauled wood, gathered trash, worked in the yard, or did something that kept them away from the hubbub. But I got stuck in the midst of all the chaos and still had to handle the guests, the store, the phone, hungry children, cooking and regular household chores. There were a few tense moments when I felt like barking at everyone and walking away.

The day Gail and family drove out the driveway to head home, I gave a sigh of relief. Once again, we had some peace…at least for awhile. Fall crept in faster, school began, and the winter tenants would soon invade our peace.

The mountainsides glowed with fall colors and the fresh snow on the peaks reflected the purity of innocence. Before we were ready, snow came with freezing nights. The season of Mother Nature, and the season of human nature, changed…winter soon overtook fall and the tourists were replaced with the long-term tenants…the season of change. Georgie moved back to town, but we agreed that she could camp in the pasture again next year and the years after.

The landscape quickly became white, laced with hibernating pines and ghostly gray aspen branches. Snow continued with one storm on top of another and it built up fast. Snowmobile business flourished and when the tourists returned, they sat in the lobby warming and re-told their high country adventure over and over. Each had something different to tell. They were consumed with the true Rocky Mountain high and the feeling of enjoyment of Mother Nature.

Sky Choppers and Powder (1972)

In January, Sky Choppers came to see Larry. Their helicopter tours gave powder skiers the joy of the virgin snow on the mountains. They liked the Sawtooth Range south of our lodge and the skiers thrilled over the wilderness slopes of pure deep powder. When the skiers came to a certain spot the chopper picked them up and took them back up for another run. Virgin snow was always ready for them because of overnight winds or a new snowfall.

The owner asked to use the field by the lodge for the rest of their 1972 winter powder tours and we approved. They set down in the field on a makeshift heli-pad that Larry had made by packing the snow down with his snowmobile. The powder skiers drove from town and parked at our lodge. Skis were strapped to the helicopter runners and the pilot flew the clients up to the mountaintop above Cooper Basin. Then, they began their long descent on the deep powdery snowfields and ended their run near the Lindley Hut and were picked up by the chopper in a flat area.

The pilot flew down to a field near the Lindley Hut to wait for them to make their descent. When the skiers arrived, he flew them up for another run, or back to Elk Mountain Lodge, if they were done for the day.

Mel made the run to the top on a sunny day for the skier's second run and then he landed at the usual snowfield below to wait for them. When they arrived, ready to head back to their hotels, the chopper engine would not turn over. Mel fidgeted with the motor, but to no avail and finally gave up after many tries.

He told the skiers they would have to ski down to our lodge and tell us he was stuck up there. He didn't have any skis, so it had to be up to them to get back on their own. He radioed for a mechanic. The group skied down our snowmobile trail and when they arrived at our camp, they told Larry what had happened.

By the time the mechanic arrived at our lodge with his gear, it had become too dark to take a snowmobile up. The rescue team radioed Mel to spend the night in the Lindley Hut and he waded to it. A few days later, he told us he found the key to the hut exactly where Fred Braun, in charge of the hut, said it would be and he quickly entered. He got a fire going in the stove and he was happy that the hut furnished the wood.

He told us, "After eating the rest of my meager lunch that I'd packed that day, I ate my apple. The crackle of the fire lulled me and I curled up in my sleeping bag. In no time I fell asleep. It's a good thing that I kept a sleeping bag in the chopper for emergencies." He said he stoked up the fire the next morning and fixed a cup of coffee. A previous occupant had left a can of coffee in the cupboard.

On that morning, Larry led the mechanic on our snowmobiles up the trail and to the hut. He told me later that Mel put out the fire, cleaned the hut, and replaced the key where he found it. Mel sat behind Larry on one snowmobile and the mechanic followed them to the helicopter. Larry knew how to stay atop the powder snow and help pack the temporary trail. "The mechanic adjusted, tinkered and fiddled, and tried different methods. He finally got the chopper to purr and the blades began their slow turn, picked up speed and soon produced a snowy circle of white fluff reaching for the sky."

Larry said that Mel saluted the mechanic as he lifted and began his voyage home. The mechanic and Larry headed back to the lodge where I had coffee and cookies ready for them. By the next day, the helicopter had been repaired and Sky Choppers came back with more skiers.

One day, after the rescue, the pilot gave Larry, Susy and me a ride in the helicopter and flew us up valley to the peaks. Susy happened to be home from school that day for some reason. Susy and I sat in the front with the pilot and the bubble gave us a view from the top to under our feet. We flew close to the mountainside and up to the peaks. Susy gripped my knee so tight that I thought I'd have a nice bruise. What a thrill to see the glorious peaks from the chopper!

Explosion (1972)

Things got back to normal for awhile. We had begun to use a commercial trash dumpster to deposit garbage instead of hauling it to the county dump ourselves. The trash company came once a week to dump it. We warned tenants not to put ashes from the woodstoves in the dumpster. Ashes could stay hot for at least a week, or maybe two, and a fire could easily erupt.

Warnings didn't work in February. Hot ashes were put in the dumpster and caught the trash on fire. Larry went to douse it and in a few minutes he came back in. "Get me a clean towel." He held his hand to his forehead and blood rushed through his fingers.

"Oh my God, what happened?" I quickly handed him a clean towel. "Sit down."

"I was dowsing the fire and suddenly an aerosol can exploded and a small fragment of metal hit me in the middle of my forehead. It'll be okay once the bleeding stops. Will you get me a cold pack to put on it?" He leaned his head back.

I hurriedly put some ice cubes in the center of a washcloth, folded it over and put the pack on the wound. He leaned his head back. Finally the bleeding stopped and I put a bandage on it. I didn't think to just go outside and grab an icicle hanging from the eave. It would have been quicker.

A couple of days later, Larry's forehead swelled up with an infection. The angry red got worse and the swelling spread down through his eyes and cheeks. His forehead swelled and pushed back and upward and his eyes became slanted slits.

Mickey Payne came to visit and laughed. "You look like a Martian, Larry, with your forehead swollen and those slanted, squinty eyes. The only difference is that you have hair and the pictures of Martians show them bald. Sit down and let me try to extract the infection."

Larry reluctantly sat and leaned his head back. She stood over him and began to press around the wound to force the gunk out. She squeezed and pressed harder and harder.

"Don't squeeze so hard," Larry yelled. He soon swatted her hands away. "Okay. That's enough. I don't want any more. Keep your hands off, Mickey." He had become more pained than angry.

"All right, all right, but I hope I got it all. Keep an eye on it."

Another couple of days showed no improvement, so Larry went to the doctor and he cleaned the wound. Larry received an antibiotic and finally the infection cleared up. It became all history…we thought.

Finally, winter faded without any big hassles and no more cans exploded in the trash. My warnings had been heeded by the long-term tenants when they broke a rule and fines were paid. Winter became much less stressful than the last, even though one tenant, Howard, in the Trout cabin greeted me with a surprise. I knocked on his door hoping to collect rent that had become past due.

"Come in," he yelled.

So I stepped inside and he came around the corner from the bath in only his briefs. I became flustered, my cheeks got hot and I stammered. I don't remember if Howard gave me the rent money right then or not. I retreated fast! Thank God I did not have any other male tenant greet me in his undies and I gave a sigh of relief when the last long-term tenant moved out.

Chapter 14

New Home (1972)

In January, my frustration came to a head while trying to clean the outdated and worn out kitchen. I'd had enough of the old log kitchen after 7 years of putting up with it. I looked at Larry, "I will not live with this kitchen another year. You have to build a new one or I'm going to leave. I'm tired of hanging blankets over the logs in the winter to keep out the cold. I'm tired of the old plumbing, and I'm tired of the old worn out linoleum that has dissolved to patches of dust here and there, plus the can lids over holes. I can't take another year with this horrible kitchen." My jaw quivered and my eyes glistened

"Okay, okay. I'll see what I can do, but it has to wait until spring." Larry knew he had said, "have patience" too many times.

In February, he began investigating the possibility of building a complete new structure. He didn't want to just replace the kitchen, he wanted to build a whole new house for us. He wrote some prefabricated construction companies for information on different types of housing

One day he plopped some papers on the table. "I want to tear all this back part off and build a two-story home which we can attach to the old living room and the lobby. These are the plans I sent away for. Let's look through them, and see what we come up with."

My eyes lit up. "Spread them out on the table. The kids are in school, so we can have some peace going through all these."

Over coffee and serious discussions, we narrowed the choices down. It took some time to go through the different plans thoroughly. We finally decided on a two-story home manufactured by Capp Homes…a pre-cut building. Sections would be delivered ready to erect. The main floor would include a new office, a large laundry room with plenty of storage space, a bedroom, a family room, a furnace room and an apartment for Glenn.

Larry pointed to the floor plans, "We'll have our living quarters upstairs. It'll have a large living room, dining room, kitchen, three bedrooms and two baths. The living room will have two huge windows facing the peaks and another on each side, and it'll have a balcony too."

"Great!" I became as excited as a child at Christmastime.

"Glenn is eager to help, and excited about his new quarters too." A couple of years earlier, we built a Panabode prefabricated log cabin closer to the creek and Glenn moved into that. It would become a nice modern rental when he moved in to the new building. Larry continued, "But in order to build this, we have to move out of here. All this old part has to be torn down. I'll board off the lobby and we'll move the office in there. We can keep the office going during the construction."

"Okay. We can move into #14 since it's about the largest modern cabin and close to the office. It'll be crowded, but it will have to work and I'll be over here every day to take care of the office." I couldn't wait for spring, but winter had to continue until worn out.

A view of the lodge showing new home being built

We lined up the financing and set the delivery date. Larry planned to have the foundation ready for a crew to erect the structure by the middle of May. He and Glenn began tearing off the old section toward the end of April, and we moved into #14. Excess furniture and items were stored away.

I was delighted to see the old kitchen demolished. The days were long and full of hard work. When they completely removed the old structure, the men dug trenches and built the foundation. Aspen Cement Company poured the concrete. Then we were ready for the crew to come and erect the structure.

Capp Homes arrived the third week of May and construction progressed quickly. They installed the plumbing, electricity, drywall and the vinyl in the kitchen and baths. The finishing had been agreed to as a do-it-yourself proposition. Larry would install the wood flooring in the bedrooms and hall. He also agreed to install the carpet in the living room and dining room and do the inside painting. That kept the cost down.

By the end of May, guests began to arrive for the other cabins. I ran the office amid the banging and clanging. I went to our temporary home to prepare meals, but I spent most of my time at the office until late evening. We placed a note on the lobby door telling where to come if a guest needed something. We hired my niece, Lynn, as our maid and she and Tina slept in a vacant cabin until we could move into our new home. That just left Larry, Greg, Susy and me for #14 and we knew it wouldn't be for too long.

Larry worked hard to get the inside ready for occupancy after Capp Homes finished their construction. Time started to run out and the outer siding would have to wait until fall. Our new home barely became ready for occupancy before guests were to arrive for #14…our temporary quarters. Then the summer business kept us busy, busy.

I loved my new, modern kitchen and brand-new, shiny vinyl floor!

Boys and Dynamite (1972)

June kept us on the run from morning until night. July sped in and the Kraus family from Texas came for their annual two-week stay at the lodge. Fred and Helga were a pleasant couple near our age and with similar upbringing and standards. They had two boys, Peter and Michael, who were about Greg's age. The boys played together almost every day. Often, Greg went fishing with the family or on their hiking trips.

They decided to stay in camp one day, and Michael, Peter and Greg took a hike along the creek. Through the years, the boys often were up on the mountainsides exploring and found old mines every so often. They crawled in a few musty entrances shrouded with cobwebs, but the beams usually had fallen in and the shaft filled with earth and rocks. This year, as I recall, they wandered off the trail, climbed high above the creek, and found an old abandoned mine. The mine shaft had collapsed and the beams protruded out of the entrance a few feet. The boys decided to finish the "cave in" and climbed above the entrance and pushed rocks down to block any possible entrance. Then about 10 yards from the mine they found a wooden box sunk into a rocky area, but the top was still ¼ above the rocks. It looked like a standard-sized crate, similar to an old milk crate, but this one contained several crystallized dynamite sticks. The boys picked them up to investigate, but decided to leave them there and climbed on down. They saw Fred and Helga hiking and told them what they found. Fred instructed the boys to wash their hands in the creek and to be careful around dynamite. When they got back to camp, they told us what they found.

"God Almighty!" Larry yelled. "You kids stay away from dynamite. Those sticks could have gone off and killed you. They're crystallized and if any nitroglycerine has leaked, just a little jostling could make it blow."

The boys told him where they found it and Larry called the sheriff. Soon, a sheriff's deputy arrived, cordoned off the area, hiked to the site, and carefully placed the dynamite in a spot to blow up without damage to anything or anyone. We all expected a big loud blast, but instead there was a distant soft rumble and a small white cloud rising above the timber. I do not know if the deputy covered the dynamite before lighting the fuse and that prevented a loud explosion, or what. In a few minutes, he walked back to the office and talked to the boys and guests and told them of the danger of crystallized dynamite.

The next week, Larry and Glenn got busy updating the House on the Hill. Larry decided to work on the electrical wiring while Glenn went to town one afternoon. Normally, Glenn did the electrical work, but Larry decided to try the wiring himself. It couldn't be that difficult.

After awhile he came home and sheepishly told me what happened. "I thought I had all the wiring figured out. So, I went inside and flipped on the light switch in the living room. The light bulb blew out with a spark and flash. Then I went from room to room and each time I flipped a switch the bulb blew. I couldn't figure out how come all of them would blow at the same time." He stopped and took a sip of coffee and grinned while he told me, "When I got to the last room and the light bulb blew, it dawned on me. I'd wired the whole house for 220 instead of 110! So, I had to rewire it and now I have to go back up with new light bulbs."

"I sure wouldn't hire you for electrical work," I teased with a smirk on my face.

"Well, I hope I can still give you a good jolt." He grinned and slapped me gently on my rear end as he walked out the door.

Later in the week, Larry and Glenn were at the same cabin working on the oil furnace. When Larry came back, he said that the pilot light kept going out. The furnace room had been added onto the back of the cabin and was a small room. It held the boiler for the hot water baseboard heat. Glenn spilled some oil on the concrete floor when he oiled it. He adjusted the settings and tried to light the pilot again, but dropped the match and the spilled oil caught fire. Larry was standing behind him and immediately grabbed the fire extinguisher. He kept it handy whenever Glenn worked on the gas lines or furnaces.

Larry said he calmly told Glenn to back up and he turned the extinguisher on the fire. He snuffed it out quickly and nothing was damaged. Glenn kept working and eventually got the boiler fixed, but Larry stayed close to extinguish any other fires. No cabin fire…this time!

Star Peak (1972)

Glenn may not have been overly cautious, but neither was Larry in some other ways. A sunny bright summer day invited adventure. During a lull in business Larry and his friend, Marv, decided to climb the 13,500 foot Star Peak that rose from the Sawtooth Range and had been a part of our daily view. The afternoon brought warmth and a cloudless day…a great day for a climb.

When they returned several hours later, they sat at the kitchen table after Larry got each a beer. They raised their beers to salute the sky. Then they told me about their experience.

Larry still had a grin. "We felt victorious while enjoying the view at the top." He described the panoramic scene of all the peaks. "Then we looked at the clouds rolling in, and the rumble of thunder got closer and we saw lightning coming pretty fast and strong." He stopped to take a sip of his beer. "I felt the static electricity buzzing and crackling back and forth on the metal frame of my glasses. My hair stood on end like I had waxed it straight up. That's sure an eerie feeling."

Marv also had glasses and had the same sensation. "I told Larry that I thought it high time we got out of there. That static electricity would draw lightning with all those charged ions."

Larry took over. "Yeah, and the buzzing got stronger. We were sitting ducks up there ready to be zapped. We needed to get the hell out of there fast."

I sat there in shock. I didn't like to hear of almost-death adventures. I finally sputtered, "Good God!"

Larry said they descended at a reasonable pace and then stopped to turn and check if the lightning got closer. "As we turned, a blinding flash and fierce, deafening clap of thunder hit the exact spot where we had stood just a few minutes earlier. A sulfurous odor crept into our nostrils. That got us moving down faster, let me tell you! Lightning almost licked our heels. When we got to the bottom and jumped into the Jeep, we were out of breath." They both laughed.

Marv added, "It sure got our adrenalin flowing, didn't it? That buzz traveling back and forth between my nose and earpieces was really something. I have never felt anything like that before."

"Well, how many more near-death experiences are you going to have, Larry? Or is one of these going to be your last?" I worried about him being injured or killed every time he took off for some adventure.

"There's nothing to worry about. Nothing's going to happen to me." I trusted him completely, but it was hard not to worry.

Shots on the Hill

There were no more climbs because Jeep tours were booked almost every day with both Larry and Glenn driving their four-wheelers. That left me alone in the office to handle reservations for cabins and Jeep tours, check guests in when they arrived and out when they left, do correspondence, visit with tourists, take care of the store and handle the household duties. If we ran out of clean linen, I had to wash and iron sheets and pillowcases, but we had acquired more linen and most times we had plenty. At least we had a modern clothes dryer by then and I didn't have to bother with the clothesline anymore. Sometimes Larry helped out in between tours. After Jeep trips, Larry and Glenn still had to split and haul wood to the cabins and do repairs. Often, we visited with the guests until late. We were busy from early morning until at least 10 at night, and sometimes later. Bed was always welcome.

The Jeep tours were out on a sunny day, per usual, and cabins were being cleaned by Lynn. The children were at the stables, or off on some adventure. Not many tourists popped in and it was a good time to get caught up on correspondence. I heard what sounded like gunshots that afternoon coming from up behind the House on the Hill near the American Lake trail. Pop after pop could be heard. I worried about the horses out on the trail. They might get spooked and buck off a rider. I locked up the lobby, stomped up the hill and yelled, "Stop shooting now. Get out of here. Stop shooting!"

The pops continued. I screamed while climbing more to search for the person or persons. "Stop before a horse comes and gets spooked. Stop it now." I got angrier by the minute.

The pops finally stopped and I walked around the hillside more to search for the culprits, but didn't find anyone and thought they must have been scared off. I was so wrought up that after a few minutes of silence, I decided to walk down to Payne's and tell Mickey what had happened. I needed to calm down and the half mile walk helped, even though I made it quicker than usual.

Mickey poured me a fresh cup of coffee. "What would you have done if you had confronted some guy with a gun?"

"I was so mad, I probably would have kept going and ripped the gun out of the guy's hand as long as he missed me. I hate people who don't think about what they are doing."

I didn't need a horse getting spooked and bucking. A couple of years before a woman had gotten bucked off and broke her arm in seven places. She had misused the horse and pushed it against a barbed wire fence. The pokes and scrapes jolted the horse and he bucked. Thank goodness she admitted what happened and had signed the release form. Another time, a girl was thrown off the American Lake trail and rolled down the mountainside because a hiker didn't control his dog and it barked and charged at her horse.

Finally, after coffee with Mickey I walked back to the lodge. My temper subsided. I never found out who was the shooter. He didn't know how lucky he was!

That night my tale was overshadowed by the national news, which centered on the upcoming election. Then shortly, June exploded with the scandal of the Watergate break-in. Washington D.C. was full of reports. The country demanded that President Nixon be impeached.

Politics and the war became the main items of interest and discussion. I thought what a mess power creates along with hate. The war still tore the country apart. I wondered if the United States would ever see peace again, and if the coming winter would be the last winter for the troops in Vietnam. No doubt, it would be for too many.

Summer continued until it wore out and faded away into the drab colors of fall, but with a promise of virgin white to soon paint the landscape. The summer guests were enjoyable and I wondered why the winter tenants couldn't be that way. What a contrast the tenants were from the summer families! The old era ruined by the new era in some ways.

Winter approached with snow piling high. It looked like we would have a good snowmobile season.

Verbal Abuse (1972)

Fran and Lynn were kept on the payroll to help with snowmobiles. The customers liked their easy manners and genuine smiles as much as we did.

Larry and Fran left to pack the trail on a sunny December morning after the previous night's snowfall. Lynn remained at their quarters until time for business. The two men drove the snowmobiles up the side of the plowed road to the trailhead and hadn't bothered to haul them up on the trailer. The road did not have traffic at that hour and the school bus had already passed. They didn't see a problem using the side of the road.

About 20 minutes after they left, a sheriff's deputy drove in, and stomped into the lobby. He towered over me and plopped his hands down on the counter. I walked to the lobby to greet him and knew his icy grey eyes revealed a great deal of anger and hate.

He began with profanity and then added, "I know that two men drove your snowmobiles on the … road. You know that's illegal. I'm going to catch them when they come back, and I'll confiscate those … machines." He laced each sentence with curses. "I hate snowmobiles! Who do you think you are running those things up here? I'm going to rip them apart."

"You…you can't do that." His outburst shocked me.

"Yes I can. In fact, I'll confiscate all of them here too. Then I'll chop them up into pieces. I'll make it so you won't be able to run them again. They're noisy, ugly and make tracks all over." He spat out more vulgarity. "Cross-country skiers can't enjoy the backcountry in peace and, damn it, you scare the wildlife too. You ought to be arrested for running this damned business and causing trouble for cross-country skiers."

My eyes widened and I didn't know what to say or do, but he scared me. After what seemed like forever with foul language, threats and hate, the officer started for the door. He probably only bellowed a few minutes, but it seemed like an eternity.

He stopped and turned back to me, swore, and yelled, "I'm going to be watching and when they come back, I'll get them. They'll be sorry then." He stomped out and slammed the door, walked to his four-wheel vehicle and drove out the drive.

I had never been verbally abused before, especially by law enforcement, and I felt tears welling up. The officer radiated such a feeling of violence and hate that it frightened me. I got on the C.B. radio to call Larry, but then realized that he had not taken the C.B. that morning. "Dang, dang, dang," I muttered.

Then I thought I should drive the trailer up to the trailhead, so Larry could load the snowmobiles when they came back. I rushed out to the Jeep and my hand shook as I tried to get the key in the ignition. When I succeeded, I backed up, but the trailer jack-knifed. I drove forward and then tried to back up again, but turned wrong and it jack-knifed again. I didn't have the concentration needed and after several unsuccessful tries, I surrendered with upraised arms and decided Larry would just have to take his lumps.

My shoulders sagged and I trudged back inside, sure that the deputy would come out of hiding and stop Larry and Fran as soon as they got on the road. I said a prayer for no violence and kept watch with my binoculars to see when the snowmobiles came down the trail through Ashcroft. After awhile, Larry and Fran came into sight and I waited with baited breath for the sheriff's car to appear when they got on the side of the road to head home. The officer did not appear and I gave a sigh of relief. The deputy must have just wanted to cause a scare and then left the valley. He'd certainly succeeded. When Larry got back, I told him what had happened.

"He had no right to talk to you that way. I don't care if I am in the wrong." There could be no denying that the snowmobiles were on the road, yet there was no excuse for that kind of behavior from a law enforcement officer, regardless of the circumstances. "Someone had to call the sheriff and demand that he do something and I'll bet I know who."

We had a busy winter season and they did not snowmobile on the road again. Snowmobile tours included the movie star, Henry Fonda, and later Ed

McMahan who hosted for the *Tonight Show* with Johnny Carson. McMahan came back for two days. I didn't ask for an autograph from these famous people, or others that I don't remember by name or group, who came through the years. It wasn't the Aspen style, or our style, and we treated celebrities like any other person.

Soon, we learned that a petition was being circulated in town to have Pitkin County ban all snowmobiles on roads. We had our suspicions of who the originator of the petition might be. We weren't worried until Fred Braun notified us that the petition grew and many were signing it. Because Fred used our snowmobiles sometimes to get to the huts or on rescues with the Mountain Rescue teams, he felt one thing would lead to another and pretty soon snowmobiles would be banned altogether. The petition turned out not to be enough for the county to restrict snowmobiles and we lucked out. Our opponent was not happy and we knew something else would come.

Later, Larry decided the time had come to apply for permission from Pitkin County to drive the snowmobiles on the side of the county road, not *on* the road, but on the shoulder. Maybe that would counter a petition that might be circulated again. Public hearings were soon announced. After two hearings and strong objections from mainly one person, the county voted to allow snowmobiles to drive on the shoulder of the roads. The opponent(s) had been adamant and even wanted all snowmobiles banned from all public lands, but the county commissioners did not agree. Finally, it was a battle won for the Brands and other snowmobilers.

Off Road Teens (1972)

On December 7, 1972, we had a different experience involving the side of the road. At 1:30 a.m., I woke to the door buzzer sounding over and over. I put on my robe, woke Larry, and went to the door. A group of high school kids stood there and I saw four girls and one boy huddled together in the bitter cold night.

The boy seemed the calmest. "We ran off the road by your drive and rolled into the ditch. A couple of the guys are trying to get the car out, but these girls have a couple of cuts. Can we come inside and get warm until they get the car out?"

I immediately let them come into the living room and Larry joined me. One of the girls had a gash on her forehead that didn't look serious, but bled profusely and went into the hairline. Another girl had a short, but deep cut on the backside of her hip just below the waistline. It looked like it needed stitches. Another had a long gash on her leg and it definitely needed stitches. The last girl seemed to be in shock, but not injured. Larry had her lie down on the sofa with her feet elevated and he covered her with blankets to keep her warm and talked to her while I put cold compresses on the cuts of the other girls.

Larry looked at me. "We need to call an ambulance and get these girls to the hospital." I started to walk toward the phone.

The boy yelled, "No! We don't want an ambulance." The girls agreed, as they shook their heads from side to side. "No ambulance."

"Then, at least let me call your parents, or you call them."

"No…no call to our parents either. We'll be okay and as soon as the car is out of the ditch we'll take the girls to the hospital." He paused and then said, "I know Kent Mace and he'll come to help us get out. Can I use your phone to call him?"

"Okay. If you won't let us call an ambulance or your parents, you need to get these girls to the hospital as soon as possible." I wondered if they had some alcohol or drugs in the car. It could have been the reason they didn't want an ambulance and especially not the sheriff who would come to investigate.

Kent Mace arrived within minutes of the call and took charge. I don't recall if any of his brothers joined him. He got the car upright and on the road by using a winch on his four-wheeler. Then the group piled in and drove away.

The next day a nurse friend called and told us the girl with the leg injury had 70 stitches. The girl with the lower back injury really lucked out. A small metal pipe, apparently lying loose in the car, rammed into her back on impact. It just missed her spine and kidney. The other girl with the head wound had a few stitches and the one who had been in shock was fine.

The boys were okay. We wondered why they didn't have any injuries. Possibly, the girls were piled in on their laps and they were a cushion… protecting the boys.

I vowed, "If anyone else ever comes here after an accident, I will immediately call the sheriff and an ambulance. I won't take no for an answer. Those kids could have really been in serious danger."

Chapter 15

Peace Agreement (1973)

Winter seemed to settle down and the rest of December and most of January were calm. The long-term tenants gave us a break and I didn't get binocularitis or have to fine tenants. I doubted that our troubles with long-term tenants were ending. I was sure trouble would come.

But there was good news: the Vietnam War would end. The international news of January 27, 1973, was all about the Paris peace agreement signed by the United States and North Vietnam calling an end to the war.

I listened to the news and had a sad feeling engulf me. We saw and read all the years of fighting in Vietnam and the horrible deaths and injuries to the troops and civilians. "Now it's over and we didn't gain a thing. Lives lost for no gain. Many others are prisoners or missing."

Larry felt the same way and nodded. "All the war protests helped the enemy because they understood our country's politics and knew American leaders would eventually have to seek a way out. North Vietnam didn't care how many of their people they killed or how long it took. Our government officials seemed more concerned about politics and their legacy."

I nodded. "This peace agreement calls for a ceasefire, the return of prisoners of war and withdrawal of U.S. troops within 60 days."

Glenn had been listening and interjected, "I read that over 58,000 Americans have lost their lives in Vietnam, and over 153,000 wounded. These figures don't include the POWs and MIAs and it's reported that at least a million Vietnamese have been killed. In the 9 years of the United States involvement, over 500,000 U.S. troops have fought in Vietnam."

Larry added, "People hoped World War II would be the end of all wars. Then we got into the Korean War…Police Action… and now this mess. War will never be over. There will always be something to fight over, or some tyrant. Power and money are the devil in disguise."

Glenn nodded. "And when the GI's come home, they are tormented by peace protesters. They're even spit on and called baby killers. There's no celebration for the return of these men. Not like other wars when the troops came home to parades and treated like heroes."

His comments made me sad. "Yeah, so many servicemen have to weather the storm of hate in the U.S. and still try to hold their heads up high. How many will instead retreat within and suffer mentally in silence?" I remembered hearing of many hateful things said and done to the U.S. military. "Soldiers should never have to come home to hate. They saw enough of it in battle. These GI's have to live with this memory of hatred from their own countrymen. They should be respected regardless of which side people are on. They fought because they were called to do so and felt it their duty. Will the U.S. ever heal from this conflict?" No answer came.

We saw the United States change drastically since this war began. Old ways were dying and our culture changing. Formal life, formal attire and formal ways were tossed aside by the new culture. Many young men no longer wore suits and ties except for special occasions, if at all. Young women did not dress up with hats, gloves, girdles and garter belts holding up their hose. They went braless, did not use makeup, wore long straight hair…no permanents for them…and high heels were tossed out. Bellbottom pants were usually frayed at the bottom and some were held up by a colorful handmade rope or a long sash. The young people thrived on the freedom of sex and drugs and they rebelled against the old social ways.

I sometimes wondered if our area drew the hippies like flies to honey. We had far too many and they were more pesky than flies, as far as I was concerned!

No Peeing Outside! (1973)

My dislike for the new culture came out full force on a cold, sunny February day. While peeling potatoes over the kitchen sink, I looked out the window and saw a pickup drive up to one of the cabins. It wheeled around and parked behind a car that sat in the drive. Three straggly-haired young men got out of the vehicle, stood facing our lodge and relieved themselves in plain view of anyone who looked that way, including me.

I muttered to myself and immediately threw my knife down, ran downstairs, out the back door, and rushed toward them yelling. I hadn't even bothered to put on a jacket, but it was a good thing that I had not carried the knife with me! Larry was in the office and as I flew out and slammed the door, he wondered what happened.

"Get out of here!" I yelled as I ran over to them waving my arms toward the road. "Get out of here!" My small figure didn't seem threatening and they ignored me.

They were done with relief and were getting ready to push the car with their pickup. A 4-foot gap sat between the two vehicles and I stepped in between and yelled, "Get off this land right now. You don't do that right out in front of everyone at our place. I have kids and they don't need to see that. Get off this land now."

A tall ponytailed guy answered, "Hey, lady, we're going to push this car and get it started. You better move…and there's nothing wrong with us peeing here."

They were all taller than me…one by several inches and the other two by about a foot. One sat in the truck easing it closer to me and the back of the car. He held the door open and his head tipped out to hear. He eased the truck closer and the space between me and the vehicles became only about three feet. I stood my ground in between with a set jaw and arms wrapped around me.

"You hippie trash are going to get in your truck and get out of here right now, or I'll call the sheriff."

One moved right in front of me with his arms hanging stiffly by his sides and his hands doubled into fists. He demanded, "What did you call us?" He scowled and his hair fell forward when his head tilted down to meet my eyes. The one in the pickup got out and stood on one side of me while the other one stood on the other side.

I raised my head to look straight up at the one in front of me. *Uh, oh, I've done it this time. I'm going to be a punching bag and land in the mud, pee and snow.* My pride took over and it was too late to back down. I never backed down.

I decided I'd better not repeat what I called them. "You heard me. You're on private land. Now you better get out of here. You're trespassing." They couldn't see my hands shaking because I kept them wrapped around me. My stomach churned, but I was ready for whatever came.

"No. I think you better move and let us get this car started. If you don't move, we'll make you move."

I glanced over to the lodge. "You better not lay a hand on me and you better move now, or else my husband is going to call the sheriff and there's only one way out of this valley and you won't get away." They saw me point to where Larry and Glenn stood watching from the back door ready for anything. Both knew my temper and they thought it might cause a fight this time, but Larry wanted to see what the group would do. He knew that hippies were not usually fighters. It would only take a couple of seconds to reach them, if needed.

They looked to the lodge, then at each other and stepped away glaring at me. "Okay, but we'll be back, lady." They reluctantly got in their pickup, I moved to the side, and they drove out giving me their meanest, hateful expressions.

I stood there until they were out on the county road and then I stomped back to the lodge. Larry just shook his head and I heard him tell Glenn, "She's never going to be tamed." He tolerated my flare-ups with the tenants, but he didn't want to battle them. His method was to talk and avoid conflict. Mine always seemed to be to fight. He worried that some day he might have to fight my battle.

I continued to peel the potatoes, but with a new vigor. Later, I told Larry I was sorry, but I just blew when I saw them. I considered their action uncivilized and immoral. My upbringing just could not accept that behavior.

Kelly's Cabin Gone! (1973)

Winter was bound and determined to give us no rest. Larry and I were awakened at 3:30 a.m. on March 12th. It was a bitter cold night and the temperature had dropped to -20°F. The banging on the door was continuous and the doorbell buzzed endlessly. When I rushed to the door, two tenants yelled, "Kelly's cabin's on fire!"

Larry came up behind me and immediately bundled up. He grabbed a hose, ran to the cabin, and hooked the hose up to the outside faucet wrapped with insulation to keep the water from freezing. He hoped to quench the fire and used his thumb over the end of the hose to help make a spray. He thought it was just delaying the inevitable, but he tried to bring the flames to a halt.

I ran to wake up Glenn and Fran and they came running. Then I asked Larry if I should call the Aspen Fire Department. He replied that it was too late.

I walked back to our home and watched from our window. I saw Fran run up on the porch and kick the door in with all the force he could muster. As the door flung open, it toppled to the side and out whooshed gusts of thick, grey smoke that engulfed him. He inhaled it deeply and then bent over coughing hard and long. Then he straightened, raised an arm over his head, and tried to peer inside the cabin, but didn't see anyone through all the smoke and flames. It was too dangerous to enter and he had to back away and just watch the flames.

Larry and Glenn had realized that the fire could not be stopped and was out of control. Larry put the hose down, turned the spigot off, and let the cabin burn to the ground.

All the excitement woke the children and they watched with me from our window. The fire consumed the cabin quickly and the red blaze soared to the sky through the gray-white smoke.

It fascinated Tina. "Isn't it pretty with all those big red and orange flames against the dark sky?"

"No! It is *not* pretty at all! I hate fire." This reinforced my fear of fires all the more. *How many more fires are we going to have? Why always fire?*

Tina watched in silence after my outburst. Fran came into the lodge while Larry and Glenn were tending to the burning embers. He didn't feel well and I noticed immediately that his skin was the color of granite. It was not from ash fallout, but the actual pigment of his skin. He had inhaled so much smoke that his skin turned gray and it caused him to become quite ill. I tried to help, but couldn't do much except let him try to get it out of his system. He finally stopped vomiting and shuffled down to his quarters. He would recover after a night of rest, but he sure had paid for his bravery in trying to save someone… if there had been someone in the cabin. When Larry came back, he told me that another tenant said Kelly was downtown.

A tenant told us the next morning, "Kelly cleaned ashes out of his wood stove and put them in a cardboard box on the floor. I saw him do it. I thought he'd take them out to a snow bank later."

Larry almost yelled, "That idiot! You don't keep hot ashes in a cardboard box on a wood floor. Everyone is warned to keep the ashes in a metal container, like a pail, and in a snow mound until the ashes are cold clear through. Ashes can stay hot for two weeks, even in the cold. How brainless can a person be?"

The tenant's hands flew up by his shoulders. "Hey, man, you sure aren't going to have to worry about me doing that. Not after what I saw last night."

When Kelly finally came back from town, he discovered that his meager belongings were now a pile of ashes. He stayed in a friend's cabin the rest of the night and again for several nights. The townspeople soon heard of his plight and gave him donations of money and goods. One store donated an expensive pair of ski pants and a parka, but Kelly complained that the store should have included ski boots. He gave no thanks for any of the gifts and even expected someone to give him a pair of skis so he could continue to ski. It seemed like all he could do was complain because he didn't get more.

Larry had no sympathy. "Life is going to be a disappointment for him, if he keeps thinking the good life is his due." I agreed.

There were still a couple of months before the long-term tenants would be gone. I wondered if we would have another fiery finish before winter ended.

Instead, frozen water pipes became the next problem. It seemed we could never get enough insulation to prevent freezing of all the cabins. Larry and Glenn did the thawing and their labor brought a few choice words.

Finally, winter was conquered by the warmth of spring and I gave a sigh of relief. It was a slow process, but what a pleasure to see the new season. The long-term tenants moved out, and we were glad to have them gone. Then the work began to ready the cabins for the summer tourists.

On Memorial Day 1973, weekend business began with a flourish. Many repeat guests were returning. Some had been coming to Elk Mountain Lodge since childhood and now were grown up, married and bringing their children along with grandpa and grandma.

Fran and Lynn had decided to go back to their hometown in Pennsylvania, so we hired new wranglers for the summer, but we made a poor choice. It became evident right off that a mistake had been made, but too late to try to find new wranglers. So, we accepted our fate.

"Those lazy wranglers don't want to work," Larry said to me. "They close whenever they want and take off for town or just laze around. I wouldn't be surprised if they were taking more than their cut too. The reports they give me don't look like enough money for the number of people I saw riding horses." Talking to them did no good.

Helicopter and Hut Lumber (1973)

June and July passed quicker than a chased rabbit and August arrived before we knew it. The director of the mountain ski touring huts, Fred Braun, decided they had enough money from donations to build another ski hut high in the backcountry. He had the bundles of lumber delivered to Elk Mountain Lodge and placed in a field. A helicopter hovered over our field on August 11th and lowered a cable. Fred, Larry and Glenn hooked a bundle to the cable and when it was secured the pilot was waved away. Then the helicopter headed to the site up on the mountain with the lumber dangling below. At the building site, another crew waited to unhook the lumber. The chopper returned for another load and continued until all the bundles of lumber were transported to the site.

The children, guests and I watched in fascination. Each time the helicopter rose with the lumber dangling, we held our breath waiting to see if the cable would break loose and the lumber plunge to the ground. Nothing happened and every load went according to plan and the operation was completed successfully. Then the volunteer crew at the site began building. The foundation had been constructed earlier. In a few weeks, the hut would be completed and

Helicopter picking up a load of lumber

ready for occupancy. The ski hut association named it the "Goodwin-Green Hut" after two mountaineers: Peter Goodwin and Carl Greene.

Fred Braun had been a main initiator in starting the hut system in 1946 and he was the director of the system for years. He maintained the huts, stocked them with firewood, did repairs and cleaned them after use. Sometimes, Glenn would go with him to help, or other volunteers, but Fred went with or without help in both summer and winter. Sometimes, a hut ran out of wood because more had been used than anticipated and that meant hauling more firewood up. Fred usually stopped at Elk Mountain Lodge and often used one of our snowmobiles to get to a hut in the winter. I really liked that remarkable man with his German accent and short, toughened body always on the move. Years were telling on him, but he never seemed to give up and was always ready for whatever came. When he took off on a snowmobile and did not return at a time we expected, we worried, but he'd make it back each time.

Summer rushed to fall too fast again. We gave a sigh of relief when the wranglers left by September. At least there were no horse rescues or injuries, but revenue from the stables turned out to be way below average. When we checked the wrangler's quarters, we saw that several days of cleaning were needed to get it back in shape. The wrangler's laziness included no cleaning.

Larry looked out behind the quarters on the last day of cleaning and got a surprise. Under the kitchen window next to the outside wall sat two large marijuana plants thriving in the sun. They were hidden from view of the lodge or the drive to the stables and we had not seen them. Larry dug them up and burned them in the field. "It's a wonder I didn't get high from inhaling the smoke. That's the worst horse season we've ever had." The end of the season proved that the horse business went down drastically. Yet we knew the demand was there.

We welcomed fall…the quiet time before winter. We enjoyed the changing colors on the mountainsides and the peaks changing from grey to swatches of new virgin snow draping the peaks like frosting dribbling off the sides of a cake. By October, the cabins were full of long-term tenants. I didn't know what would happen, but I hoped winter tenants and snowmobile tours would give us some peace and quiet. Hope springs eternal.

Chapter 16

Thieves and Hitchhikers (1974)

Aspen embraced the ski season, but so did thieves. When the skiers came down off the mountain runs and into town, they propped their skis and poles in an unlocked rack. Then they walked to a bar or café nearby for an après-ski social. A thief had easy pickings during the busy season. He watched to see who just arrived and where they'd gone. After 10 or 15 minutes, he'd pirate the skis and poles and walk away as if he were the owner. The thief usually transported the skis to another area to sell…if he was smart.

A sheriff's deputy arrived at our lodge one January afternoon and asked which cabin Randy rented. I pointed to the Buckskin and when he left, I quickly grabbed my binoculars and saw the deputy hand Randy what must have been a warrant and he entered. They came out in a few minutes with Randy in handcuffs and placed in the back seat of the sheriff's car. The deputy put several pairs of skis in the trunk before driving off.

I told Larry and Glenn over lunch, "I talked to Connie, in the Homestead, and she said her skis were stolen a couple of day ago. Randy approached one of her friends to buy some skis cheap. Her friend recognized Connie's skis and Randy, but he didn't recognize her. She called the police. The search of his cabin also turned up several additional pairs of stolen skis."

Larry laughed. "He's not too smart. How dumb can you be to try to sell the skis in the same town?"

I agreed. "We're going to evict him. We don't want a thief here."

When Randy got out on bail, he received our notice to vacate and he did not argue. He packed his belongings and left while I watched with my binoculars. I wondered if he would skip town or wait for the trial. Upon checking his cabin, we found the usual mess and dirt, but no damage. *He must have been too busy stealing to stick around and damage his cabin.*

More ski troubles came. About every day, a few ski groups schussed down the backside of Ajax Mountain, instead of taking the ski runs back into town. They enjoyed the powder and ended up on the Castle Creek Road at Little Annie hill between our lodge and Aspen. If a friend did not pick them up, they attempted hitching a ride back into town.

Over coffee one evening, Norm Payne said that he saw more and more skiers hitching on the road. "I don't stop for them, but I sure receive four-letter words and obscene gestures as I drive by. This happens almost every time I go to town. I hear other people get the same treatment if they don't stop."

"Well, let me tell you what happened to me." I slapped my hand on the table. "Yesterday, I decided to be nice and I picked up four skiers. They put their skis in the back of the station wagon, but hung them over the back seat. I took them to the front door of their hotel. They got their stuff, slammed the car doors and walked away without a single thank you. I didn't think about it when they pulled their skis out, but later I saw a rip in the top of the back headrest. I know it was from those skis."

"So, are you going to pick up anymore now?" Norm asked.

"No. I'll wave as I pass while they cuss me and give their gestures. Lord! Where is decency anymore! Can it get any worse?"

The next week, I drove to town and saw four skiers thumbing a ride close to the turn off for the Music School and I was not about to stop. Just as I started to pass them, one of the guys swung his skis, like a baseball bat, right at my headlights. I swerved to miss and pulled back into my lane before the oncoming car got too close. The skiers yelled their usual nasty comments and gestures. My answer was kept in the car, but that swing scared me. When I got home, I told Larry, "I wished we had an ax in the car. I would have stopped and chopped that guy's skis up. They could have caused me to crash!"

Winter continued, but I never put an ax in the car. Neither did I run into anymore skis being swung at my car as I passed. Nasty yells and gestures continued, but I kept going.

Rescue at Lindley (1973)

Our snowmobile business flourished. Cross-country skiers also enjoyed the Sawtooth Range on day trips and some rented the ski huts for more than a day venture. They would ski the surrounding area enjoying the powder and Mother Nature.

Late in the afternoon on March 16th, two men skied from the Lindley Hut to our lodge. One told us, "Our buddy crashed into a tree and we think he broke some ribs. He needs to get to the hospital, but we didn't have a way to get him down here. He's really in a lot of pain. Will you help us?"

By now, Larry knew the sheriff's phone number by heart. "I'll call it in." It would be another rescue with Elk Mountain Lodge used as the base.

Aspen Mountain Rescue came and borrowed our snowmobiles. They hooked a litter sled on behind one machine. Fred Braun, Glenn and three other rescuers left at 6:30 p.m. Upon returning, Glenn told how they handled the rescue.

They were able to snowmobile up most of the way on our trail, but there was no packed trail over to the injured man and the machines and a litter would get stuck in the deep powdery snow. So, they put their snowshoes on and duck-waddled the last yards to the injured skier. After giving emergency medical treatment, they tightly strapped the man in the litter-sled. The rescuers tugged and pulled the litter through the deep snow and finally got back to the snowmobiles. They hooked the litter sled on behind the one machine and the driver cruised slowly so it wouldn't bounce too much.

Lindley hut in it's glorious setting

They arrived back at our lodge at 11:00 p.m. and hoisted the litter into the rescue van and it headed to the hospital. The other rescuers, including Fred and Glenn, stayed for some food and coffee. They relaxed and warmed up a little before heading home. I wondered if any rescuers were able to get a good sleep and be ready for another day, even if it meant another rescue immediately. They never knew what would be next.

That was the last excitement for the season. There were no more rescues or arrests at Elk Mountain Lodge. Winter expired, snow disappeared into the ground, and sprouts and buds began to peek out for the sun to nourish. It seemed to bring new hope and appreciation for the alpine glory. Something new came with each season. The long-term tenants moved out by the end of May and left the cleaning to us. Snowmobiles were put to bed and all cabins were scrubbed and prepared for the summer tourists, including more firewood from the high country and the wood racks stocked. We also re-stocked the store and put up the sign to come to the office for service.

The summer season got off to a bang. Tourists kept us on the run all summer, but it was nice to have the repeats back. We enjoyed visiting with our "summer families" and hearing about their lives. Those who lived in cities made me realize how thankful I was that I lived in God's country while Aspen gave all the culture a city could. There was the Aspen Music Festival, lectures by many famous people, conferences, concerts, ballet, art galleries, exclusive restaurants and, of course, folk musicians at all the lounges. To top it off, Aspen was surrounded by mountains and peaks for a daily view of glory.

Cathedral Peak from Pearl Pass

Cathedral Peak Rescue (1974)

Before our busy July 4, 1974, dwindled, it brought another rescue. At 2:30 p.m., Glenn got a call that a girl climbing Cathedral Peak had fallen and broken both legs. Her companion hiked out to notify Mountain Rescue, but couldn't describe the exact location of the girl. Glenn and a rescue crew started to climb up to Cathedral Peak. By 6:00 p.m. a helicopter located her and dropped three rescuers nearby because Glenn and the other rescuers were not close enough at that time. They climbed to her and gave her what medical treatment they could and then started to transport her to a location safe for pickup by the chopper. Darkness set in before the girl could be lifted up and into the helicopter.

The rescuers hiked out and arrived back at our lodge about 10:30 p.m. tired and hungry. I made sandwiches and coffee and set out cookies, which were devoured in minutes. My notes state that one of our guests and a Dr. Pieper also helped, but I don't know how and I don't remember these two men. Apparently, they helped when the patient arrived at the lodge. The rescuers left about 11:00 p.m. for home and rest.

It had been a very long full day with the phone ringing off the hook, cabin cleaning, cabins checking in and out, store purchases, and then the rescue. Larry and I plopped in bed about midnight and immediately fell asleep. We did not have our July 4th fireworks at Elk Mountain Lodge. The kids had gone to town to see the fireworks with friends, so they didn't miss ours. Some of the guests may have been disappointed, but when they learned of the rescue, they agreed it was more important than our celebration.

Meal Rides, Worms, Walk Home (1974)

By this time, Tina was old enough to earn more spending money. She had become our part-time maid helping the full-time maid. She also babysat for the guests and worked at the stables as often as possible. In the early evenings, she and Greg helped with the children's wiener-roast rides. They were held separately from the adult steak rides, but at the same time. The parents could enjoy themselves with other adults, and the children would be taken care of while having fun.

The wranglers had a special location for the steak rides and the tourists sat on logs arranged around the fire to eat and visit. The wranglers brought a grate for the top of the rock firebox and steaks were grilled to perfection on the open fire. After dinner, the adults sipped their coffee perked over the open fire. They shared experiences and talked about their city lives.

The children's wiener roasts were at a completely different location and led by Tina and Greg. The children gathered wood and helped make the fire. Then Tina and Greg helped them cut a branch from a tree or bush and carve a point at the end to spear the wiener and roast it over the open fire. The same stick was used to make S'mores over the flames. There were always a few wieners or marshmallows that fell into the fire, but they were replaced and tears dried.

Greg, also, had other means to earn spending money. He decided to sell worms to the fishermen who always wanted good bait. Larry ordered a supply of containers in large and small sizes. The container cost was deducted from Greg's first proceeds to teach him the realities of business. The worms were kept in a large 2-foot x 8-foot wooden box that Larry built and filled with soil and Greg dug for the worms to be kept in it. The rich soil by the ponds produced

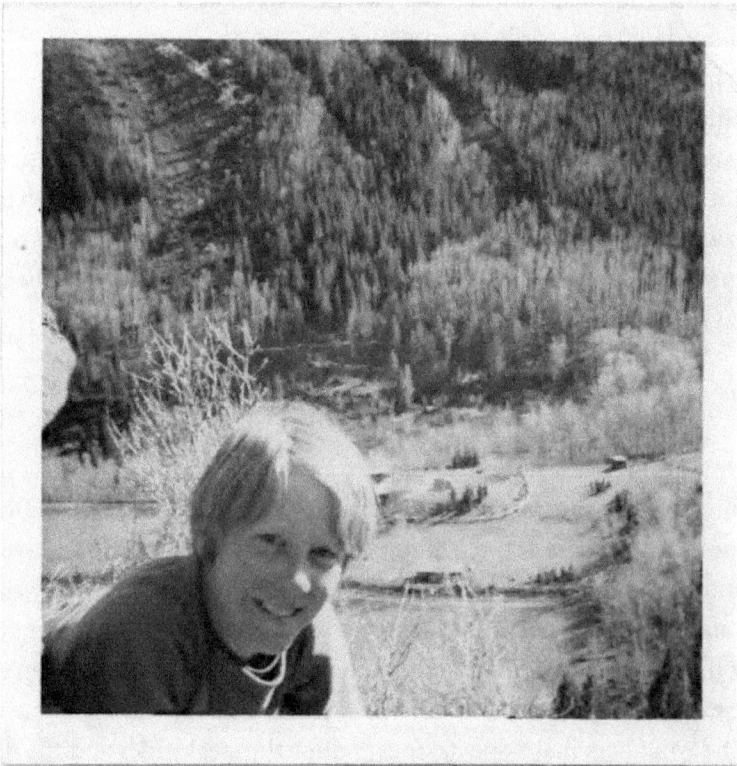

Greg on one of his excursions

plenty of worms. He made signs for the lobby, the store bulletin and the entry post by the road. Some evenings, Tina helped him catch night crawlers. His business quickly flourished, but I became the unwilling salesman for him.

"Greg, you have to fill several containers each morning so they will be ready for selling. You'll need to fill both the large and small sizes. Don't forget." He had forgotten the day before.

"I will, Mama. But if I'm fishing, or not here, will you sell them for me, pleeeese?"

"Okay, I guess." He knew how to work me.

Often he forgot and disappeared on excursions. When a fisherman wanted worms, I reluctantly dug through the dirt box, grabbed the worms and quickly dropped them in the container. I wrinkled up my nose in disgust through the process. Then I wiped my hands on a rag, put the lid on the container and gave it to the buyer. I hated this task and couldn't help but think that the night crawlers were almost big enough to be snakes. I hated snakes…any kind or size! The city girl still lingered in me at times and I still hated worms and mice.

I scolded Greg one day. "Greg, you forgot to fill your worm containers again today. You have to remember. I may not sell worms for you, if you don't have them ready."

Tina and Greg were always busy somewhere, working or playing…or arguing. It seemed like Greg and Tina were determined to injure the other physically or by insults and teasing. Fights erupted often, but Larry and I had a hard time figuring out which child started an argument. Susy stayed on the sidelines and out of their spats.

Coming back from church one nice warm Sunday, Greg and Tina picked on each other and poked, hit, teased and yelled. I could only turn around from the front seat and order them to stop with repeated strong requests. Finally, about a mile from the lodge, I told Larry to stop the car. He pulled over to the side of the road and I bounced out. I opened the back door and said, "Get out, Tina and Greg."

The two got out of the car and stood there facing me. Their eyes were big and the two fell silent while waiting for my hand to land on their behinds.

I didn't. "Now you two walk the rest of the way home and see if you can quit your fighting." I got back in the car. "Drive home, Larry." He did, but with a grin on his face.

Susy stayed silent and just took in my action. When home, I watched for Tina and Greg out the window, hoping to see the two walking up the road, but there seemed no sign of them. Larry said he needed to check something at the House on the Hill. I suspected that he walked down into the back field and secretly watched the children to make sure they were all right.

It seemed like hours, but probably only half an hour passed when the two came into sight, walking at a leisurely pace and laughing. I knew the punishment had been worse for me than for them.

Chapter 17

The Old Pickup (1974)

Summer continued and plenty of guest's children scampered around as well as my own. They often joined Larry or Glenn when they used the old 1938 pickup to drive around camp and pick up garbage. The pickup, almost void of any color, had some dents and plenty of scratches, but it somehow had character. Maybe the sturdiness of a well-built product revealed its history of perseverance while battling the wars of the seasons and age. Our children and guests' children sat on the bed walls and considered it fun to be bounced around on the bumpy drives. After all the cabin trash containers were dumped into the pickup, the men loaded it into our dumpster. When full, the trash would be transported to the county dump.

On July 26th, we sold the old pickup for $100.00. It felt like we sold a part of the history of Elk Mountain Lodge. That old 1938 pickup had been on the property for years servicing the lodge and suddenly it was no more. The children would miss the fun of riding in that old beat up truck while bouncing around the grounds. The new pickup didn't have the character or seasoning.

Fall swept in with brisk winds tossing the golden leaves to the ground. Snow began to paint the peaks to enhance the surrounding mountains' vivid hues.

Picnics and Partying (1974)

I looked at the reservations and told Larry, "Dorothy and Jack Warriner are coming tomorrow. Their cabin is all ready. I'll fix a roast beef dinner and we can discuss our plans." They had become regular guests every year in September and we looked forward to their two week stay.

"Okay. It will be good to see them again. I'd like to know what the Texans have to say about the war, all the protests, and the hippies."

Jack stood a couple of inches shorter than Larry, but he was lean and brawny. His white crew-cut hair showed his late 40-some years and his pale blue eyes sure caught the breath of the women. Dorothy's cropped red hair topped her small frame and her mouth seemed to always be moving. Their Texas accents were so thick that once in awhile I felt I needed an interpreter.

When they arrived, we planned our annual picnic for that coming Saturday at our favorite spot across the creek from the lodge.

I warned the children on that day, "When Dorothy and I are on that swinging bridge crossing the creek, don't you kids dare start bouncing and swinging."

"Ah, that's no fun." Tina and Greg said in unison and grinned at each other.

After a stern look from me, the two decided they better not do anything. We adults and Susy, holding tightly to me, crossed the old narrow swing bridge. Each of us held onto the rope hand railings for balance as the bridge swayed high above Castle Creek. Then Tina and Greg had their fun bouncing up and down and swaying to and fro before crossing over. We all hiked down the other side to the picnic area by the creek.

Glenn brought the 18-inch diameter iron skillet that the wranglers used for cookouts and camping trips. An antique iron floor grate, from an old Victorian home, sat on top of the rock walls laid in a circle for the fire pit. It sat in an open spot near the creek.

"Okay, you kidlets," Larry said. "Start gathering some small dry branches for the firewood. We'll show you how to place the pieces cross-ways, piling them on top of one another, to get a good fire going."

The children scattered. Soon, they came with arms full of little twigs. Larry and Jack had gotten some larger wood and they started the fire while the youngsters observed.

"Now that the fire is going strong, we'll get the skillet hot and then the hamburgers can go in," Jack said in his Texan drawl.

Dorothy and I had previously molded the hamburger patties. Each child was allowed to plop a couple into the skillet. We set the rest of the food on the wooden picnic table with attached benches. It was placed there many years ago. It sat among the tall pines near the small gurgling offshoot of Castle Creek. We opened the bowl of potato salad and set out fresh sliced tomatoes, onion slices and hot spicy Texas dill pickles canned by Dorothy. After indulging, we

Jack Warriner and Tina washing the skillet in the creek

adults sipped beer and visited while the children played around the towering pines and in the stream winding around the picnic site. Then time came to clean up.

"Come here kids," Jack called. "I'll teach y'all how to clean the skillet using sand and pebbles and then rinse with the fresh stream water."

The washing delighted the children and they couldn't believe that dishes or pans could be cleaned with dirt, pebbles and cold water. They also learned the importance of dousing a fire with plenty of water when camping or picnicking. They were taught to burrow under the top pile of ashes and stir them to be sure all were soaked and cold and then to pile dirt on top. When they finished, we climbed up the bank to the swinging bridge, crossed and headed home through the field. We felt the pleasure of a perfect day with friendship.

Later that week, Larry came in. "Remember, we're going on another Jeep trip with Jack and Dorothy tomorrow."

"Yeah. Dorothy is frying the chicken. I'll make the baked beans and bring potato chips."

The next day, we climbed in our two Jeeps and headed up the trail. At a pleasant spot high in the Rockies, we stopped and set up the picnic amidst the pines and aspens. A stream gurgled through the rocks nearby. The aspen trees were gilded in gold, mandarin orange, yellow and fading grey-green. Some leaves were trimmed on the edges with deep brown caused by frostbite. The surrounding mountain vistas seemed closer with the fresh new snow sitting in the crevices. It could have been a picture out of a photographer's magazine or on a postcard.

We had our picnic at an old mining claim. A dilapidated log cabin sat on the hillside with its sod roof still intact, but it sloped down on one side touching the ground. It had lost its support beam to decay. I knew it wouldn't be too many more years before the cabin completely fell in and would be covered by brush.

Larry gathered the children. "You kids listen to me. You are not allowed to venture into that old mine." The entrance on the hillside by the cabin brought temptation, but he knew the dangers of mine tunnels. A shaft supported by decades-old timber could collapse at any time with just a slight push or shift of the earth. He saw that this one had already caved in near the entrance.

The children reluctantly agreed and knew that his deep, strong voice meant no challenge. They played around the old cabin until it was time to head home.

Joanne and Larry dolled up for night out!

Then the Warriner-Brand annual night out on the town arrived. Mickey Payne sat with the children. I wore my long sleeved floor-length black dress trimmed in white around the neck and I wore my wig because I didn't have time to set my hair in curlers. Larry wore his sport jacket over a white turtleneck which accentuated his deep tan. He was a handsome man when dressed up, and I told him so. He joked, "Well, guess I'll see how many young gals I can catch tonight."

"You better not, or they'll have me to contend with." I raised my fist. Larry laughed.

We enjoyed dinner at the Crystal Palace, a popular dinner theater in Aspen, and we loved the singing waiters and waitresses. The owners, Mead and Joannie Metcalf, made everyone laugh with the humorous and political satire songs. Later, we toured the lounges around Aspen listening to the folk singers. It might have been this year that we also enjoyed the Nitty Gritty Dirt Band, or maybe the Drifters, or another popular group. I don't remember the years, but we listened to several famous folk singers through the years. We liked folk music over rock music.

Later that November, Larry's forehead swelled up again and became an angry infection. The same piece of aerosol can that exploded in 1972 once again plagued him. An x-ray showed a small dent in Larry's skull and a metal fragment imbedded. The doctor made an incision to drain the poison and gave him an antibiotic. In no time, his forehead resumed the normal size and the infection died. He would not let Mickey Payne touch his head this time.

Close that Pass!

Thanksgiving came, but with a lack of snow. Independence Pass still remained open on December 4, 1974, and the mountains had little snow. The pass is on the Continental Divide and stands 12,095 feet high. The road from Aspen to Twin Lakes is narrow and at some spots it clings to the side of the mountain with hundreds of feet of drop offs and there are no guard rails. Drivers have to be cautious and on some curves the road narrows to one lane. If another car comes the opposite way, the driver heading up must stop and find a wide enough spot to let the other vehicle pass. Independence Pass is normally closed by early winter, sometimes in October and sometimes in late November, just depending on the snowfall. Drivers could go over the pass in

1974 until December 15th. Then finally, snow came and the State closed the Pass.

Skiing and snowmobiling were in as sad a shape as Independence Pass until the mid-December storms began. Then, business perked up and the snowstorms gave the needed base. At last, morale perked up. It would be a good year as far as snow after all, but we expected our usual problems with the long-term tenants. I'd keep my eye on them.

My binoculars got a workout and on a December morning I counted 22 extra people in cabins and the next day there were 26 extra people. Twenty of those came from the Homestead cabin. I made out the bills and collected the $3.00 extra per person per day. *They must be stacked in like logs in the wood racks.*

My fines stopped the extra people, but we were just beginning the season. Per usual, I would be the one to pass out the bills, warnings, or evictions. Larry and Glenn were the nice guys, but the tenants knew me as the wicked old witch. So I lived up to the image when necessary.

Frozen Vehicles and Pipes (1975)

After my crackdowns, the tenants were quiet the first part of the new year, but the weather wasn't. On January 9th, the Forest Service warned of avalanche danger. Melting snow refreezes and is like sugar crystals, that form a weak bond. Each new layer is weaker than the snowpack found on less steep terrain. Even a slight vibration or a weight change can trigger a slide. Larry checked the trail and knew the danger was too high and we cancelled snowmobile tours. I wondered if he had ever come close to being caught by an avalanche. He'd not told me, but I knew it could be a possibility.

A few days later 8-inches of new snow greeted the mountains and the morning low of -30°F greeted us. The high for the day only made it to -6°F. The wind chill factor dropped the temperature even further, so snowmobile tours were once again cancelled. It became just too cold to zip along on a machine while the needle-pricking icy air blasted through to the bones. The wind chill factor would be at 10°F to 20°F below the standing-still temperature, depending on the speed.

The bitter cold day became a bitter day all around. Vehicles refused to start...the freezing temperatures had conquered their innards and the sun did not warm enough to help. Larry and Glenn came in frozen to the bone.

They brushed off the dripping ice from their eyebrows, and from their hair which sneaked out over the forehead below their ski caps. I poured a cup of hot coffee for each of them.

Glenn wrapped his hands around his cup. "I coaxed and coaxed, until ol' Nellie Belle finally chugged and sputtered to life. She had been plugged in all night, but took her time to turn over."

Larry added, "After she was purring, we jump-started the tenants' vehicles." He took his last sip of coffee, "We needed a jump start to warm up before we thaw the Montezuma and Trout water pipes." He rose and put his parka on. "The sooner it's done, the sooner we can sit by the fire." Glenn followed.

After a couple of hours, the pipes were thawed with a torch and the cabins had running water once again. Larry and Glenn checked inside and found no leaks. They were almost icicles when they returned. Their fingers and toes must have been close to being frostbitten. The fireplace crackled and the two sat on chairs pulled in front of the fireplace, leaned forward, and let the heat warm their outer bodies while coffee warmed their insides.

Frigid air almost froze time. The children peered through the white diamond-sparkly, spidery-iced webs clinging to the windowpanes. They had no desire to venture outside and neither did I.

Chapter 18

Sandy Gulch Avalanche! (1975)

Finally, the weather turned back to bearable. Vehicles started in the morning and snowmobile tours were back in swing. On January 15, 1975, while Larry guided a tour, a frantic man ran into the lodge. Almost out of breath, he blurted out, "I need help!"

I jumped up from my office chair, heart beating fast, and knew it had to be bad. "What happened?"

"There's been an avalanche at Sandy Gulch and my friend's son was caught in it."

"Oh Lord! Wait just a minute. The Forest Service is here talking to my brother-in-law. They're rescuers and will call it in right away." Dick Cerise had been measuring the snow depth in the high country for the Forest Service records and he stopped in to visit. I ran to the kitchen where he and Glenn were enjoying coffee. They came to the office and Dick asked what happened.

"My friend, his son, and I were cross-country skiing. When we skied across the open gully, about halfway up the mountain the snow shifted. We heard it like a whip snapping and all of a sudden the crest on top cracked and in seconds an avalanche started to pour down." He stopped and wiped his face to give him time for more control. "We tried to out-race it by skiing across the gully as fast as we could. Chuck and I were ahead. We made it, but his 14-year old boy didn't." His voice cracked, he lowered his head and his fingers burrowed into his eyes trying to halt the tears.

"Do you have an idea where he may be?"

"No. At first, we saw him being tumbled over and over. Then we just saw the skis. He may be close to the bottom, but I don't know. When everything became still and quiet, we yelled and yelled trying to find him, but he didn't answer. We searched for any sign of him, but didn't find anything. Paul stayed to probe and dig." He swallowed hard and his shoulders sagged. "Can you help us?"

Immediately, Dick called for a rescue. He didn't want to say, but he felt pretty sure they were too late to find the boy alive. At least 15 minutes had already passed. Glenn quickly gathered equipment from the storeroom. Dick had probes in his truck.

Glenn had a somber face when he returned about 4:30 p.m. and slumped down in a chair. He and Dick started searching before the rescue crew arrived. He said the air smelled like fresh-chopped wood mixed with dirt and ice water. There wasn't even a sound of a bird chirping. The only life seemed to be a frantic father digging in the packed snow yelling and yelling for his son, but no answer came.

Glenn said, "The searchers came with their probes and the search dog and it became a recovery mission. It took a couple of hours to find the body." He stopped for a minute and took a deep breath. "The heartbroken father accompanied his son's body back to town and to give his wife the devastating news."

He remained quiet for a long time sipping coffee. It had to be hard to recover a body, especially the body of a 14 year old. So far, 1975 had eight avalanche deaths in Colorado and we were only in January. We hoped there would be no more.

Bobcat and Rabbit (1975)

Another film crew arrived in February to ask for permission to use the pasture field for a documentary about bobcats for a wildlife segment on TV. The snow sat about 6 feet deep in the field, but less around the trees. The day before the shooting, the crew fenced off about an acre of land with 6 foot high dense chicken-wire fencing. They anchored the fence posts in the deep snow. Filming would begin the next day.

"Can we watch them, Mama?" Susy asked on filming day and Greg also echoed the question.

"Okay. We'll walk down on the road and stand outside the fenced area. But you will have to be quiet, stay out of the way and not upset the filming."

When they walked to the site, they saw a bobcat in a cage sitting on the backend of a pickup. In a second pickup, another cage held a rabbit.

Greg saw the rabbit. "What's the rabbit for, Mama?"

"We'll see. Remember, this is a film about animals and nature." I had a pretty good idea what would happen.

When the crew had all their cameras set up, they took both cages into the fenced compound. First, they slid up the gate of the rabbit cage and it bounded out. Instantly, they opened the bobcat's cage and he burst out pursuing the rabbit. I noticed how graceful and quick the bobcat moved on the snow. His large paws acted like snowshoes and his pointed ears positioned forward caught the sounds of the prey trying to escape. The rabbit hopped and leaped exceptionally fast and used good evasive tactics. Soon both the rabbit and bobcat were in the trees. Cameras had been set up everywhere to film all the maneuvers of each animal.

We could not see them and waited. Then we heard the cries of the rabbit so plaintively asking for mercy. It sounded almost like a baby being tortured and screaming pitifully for compassion. Then dead silence came. I shivered.

"Oh, Mama, how horrible!" Susy wrapped her arms around herself and I gave her a hug.

The bobcat had won the chase and silenced his prey: however, the children did not feel it fair because of the fencing. Who knew what the end result would have been, if there were no fence?

I tried to explain that the filming would show how nature worked. "There is a reason for all animals to be on this earth and food for another species." The children shuffled home with their heads lowered in sorrow. When we got home they told Larry about the filming.

"It wasn't fair! The poor rabbit didn't have a chance," Susy said.

Larry tried to explain again. The children pouted, but soon went to their room and started to play a game. The incident faded in their minds in a few days.

I'm Not Moving! (1975)

No more filming, and life went back to the normal lodge business, including more trouble. Long-term tenants hadn't changed. I monitored them closely. Paul became past due on January rent and I posted an eviction notice on his cabin door after our reminder notices were ignored.

Paul stomped up to the lodge. "I'm not leaving. I'm expecting my folks to come through with some money anytime. You'll just have to wait."

I couldn't accept that. "Nope, either we get the money by tomorrow, or you will have to move out right away. No point in arguing. It won't do any good…either the money or out."

He stomped out with his eyes squinted menacingly.

The next day I picked up Susy from school and headed back home on the well-plowed Castle Creek Road. The snow had been piled high on the sides of the road, or pushed off the mountainside or down a slope.

About 4 miles from home I saw a car coming the opposite direction, but straight at me on my side of the road. I yelled, "My God! Pull over, you idiot."

My one hand pumped the horn and the other held tight to the steering wheel. I would not drive off the road and roll down the slope on my side. If I tried to swerve over to the other side, he could suddenly move back and we would collide. "He's got to move over," I said softly through clenched teeth. Susy leaned over from the back seat with arms propped on the headrest of the front seat. She looked at the car coming straight at us and asked, "Why is that car on our side of the road?" I couldn't answer.

I persisted with the horn blasts, slowed down more and the car continued straight toward us. When it came about 15 feet from my car, I recognized the driver. It was Paul, the one we were evicting. I saw the "whites of his eyes" glaring at me with a devil-bent-for-hell look. I knew that he intended to run me off the road. "I'm *not* driving off the road. You get out of my way," I yelled and glared back at him and continued to honk my horn.

Suddenly, I saw a flurry of snow and Paul swerved at the last second. He missed me and continued down the road. I thought my guardian angel must have taken over. Or, maybe Paul just didn't want to have a head-on collision and swerved on his own. I slowly drove home trying to stop shaking. When I came in, I asked Larry, "Is it against the law to try to run someone off the road?"

"Well, sure. What happened?"

I told him about Paul through tears running down my cheeks. "I just knew he would hit me if I didn't run off the road. Susy could have flown through the windshield, if we hit. And we might have been killed."

Larry gave me a hug. "You need to call the sheriff." I did when I calmed down and gave my statement.

Paul returned to his cabin and later the sheriff's deputy came with an arrest warrant. Larry and I watched as the handcuffed Paul was placed in the back of the car and they drove away. The next day he posted bail and returned, packed up and moved out.

I didn't hear anything from the District Attorney's office about my complaint and called after about a week, to see if Paul would be prosecuted. The District Attorney's assistant told me that a felony charge couldn't be proven. He said Paul told them that his steering did not work right and they would possibly only charge him with careless driving. I said that if the steering didn't work properly, Paul should not be allowed to drive the car. They only hemmed and hawed. My further complaints did no good. Months later, I finally gave up on any action being taken even though I had called the DA's office repeatedly. I constantly heard, "We'll get to it, but we're busy," or other excuses. I felt the DA had shirked his duty to Susy, me and the public. I was not a happy law-abiding citizen and the DA did not gain my respect. Paul eventually disappeared without any charge. I wondered if he would ever have to face up to responsibility. I'd never know.

Time moved on and winter slowly inched toward spring. Dirty snow clung to the side of the roads and a slushy, muddy drive replaced the snow packed lane. As the snow melted, warmth followed and spring blossomed. Season to season, each seemed to bring new adventures and new challenges.

At least we had good wranglers for the summer and more tourists came for rides. Jim and Robins handled so many horses that our pastures became over-grazed and more supplemental hay was needed. Sometimes, a section of fence needing repair did not seem to be noticed or left on the back burner for later. The horses generally found that spot and wandered onto Forest Service land where the grass was abundant. Supplemental hay was not as tasteful as the fresh pastureland. In a bad growing season the cost of hay rose and this year, if I remember right, it became $85.00 a ton—a steep price then.

When the horses escaped the pasture and grazed on Forest Service land, Robins drove their pickup down the valley in the mornings to look for the stray horses. When she spotted them, she honked her horn. The horses learned that when they heard her honk, it meant oats and time to come home. She didn't have to round them up on horseback like all the other wranglers. Jim planned to look for the fence break and fix it. I'll never know how Robins could get the horses to come back to the stables with only a honking horn. Did she have a technique similar to a horse whisperer in some way? Whatever, it told me the horses knew they would be rewarded at the stables.

Bear Cub (1975)

Summer of 1975 brought another film crew. This time they were making a TV film about a bear cub raised by a mountain man. They asked to use the Groundhog cabin, near the creek, for the man's mountain home with the cub.

The producer talked to Larry about their plans. "We'll set everything up to make it look like the cabin is high in the mountains and secluded with a stream running close by."

Larry nodded. "Sounds good to me. We'll let all the guests know to stay away from your shooting and from the cub."

"Thanks. This is just one part of the segment and the rest of the story will be filmed elsewhere. But we needed a cabin for the home and this is great." He registered and left to get the equipment set up. The Groundhog was one of the original old log cabins near the creek. The porch sat all across the front and an old deer skull hung above the door which was in red, the same as the window trim.

The guests were thrilled to watch all the action. The film crew kept the cub in a cage when not being filmed. Even with him caged, the wranglers had to make sure the horses did not go near the area. If they smelled bear, they would get panicky and a rider would possibly be thrown.

Larry grinned that night and said, "I wonder if that cub is a distant cousin to the one Glenn and I ran into a few years ago."

The filming did not seem as chaotic as some we had watched. I got too busy with guests, though, to watch much of it. None of the guests or children caused any trouble. Filming ended in success and there were no surprises or problems. We would not be able to see the film because it would be shown on a TV channel that we did not receive in our valley. It was too bad that we couldn't see our great old log in the movies!

Summer moved by far too fast and soon the season began to die. Sunny, warm days were replaced with cool days and cold nights. All the tourists were gone and the mountainsides displayed their glorious fall colors. I knew the fun would begin when the cabins were once again rented long term.

Gas Leak!

The winter tenants gave us a break and no warnings had to be given…at least for a few months. I always had the binoculars at hand and would be the wicked witch again, if needed.

In early November, Larry and Glenn began to remodel our old three bedrooms attached to the lodge. They would work on it when there was no snowmobile business. No longer used by our family, they wanted to convert the bedrooms into two separate studio units with a wide porch facing the peaks.

After lunch on a Saturday, they were busy on the units when I left to take the children to a matinee at the Isis Theater in Aspen. A snowstorm swooped in while the children were at the Isis, and I shopped, got mail, and the newspaper. I picked up the children after the movie and slowly drove up the mountain road for home. Wind whipped the snow furiously and made it difficult to see and I inched along trying to stay in what seemed to be the middle of the road. I didn't want to drive off and roll down the mountainside, especially on Little Annie Hill.

Finally, we arrived home. When Larry came in, I started to tell him how bad it had been driving back from town. I was proud of arriving home safely.

He poured a cup of coffee, took a sip and said, "Well, we had excitement too. While you were gone we had another fire."

I stopped short, sat down, my eyes widened and my mouth dropped open. By now my greatest fear had become fire. I hadn't noticed any burned buildings when I drove in. "What burned, where, how?"

"Glenn thought he had all the gas pipe connections soldered in the new units. He said he'd checked all connections with sudsy water to see if any gas was escaping. The suds make bubbles if there's a leak. Guess he missed one. He lit the stove burner and flames immediately traveled right to a leak inside the wall. We ripped out the wall as fast as we could." He stopped and laughed. "Then I grabbed the fire extinguisher and quickly killed the flames, but now we have a wall to repair. Man! For a few minutes I thought we were going to have to call Aspen Fire again."

"Good Lord, are you two ever going to learn?" My hand shook as I poured a cup of coffee. Another fire! A stiffer drink may have calmed me, but coffee sat ready.

Larry just chuckled. "It's no big deal. Just a little more work than planned. It's okay." He finished his coffee and went back to work.

The winter days and nights became brutally cold and we were glad our furnace kept pushing out heat. In late November, the day temperature was -15°F and had been below zero for several days.

Kristy, renting a modern cabin with her boyfriend, came up to the office and complained, "The heat has been off for two days. My plants are freezing and dying, and now the water is frozen too. That Ben Franklin wood stove isn't enough to keep us warm. Why haven't you got the heat going? It should have been done by now. You have to fix the heat right away and you have to get the water on. You're killing my plants!"

I stared at her a moment and tried not to explode. "Why did you wait two days to tell us the heat was off? How were we supposed to know? You're the one who lives there. It is up to you to let us know if that happens." *Her plants? What are they, marijuana plants?*

"Well, you should have seen that the heat is off."

"How could we tell? The furnace isn't hooked up to a red light to flicker when it's off, or set to an alarm. You live there, not us. You are the one who knows." I paused to take a deep breath and sighed. "I'll see if Larry and Glenn can get it going."

"Well, get them on it fast." She turned and stomped out the door.

Typical winter

188

I almost threw a book at her, but instead I went to find Larry and Glenn. They relit the furnace, but couldn't thaw the water pipe. It froze somewhere underground from the cabin to the main line. We had to call a welder from town to thaw the pipe. A couple of hours later it arrived and soon water was flowing again in the cabin. Later, I presented the bill to Kristy for payment.

"You're crazy. I don't owe you for that. You should have kept the water from freezing."

"You owe it. You didn't accept your responsibility and you didn't tell us right away that the heat was off. You pay, or out you go. We wouldn't have had to call a welder, if you had let us know right away. It's your bill."

They grudgingly paid and I made sure that they knew enough to tell us if the heat went out again. Another thing to put in next year's lease: if the heat goes out, notify the office immediately. I felt that these young kids must not have been taught much about living on their own and maybe they had lived pampered lives. Even I would have known to call the landlord, if the heat went out when I lived in the city.

We stayed home on New Year's Eve and by 10:00 p.m., Larry and I gave each other a toast to 1976 and went to bed. We snuggled under the pile of blankets and fell asleep before midnight.

Chapter 19

A Frozen New Year (1976)

Icy wind blew through the night and New Year's Day came with the morning low temperature of -25°F and none of the vehicles would start again. Our Jeep had been plugged in to keep the engine warm, but it rebelled and only grunted and groaned. No vehicles in camp would start. Larry finally gave up and called a wrecker from town to come and jump-start our vehicles and then he jump-started the tenants' vehicles.

The winter continued to be bitter cold and two more cabins fell victim to frozen water pipes. At least the tenants let us know right away.

When the sky became clear and the full moon came out, it meant a bitter cold night because there were no clouds to hold the warmth close to earth. I loved to get out and walk on those starry nights. I put on my insulated snow pants and donned my felt-lined boots and my parka over my sweater. I wrapped a scarf around my neck, tied the lace of my furry winter hat and put on my thick insulated snowmobile mittens that reached to my elbows. Then, I ventured out into the icy night and breathed in its crisp pure Rocky Mountain air. The quietness gave me a feeling of peace in a world of mass confusion. The bright stars twinkled and moon shadows on the fields were long streams of varying degrees of blue-grey. They rippled over the snow and often took on their own form resembling animals or all sorts of objects. The light shining from the cabin windows gave a warm golden glow to the snow and made a picture-perfect setting. Sometimes, I could hear music filtering out into the icy atmosphere. Some nights, I walked to the Payne's cabin a half mile down the road. We visited over coffee and then I walked back enjoying the peaceful night.

All Rise (1976)

Winter peace was finally broken. We discovered that "Hairy Gary" moved out without any notice. We charged him rent because his lease required a 10 day notice of vacating. It would be hard to re-rent quickly in January, especially because we needed time to repair and clean the unit.

He came to the office two days after moving out. "I'm here to get my deposit back. Is my check ready?" There was no "please," only a demand.

I handed him the letter I was ready to mail. "I was going to mail this, but here. You aren't getting any money back. You damaged the floor and the sofa, and you left without a 10 day notice. Here's our list of the damages and rent due. You owe us."

He glanced at the letter and looked at me with angry squinted eyes. "You can't do that. I want my money. I need it."

"Nope. You are not getting it and that's that." I gave a sigh. *Am I going to have to be the parent again?*

Instead, he surprised me with, "Okay then. I'm taking you to court," and he stomped out. The door slammed shut with a bang.

Soon, Elk Mountain Lodge received a summons to appear in court. The trial day came and testimony was given. Gary had no evidence other than the receipt for his deposit. He stated he didn't need anything else and he should get his deposit back.

Then our turn came, and we presented the judge with a list of the damages along with the lease. I underlined the clause about a 10-day notice required to vacate. After all evidence was presented, the judge ruled in favor of Elk Mountain Lodge. It had been a simple and straightforward case.

Gary raised his fist and shook it at us. "I'll get even with you. I'll show you for keeping my money."

The judge quickly rapped his gavel. He strongly recommended that Gary be quiet and stop the threats, or he would land in jail. A deputy escorted Gary out of the room and probably had a serious talk with him. That ended the "Hairy Gary" problem, but we kept a wary eye out for him anyway.

The same month, binocularitis about got me. We had rented the modern House on the Hill across the road to "Benny the Brainless". I saw people in vans painted with hip art, old pickups, or little VWs, arrive at odd hours of the day and night, and leave very shortly after they came. He turned off the porch light and the people always stepped just inside, leaving the door open to emit a glow from the house lights. They left in a few minutes. I suspected Benny of being a drug dealer, but I couldn't see any exchange of drugs or money and had no evidence to notify the law. But I just knew what was going on…why else would the people come and go like that? Larry thought I might want to give the binoculars a break and forget it because I couldn't see anything. I guess I still had that feeling of guilty until proven innocent, but maybe I was right this time. I finally gave up.

On a bitter cold day, "Benny the Brainless" came to the office. "You have to fix the fireplace hearth. I chopped wood on the floor, but my stereo shook and my music got ruined. So, I've been chopping on the hearth, but now the brick is cracking and breaking into pieces. You have to fix it."

A fire began to brew inside me. "The rules state no chopping of wood inside and you are supposed to chop it outside on the chopping block. You're responsible for the damage and you'll have to pay for the repair of the floor and the hearth."

"Well, it's too cold to chop the wood outside. Anyway, you still have to fix the hearth."

"You can always turn your heat up if you get cold. You have hot water baseboard heat, you know. Quit chopping inside!" I gave him my witchy scowl.

He just turned and left. Two days later he moved out, leaving the cabin in the usual hippie disaster and no forwarding address. The hearth bricks had to be replaced and the wood floor had to be repaired and refinished. Many hours of elbow grease were spent getting the cabin back to normal. We sent a notice of the damages to General Delivery in town, but "Benny the Brainless" had disappeared and our letter was returned later marked undeliverable. At least my binoculars could rest.

The winter of arguments, cleaning and repairs ended none too soon for us, but somehow we had survived. We only had one last cold snap, but no frozen pipes. Soon, the weather dribbled into spring and snow began to melt, mud followed and virgin growth was fighting to push through the earth. Then it was time to prepare for the summer business again. The repeat guests would return and brighten our days.

Spring gave us a renewed hope for a season of peace and normalcy.

Beaver vs. Mace (1976)

By late May, the mountains displayed a new rich green and the wildflowers gave abundant pinks, reds, blues, whites and yellows. Many afternoons, rain dowsed the valley and gave a sweet scent of fresh moisture from the heavens.

I walked down by the creek one day and enjoyed God's nature. I treasured a spot with tiny delicate pink flowers, in the shape of an elephant trunk and ears. We called them Elephantella. Most people missed these dainty flowers, because they were so well hidden in the willows and amongst the tall moist grass next to the creek. That flower became my second favorite followed only behind columbine. Next were paintbrush, blue bells, buttercups and wild roses. Dandelions were last on my list even though my children, as toddlers, picked them to present to me as a gift. I graciously put them in a vase to admire.

Another film crew approached Elk Mountain Lodge in June and talked about their plans. I went to find Larry and told him, "They want to make a documentary on beaver and they asked to rent our land by the creek and the Groundhog cabin to store all their equipment. They brought their own special breed of beaver and said they'll keep them in cages at the edge of the creek."

"Okay. Since the Groundhog isn't rented and near the creek, it'll work."

"The guy said the beaver will only be out of the cages during the filming and they'll be close to the bank. He said that they are very expensive animals and they have special handlers."

Larry discussed the details with the men. Soon, the professionals began to set up their equipment and cages. Nothing appeared make-shift and by that afternoon filming began. It wasn't long and they encountered Stuart Mace. He seemed to never miss a thing that happened in the valley and he stopped on the road near the filming.

I saw him talking to the crew over the fence. Then the photographer came to the office and told me, "That guy stopped and asked what we were doing. After I told him, he yelled for us to stop and that it's against the law to have our beaver in the creek. I said that we were going to film and added that if it's against the law, to go get a warrant."

Later that afternoon, the Forest Service arrived. They had a complaint that the valley's environment would be endangered by these foreign beaver. They might mate with the native beaver, or give them a virus or some disease. The complaint demanded the Forest Service cite the documentary crew for inhumane and unhealthy conditions. Reluctantly, the Forest Service checked, but didn't find anything wrong and all the health certificates for the beaver were in order. The film crew received permission to continue.

That evening, the photographer told me that they had received a threat that their beaver would be killed, if they didn't stop. I told them that no one would set foot on our property without permission, but they decided to hire a night security guard to protect their beaver.

During the next days of filming, no incidents occurred and no night raids. Mace was the ever-ready vigilant environmentalist and drove by slowly a couple of times every day. When the filming finished, the crew headed back to the Big Apple. All was tranquil in the valley again…at least until someone howled about something else.

Rumors Hit Hard (1976)

The early summer progressed with a continual parade of tourists. Then trouble came on June 19th. Bubonic Plague was discovered in two gophers in Ashcroft and the State Health Department quarantined the ghost town. An inspector came to talk to us and make sure we kept our horses and guests away from Ashcroft. We talked while out on the porch. Right at that moment, our old tomcat pranced up and deposited a mouse at Larry's feet…not an unusual occurrence. We had just told the inspector that our camp did not have any signs of the plague.

When the inspector looked down he frowned, "What's your cat got?"

"Oh, it's just a mouse. He probably caught it up the trail. I saw him coming from down there." Larry pointed to the trail leading to Ashcroft. The wrong thing to say!

"Hey, we have to test that mouse. It may have the plague." He carefully dropped the mouse in a paper bag and placed it in his car. Then he headed to town.

We got a call later that day from a friend. He said when the inspector got back in town, he carelessly mentioned that the mouse came from our lodge and we probably had the plague. Word got out of the possibility and the news media picked right up on it. By that night, it was reported that Elk Mountain Lodge had the plague. Rumors changed to disaster and it shut down our lodge like a prison…quarantined without reason or evidence. By the next day, our camp became quiet and non-touristy. Only a few old-timers remained.

I complained, "Larry, all our horse business has died and the cabin reservations are being cancelled. Why did that inspector say that? He doesn't even know the results of the test yet."

"There's not much we can do about it until they find out about the mouse. That health inspector sure fixed us, if it isn't the plague." We lost part of our summer income because of one remark.

The test result came back on June 22nd and Larry got the call. When he hung up he growled, "That damned inspector. The test came back negative and there's no plague at our lodge. It will come out in the local news today or tomorrow, but it doesn't pay for the lost income."

The damage had been done. It took a couple of weeks for our business to recover.

Pass Folly

We just got business flowing again and then another careless act occurred. A couple from Houston parked their truck and horse trailer at the trailhead to Cathedral Lake on July 2nd. They unloaded their two saddle horses and a packhorse and headed up the trail.

I happened to be down at the stables talking to Jim and Robins that afternoon, when the woman raced into our stables on her horse. She dismounted and asked for help between quick breaths.

She told us what happened. "When we were crossing the loose shale on Electric Pass it began to slide away. I lagged in the rear and then I saw my husband's horse and the packhorse lose their footing." She stopped to take a drink of water that Robins had given her. "Dennis jumped off his mount and clung to the edge of the trail. He slipped and slid a few feet before he could dig his heels in and stop. The horses couldn't catch their footing and rolled and bounced down the side of the mountain."

I imagined the horrible sound of horseflesh and bones hitting and bouncing off the rocks. It must have resounded through the mountains.

"Finally, they came to a stop and Dennis said he'd slide down and see if they were alive."

Jim stopped her and asked if they hadn't seen on their maps that Electric Pass was marked as a foot path only. She only shrugged and said the pass looked okay. Then he sighed, "Where's your husband now?"

"When he started to slide down to check on the horses, he told me to go back to a wide spot and wait. I couldn't see or hear him and after awhile I began yelling for him, but he didn't answer and I didn't know if he fell or what. So I decided to come here. Can you help, please?" She let out a long sigh, wiped her eyes, and sunk further down on the wood bench by the tack room.

"We'll see about a rescue. You walk your horse and cool him down."

Jim called Mountain Rescue and immediately rode up the trail. A helicopter had been quickly dispatched and soon radioed that they spotted the man. He seemed okay and was climbing back up and had almost reached the trail. The pilot added that both horses appeared to be dead. They had crashed down the mountain about 1,000 feet.

Dennis gradually made it back up on the trail and then headed down. Jim met him and learned that both horses had indeed perished. He told Jim that he couldn't bring out the pack gear or the saddle and could barely make it back up on his own. Exhausted, he slowly followed in silence. Jim used the C.B. radio to confirm that the man was okay and to abort any rescue.

The wife tearfully met Dennis at their trailer parked at the trailhead. They went back to town to board her horse and to rent a room. The two dead horses were left with all their tack and equipment on Electric Pass...their burial ground.

Disgruntled when he got back to the stables, Jim said, "Danged people just don't pay attention to the warnings. Why don't they believe the maps? Or, at least, check with the Forest Service." We had no answer.

That day also marked the opening of Pearl Pass. It did not open at all some years, but this year Glenn was determined to get it open for Jeep tours. He and some other eager four-wheelers drove up every so often to shovel snow and pour stove ashes on the trail to help melt the snow. July would be about a month earlier than usual for the Pass to open, but all the shoveling labor paid off. Stove ashes were also used on the American Lake trail sometimes so horses and hikers could get to the lake earlier than nature allowed.

We were only into July and the summer wasn't calm, like I had hoped.

Murder? (1976)

Summer did bring a different excitement, though. First, back a few months…news erupted on March 21, 1976. Olympic medalist, skier Vladimir "Spider" Sabich, had been fatally shot in his Aspen home. A pistol discharged while in the hands of Claudine Longet, a famous singer.

A full investigation commenced, and the grand jury couldn't conclude it as an accident, as Claudine Longet had testified. In July, the county prosecutor, Frank Tucker, ordered her arrested and charged with the murder of Spider Sabich. She denied the charge and her defense maintained that Spider had been showing her how to use the gun when it discharged accidentally. She said that she would never have hurt him and swore it to be an accident. Bail was posted and she was released. The trial was not scheduled until late fall.

Rumors flew around Aspen and the world. Speculation turned rampant about what could have happened. Some townspeople were vicious with gossip. Media had covered every detail they could possibly uncover—real or imagined. Claudine Longet could not get away from the cameras or microphones and must have felt that her every action, appearance and demeanor were judged harshly. Many people became adamant that it was cold-blooded murder. Could some gossip have been because of jealousy? After all, Spider represented the dream man of many women. Who knew where all the rumors came from? Maybe people just had to blame someone…not a gun. Of course, the media had to come up with any kind of sensational tidbits that they could discover… true or not.

One morning, Claudine secretly sneaked away to Elk Mountain Lodge and rented a cabin under her former name, disclosing her identity only to us. She requested that we not tell anyone of her presence at our lodge and we agreed. Claudine seemed prettier than I had imagined after looking at the latest pictures by the media hounds. They purposely seemed to find photos that did not show her beauty. Her smooth skin looked flawless and her hourglass shape probably was envied by many women. A bright yellow headband held back her dark shoulder-length hair and accentuated her bewitching brownish-golden eyes (as I recall, they were that color). Her likeable personality put us at ease. She asked to stay for almost a month, but we told her that she would have to move from one cabin to another in order for us to honor long-standing cabin reservations. She agreed and it meant a total of four cabins, two of which were rustic.

After she settled in a rustic cabin, she told us she enjoyed building a fire in the woodstove and using the kerosene lamp rather than the electricity. Maybe it relaxed her and kept her mind off her present troubles. We did not discuss the incident or trial with her and she offered no information.

Our famous guest rode horses, hiked the trails, and enjoyed having some friends in, who discreetly arrived from town, for her home-cooked dinners. A bottle of wine seemed a must with the meal, but she could not risk a run to town for wine and have the media find her. Several times she came to the office and Larry greeted her. She asked sweetly in her sultry French-accented English, "Please, Larry, can I borrow a bottle of wine? I'll pay you back when I get to town to buy some. Please?"

Larry appeared enchanted each time and asked if she wanted red or white. He eagerly complied with her request. Her friends would bring a new bottle for replacement later. We usually had wine with our Sunday dinners and our supply never dwindled. I decided to let Larry be flustered over her attention, but nighttime was my time with him!

A few days after she had checked in, a guest came to the office. "I'm sure that's Claudine Longet staying in that cabin. It's her, isn't it? I want to get her picture and autograph." He looked like someone who buttered up to his boss and socialized to get ahead. Whenever he spoke, he dropped the name of some well-known person to make an impression. Or, he did his best to make it sound like that person must be very important. His attitude and turned-up nose seemed to have an air that he was above others. It didn't work with us and I considered him one of the least-liked vacationers at the lodge. I often wondered whatever brought him to our lodge because he talked like he had money and was only good enough for the best accommodations. Maybe his wife demanded that he get away from trying to climb the ladder and quit pretending.

The man added, "I think she killed Spider. I saw him once and we visited."

Yeah. I'll bet! You probably visited with his group, or just saw him across a room. "She does look similar, but I sure don't have anyone registered by that name. Besides she isn't as pretty as Claudine Longet, is she? It's not her." I would disclose absolutely nothing to "Snobby Steve," as we called him.

"Oh shoot, I already called a buddy back home and told him that it's her. Oh well, he won't know the difference and it sure looks a lot like her. I'll still say it's her." He strutted out with his nose high. What a blowhard!

When it became about time for her trial, Claudine moved back to town and faced the media and jury. I admired her outer appearance of a non-flustered manner with all the camera flashes and microphones pushed at her. Andy Williams, her ex, stood by her side for support. I had taken messages from him for Claudine when she stayed at our lodge. A perfect gentleman.

The trial became a long and vicious battle between prosecution and defense. Apparently, proof beyond a reasonable doubt did not come forth and there were several mistakes made by the law enforcement with the evidence. The trial ended with Claudine Longet being convicted only of a misdemeanor—criminal negligence. She received a $250.00 fine and ordered to spend 30 days in jail at a time of her choosing, so that she could be with her children.

We never saw Claudine Longet again, but her stay at Elk Mountain Lodge remained in my memories. She was always courteous, respectful, and kept her smile.

Chapter 20

Saddle Sores and Sore Doctors (1976)

On a warm morning, I walked to the stables to check on a guest's bill. While there, two hippies rode in on horseback and dismounted at the stables.

"Hi there. I'm Will Jankins. Can we board our horses here for a couple of weeks? The Forest Service ran us off their land. Me and Cassie here, decided to do some climbing, but we don't want to take the horses." He put his arm around her and grinned down at her.

Jim looked over the pair and then examined the two horses. "I can see that a vet is needed for these horses. If you're willing to pay for the vet, we'll keep them for you."

"Sure. No problem, man." He dug into his worn jeans pocket and said, "Here's some money right now. That should take care of things. Okay? We want to get going."

Jim counted the wad and agreed. Will and Cassie were soon on their way to American Lake. Each had a sleeping bag tied on top of their backpacks.

Jim removed the saddles and blankets and examined the saddle sores. "Damn kids! I'm getting the vet up here as soon as possible."

The veterinarian arrived that afternoon. "Both of these horses are malnourished, but worse are the saddle sores, especially on this one." He pointed to the mare's flank. "This large, deep sore is from the saddle rubbing on bare flesh. It began as a blister, broke, and then the rubbing kept irritating it. Now it is a necrotic ulcer, which has gotten infected, festered and keeps getting bigger, deeper, and worse. Those kids sure didn't medicate it or keep it clean."

He pointed to the bloody, hideous cavity full of pus and decaying flesh. "The other saddle sores are more treatable, but this one is bad."

"What can you do for this badly infected sore?" Jim asked.

"I've got to debride it and that's painful. Someone will have to hold her while I cut away the infected, dead tissue and clean the wound."

Jim held the mare tight, but the pain of the surgery made her flinch and whimper with each dig and snip. After the debriding, a big gaping, inflamed, ugly, fist-sized bloody wound remained. Doc applied ointment on it, covered it with gauze and gave the mare an antibiotic shot. Then he petted her nose with his caring hands.

"Dang people who don't take care of their animals! It's a good thing they aren't here. You keep doctoring it like I showed and I'll be back to check in a couple of days."

The horses stayed long enough for the wounds to receive constant cleansing and doctoring and began to heal nicely. When Will and Cassie came back, the wranglers instructed them on how to care for the wounds.

I heard that Will just said, "Yeah, sure. Thanks." He and Cassie saddled and mounted their horses and headed down valley.

A few days later, tempers became tested again. A local doctor arrived at the stables and rented Sugar for a half-day trip to American Lake. After an hour he brought Sugar back sweating so excessively that it dripped off her like raindrops. She wheezed in fast, short breaths and could barely stand due to exhaustion. Her pitiful dull-brown eyes seemed to ask for mercy.

Jim asked the doctor what the devil he thought he was doing. Sugar had been rented for a 3-hour ride, but came back in one hour. He knew that the doctor raced up and back on the steep trail and said he would charge double for a half day ride and for running Sugar.

When I stepped out the back door, I heard the doctor yelling, "You can't charge me double. I didn't race that horse and I'm not paying double or for a half-day rate. I only rode for one hour. Besides that, I'm a doctor in town. Don't you know who I am?"

Jim yelled back, "I don't care a rat's behind who you say you are. You're paying double. You ran Sugar, or she wouldn't have come back in this condition. Her lungs are probably damaged for good."

After several minutes of arguing, Jim gave up and said they were coming up to the office for the owner to settle the dispute.

When they came, I was still on the back porch and Jim showed me Sugar and explained. The doctor scowled and shifted from one foot to the other. Immediately upon seeing Sugar, I lost my temper. "This poor horse is still dripping sweat and panting for air. You are going to pay double for a half day rate. That's a half day trip up to American Lake and you ran this poor horse to make it in an hour." I could smell the sweaty drops and hear Sugar's labored breathing. "Can't you see what you've done? Just look at her!"

"This is ridiculous. That horse will be alright and you know it. Do you know who I am? I'm a doctor in town. I can send you customers or not."

"I don't care who you say you are. This horse may not be able to breathe right again. I don't call that ridiculous. You will never be allowed to rent a horse from here again. And if the people you would send up here are like you, we sure don't want them. Now pay what you owe."

"I won't pay double."

"Yes, you will. If you leave here without paying what you owe, you'll read the headlines in the *Aspen Times*. I'll get my camera and take pictures for proof too. Shouldn't help your image, should it?"

Visualizing headlines, the doctor finally gave in and reluctantly paid, but left muttering obscenities. I made a note to be sure and not go to that doctor for any medical treatment!

Jim worked for an hour to cool Sugar down while exercising her so she wouldn't stiffen up. He wrote the doctor's name in the "Do Not Rent to This Person" list, which had only a few names over the years.

After 4-days' rest, the wranglers were able to rent Sugar again for short rides. They told her story and warned everyone who rode her that they would be shot, if they ran her. The point was made.

Summer finally galloped to the sunset with a brisk wind and aspen leaves turning Picasso orange and yellow. Then all the guests left for home. Again, we tried to select decent long-term tenants for winter, but knew there would be some problems. The tenants never failed to come up with something new every winter and it added another do or don't to the lease rules. Ahh! Another "Dippy Hippie Season" to endure! It sure kept us on our toes.

October ended and November sailed in with long-term tenants, snow-mobiles and plowing the drive. It looked like we might have picked more responsible tenants and maybe we were going to have a quiet season. We would find out.

Stove Party (1976)

All the rustic cabins contained wood burning stoves for cooking and heating. They had been installed when the cabins were built and many had been purchased as used at that time. Rick, renting the Paintbrush, came to the office and announced, "I found a small metal plate on the back of my wood stove. It says the manufacturer is Monarch, and the date stamped on it shows November 21, 1881."

Surprised that he had paid any attention, other that putting wood in the stove, I said, "That's pretty neat. No modern appliance could last that long,"

"Yeah. Next Monday, on November 21st, I'm having a stove party to celebrate the 95 years of service by that range. You're welcome to come." Rick gave a mischievous grin.

"We'll see. You just have fun honoring that stove." Larry and I didn't want to get too friendly with the tenants. We liked Rick, but he still had too much of the new ways. His likeable personality, though, bought him leeway with us.

I knew that wood stove well. It had a warmer with two doors held by chrome handles. The shiny chrome ornate curly brackets on the sides anchored the warmer to the stove above the burner plates. The same curly-cue chrome design trimmed the oven door below and it had a small round thermometer encased on the outside of the door. Its claw feet and the plate lifter handle were also chrome. The stove might have been one of the top models in its day.

The next week all his friends gathered for Rick's party. We did not go. Some sang along with a guitar player, but no loud music or yelling disrupted the camp. I felt sure, though, that "Mary Jane" joints were being passed around. Marijuana always seemed to be available. There might also be some other drugs, but I didn't think so with this group. The party dwindled by midnight and everyone dispersed. I felt glad that they had a quiet celebration because I had threatened to evict a tenant the previous year for his loud 2:00 a.m. party noise. I didn't want to evict Rick.

Log Gone!

The Elks Lodge held their annual Turkey Bingo on the Saturday night before Thanksgiving and we planned to try our luck. Tina and Susy didn't want to go, but Larry insisted, "It's a family night, and you're going…period." That ended any discussion.

The two girls were grumpy at first, but soon got into the spirit of the game in hopes of winning. Even though we could not seem to win a turkey, we all had fun playing and visiting with friends. Nearing midnight, we were about ready to head home when the town fire siren blew. Those who were volunteer firemen rushed to the firehouse. Word got back to the Elks that the fire was 10 miles up Castle Creek. Immediately, we knew it had to be Elk Mountain Lodge.

My heart began to beat rapidly. We rushed the children into the car, and Larry sped out of town and up Castle Creek Road. Glenn left just ahead of us in his pickup. When we were 5 miles from the lodge, we saw and smelled the thick smoke. I began shaking. Fire again!

Larry's voice came deep and strained, "It must be our house. There's too much smoke for a little cabin. Thank God the kids are all with us." He kept his eyes straight ahead willing the car to go faster. I saw his face muscles drawn tight.

Tina cried, "Missy and my cat are in the house! They'll be killed. Hurry Daddy. Maybe we can save them." She loved the dog and cat, almost as much as her brother and sister.

"It'll be okay," Larry answered, as his fingers tightened more on the steering wheel.

I couldn't talk. I just stared ahead. *Why do we have to have so many fires? Is it our house this time? Why, why, why?*

When we rounded the last bend, we saw the Groundhog cabin in flames furiously reaching for the stars, lighting the dark night. We gave a deep sigh of relief that our home had been spared and Larry drove down by the burning Groundhog. He and Glenn talked to the firemen while I stood back with the children staring in silence at the flames. I couldn't quit shaking. Fire did that to me.

The firemen were trying to get water on the flames, but had only one outside water spigot to hook up to and it only gave a small stream of water that hit the fire like a spit on a bonfire. They could not bring the fire truck with the water tank and there was no hope of halting the flames. The interior was engulfed and the fire consumed the 16-inch to 18-inch diameter decades-old dried logs like kindling wood. A renter from another cabin came up to Larry and said that the tenant, Terry, had gone to town. That brought another sigh of relief.

Larry and Glenn told the firemen, "Let it burn to the ground. It's not a threat to any other cabins, and the wind isn't blowing. It'll be less to clean up if it all burns down."

The Groundhog had been one of the original log cabins near the Homestead. The hungry flames rapidly devoured it. I hated to see it destroyed and take all the memories of past residents of that sturdy cabin.

Finally, the flames died…no more fuel for them. The firemen determined that the fire had started with the wood stove. They could see that wood had been stacked against the stove and also the stove pipe was separated at the joint close to the range. Both were a sure-fire way to get a fire going. After they left, Larry and Glenn stayed for a little while to make sure there was no flare up from the rubble. A burned, blackened stove with the attached pipe still upright, and the remains of a small refrigerator were the only things that stood. Ashes surrounded it along with the charred and crumbled logs.

We were glad that Larry had built the new lobby so it could be locked off from the rest of the house. That way the lobby stayed open if someone wanted to use the pay phone when we were not there. This time they sure did. One of the tenants had called in the fire.

Terry came back from town while Larry was still at the site and they talked. When he came home, Larry told me, "Terry admitted he'd stacked the wood next to the stove. He also said that he had tried to clean the chimney. He took the pipe apart and then didn't get it set back quite right, but figured it good enough even though it remained off kilter at the junction. He knew it and admitted to it. He left the cabin with a roaring fire going so it would be warm when he came home. Well, he sure came home to a mighty hot place. Anyway, I felt a bit sorry for him and agreed to loan him $200.00 since he was out of a job and said he lost his cash savings in the fire. He said he'd stay with the Homestead tenants tonight."

"His deposit isn't enough to cover the loan let alone for anything else. What if he doesn't pay?"

"Well, I felt sorry for him." Larry always trusted people and gave the benefit of the doubt to all.

Sleep remained difficult and I kept waking up and checking to make sure the fire hadn't started up again. My body became stiff from shaking so hard, but I gradually loosened up by daylight.

Terry came to the office mid-morning. His hands landed on the counter and his thin dark hair fell forward over his eyes. "I want my deposit back. I need it."

Per usual...no "please" given. I looked him in the eyes. "We aren't refunding your deposit. You caused the fire and we lost a cabin. Besides you owe us $200.00 too."

"Your husband didn't say I had to pay it back and you can't keep my deposit. I lost all my belongings. I have a right to it. Besides, that ol' cabin can be replaced."

"Take us to court if you want, but you won't get it. You burned our cabin down." I tried to look as threatening as he did, but didn't have those devil eyes. Mine just blinked faster when I got angry. His eyes seemed to be red with flames of hate.

"You bet I'll take you to court...I want my money." He yelled profanity in between his statement. When he opened the door, he turned and looked at me. "You better watch it, because sometime when you and Larry are gone and your kids are in the house alone, there could be a fire and your kids could burn up." He stormed out the door using more profanity. His threat scared me and I shivered.

Terry came back a few days later to see if we had changed our minds. I said no again, and he once again threatened our children with fire. Then I really got frightened and would not allow the children to be left alone in the lodge. I told Larry about the threat, but he thought I had exaggerated.

In a couple of days, we got a summons and the court date showed January 12, 1977. Terry was suing us for his deposit. Apparently, the holidays interfered with the court, or a lot of people were using the small claims court. Who knew?

When the court date came, Larry and I sat on the bench in the Pitkin County Court House and waited for the judge. Terry stood, leaning against a wall. He glared at us and I saw that his threat remained evident. He sneered at us and raised one hand and rolled it upward, as if to indicate a puff of smoke, while his mouth formed a circle which almost said, "Poof." When the judge appeared, he began with Terry's testimony.

I can't remember exact words, but it may have been similar to this. "They are at fault for having that ancient stove in the first place. I had a good fire going when I left for town and I don't know what happened after that. Someone else could have started the fire somehow. I didn't lock my cabin and anyone could have gone in. I lost all my clothes, my skis and my cash. I need the deposit back to rent another place. They can't keep my money when it wasn't my fault their stinking ol' cabin burned up. Besides, how'd they feel if their place burned up?" He turned and glared at us in his threatening manner. "I have a right to my deposit." He didn't mention the $200.00 Larry had loaned him.

The judge asked, "Do you have a receipt showing your deposit?"

"Yeah, I sure do. Here it is." He pulled it out of his billfold and gave it to the bailiff.

"Is that all?" the judge asked. He did not seem impressed with Terry.

"That's it. I'm due my deposit and that's it."

The judge then asked us if we had anything to say in defense. He sensed there had to be more to the story.

Larry had seen the look in Terry's eyes. Now he also feared for our children's safety. The deposit wasn't worth the risk. He looked at me and then we both looked at the judge and just shook our heads "no".

The judge looked hard at us. "You have nothing to say in defense?"

"No, Your Honor." Larry had answered in a controlled voice and his jaw muscles tightened. I squeezed his arm for restraint.

Once again the judge tried, "You're sure you don't have anything to say? I feel there is more to this, but without any additional information I'll have to rule in favor of the plaintiff. Speak up if you want your side heard."

"There's nothing to say, Your Honor," Larry replied. His arm muscles tightened while his hands became white knuckled fists. I knew he wanted to walk over and beat the tar out of Terry. I shrunk further in my chair. I had to be quiet and not cause any trouble, but I wanted to more than beat the tar out of Terry.

Reluctantly, the judge shook his head and ruled in Terry's favor. He had no choice without further testimony.

Terry clapped his hands and laughed. He turned to us and said, "You better have my money today when I come for it."

Late that afternoon, he came to receive his check for the deposit refund of $100.00. I asked if he would endorse it back to us to pay for part of the loan Larry had given him. He just sneered at me and said, "Take me to court." I knew that we did not have a signed promissory note and would get nowhere. Besides, he would threaten our children again.

When he left he grinned and waved our check in the air. "Told you I'd get it."

I didn't say a word as my body stiffened and I glared at him. I never backed down, but I had to this time. I feared for my children and knew my pride had to give in although I hated it. I held my tongue. He got away with $300, burned down a cabin, and he threatened the lives of our three children!

For months Larry and I would not let Tina, Greg or Susy be left alone. The fear had not yet subsided and it rumbled in our stomachs. Anyone vicious enough to threaten someone's children could not to be trusted, and revenge could still come. Fear took a long time to fade from me.

Terry was different from most of the hippies we dealt with through the years. He was vicious, while most of the others heeded warnings and the threat of my calling the sheriff usually scared them. Most just needed to know where they stood with us after a strong notice…not all, but many. But Terry was different. He did not fit in the usual non-violent category of most hippies.

I hoped we would not run into anymore like him.

Joanne Brand

Chapter 21

Where's Our Snow? (1977)

Terry and snowmobile business had started our winter season off to no good. December had turned dismal for business in Aspen and for us. Snowstorms were scarce, and finally the drought brought ski and snowmobile business to a halt.

January 1977 came and did not change the picture. On the 2nd Highlands Ski area had only 11 inches on top, 7 inches midway, and 4 inches at the bottom of the run. Aspen Mountain showed about the same, but had 18 inches of snow at the top. Independence Pass remained open on January 11th, but by the 17th it finally closed for safety even though it didn't have the usual amount of snow or slide danger. If you have ever driven Independence Pass, you know how narrow the road is, especially when it becomes a one-lane road around a curve. It is dangerous enough in spots without snow, but the beauty of that drive is glorious…if you can take your eyes off the road!

Finally, a full-blown snowstorm arrived and dumped about a foot on the lower altitudes and more in the high country. It was a welcome sight, even though that meant plowing more than once a day to keep the eggbeater wind from whipping the snow into the driveway. At least the drifts piled rippled waves against the cabins and provided insulation. More heavy snow came in the next few days and it finally gave enough to get the industry in full swing. Celebrations began when ski slopes opened and the town got busy. Our snowmobiles were readied and reservations for tours began once again. Dull days turned into busy tourist days.

January 19th was part of the Aspen Winterskol activities, which included Ashcroft Day. We agreed to not have our snowmobile tours that day so that skiers could enjoy the Ashcroft area and participate in the celebration without our snowmobiles interfering. Our loss of income that day did not bother the skiers, but we would rather have peace than the money. Winterskol always included the torchlight descent down Aspen Mountain, a delight to everyone. In the dark of night, only the torches were visible and it looked like many small fires slowly weaving back and forth down the mountain. We went down to Aspen that night and watched the descent. The icy cold bit into everyone, but it did not stop everyone from enjoying the festivities.

Canyon Impact (1977)

I walked toward the shower house to clean it on January 23rd. I saw two of our tenants rushing to their VW bug. I smiled and said, "Hi. You seem in a hurry."

"Yeah, we want to get to the lifts and hit the slopes while the powder is fresh. Got to beat all the tourists." Bobby had a big smile. The two hopped in the VW bug and drove off.

Bobby could only be described as handsome with dark brown, wavy hair and big brown eyes. His long, dark eyelashes made his eyes even more enticing. He could have been on a fashion magazine cover and had a great physique to go with it. John would not be magazine material, but had a pleasant face with a smile that always came up a little higher on one side when his humor came forth. Larry and I liked them both and they had not caused any trouble.

Later that day, I received a call that brought shivers down my arms. The sheriff's office wanted to know if I had a phone number or address for the boys' parents. I gave the little information that I had and learned of the tragedy. The scene had been described to me in considerable detail. John apparently sped down the road to make up for lost time and suddenly he lost control on a tight curve in the canyon about 4 miles from town. Possibly he hit a patch of ice. The little VW bug swerved up onto the canyon wall and then tipped and rolled over. When I heard this, I could almost hear the sound of metal on rock give a deep scraping groan. The vehicle landed bottom-side-up on the road and then the force of the roll carried it down into the swampy area by the creek and it came to rest on its side. Silence would have been broken only by the sound of the creek rushing by and the sizzle of the motor.

Later, we heard that in a few minutes a passing car discovered the wreck and pulled over. As I recall the story, two people waded to the wreck and then yelled for the others to go get help. They sped to the nearest home about a mile away and called the sheriff. When they returned to the crash site, the two bloody, broken victims had been pulled up and onto the side of the road. Another car stopped and covered them with blankets. One man tried to find a pulse on one, but couldn't find a beat. The other victim looked badly mangled and in serious condition.

The sheriff and ambulance arrived and transported both victims to the hospital. Then it was confirmed that John did not make it. The skid marks provided a clear picture to the sheriff of how the accident had occurred. Too much speed.

Bobby remained in the hospital for a month with head wounds, broken bones and internal injuries. After he was released from the hospital, he came to the lodge, accompanied by his parents. He needed to pack his meager belongings and say goodbye. He told me that he would be going home to stay with his folks and he needed a lot of physical therapy. I also knew that he needed to deal with the loss of his best friend. His parents were very supportive and I felt they would help him through this tragedy.

I could hardly believe the transformation of Bobby. He was no longer an exuberant, handsome young man. His face sat a bit off-kilter and scars crisscrossed his face, and his eyes no longer had that familiar sparkle. He had a limp and with the help of a cane he walked in a bit of an awkward, stiff hobble. I felt dreadfully sorry for him. I wondered how his life would turn out. I hoped he would have a good future, but I never heard.

After that tragedy, winter continued with more tenants coming and going. No more were killed, thank God. None were evicted, but some had a hard time paying their rent on time. We granted some leeway to those who seemed to really try. It had been an easier season than most in the past. I thought that maybe some of the hippies were rejoining the mainstream, or maybe we had just picked better tenants. Or, maybe I was becoming more understanding of the young people and giving them the benefit of doubt. But the season wasn't over yet and there would be plenty of time to see what would happen.

Here We Go Again! (1977)

Late February of 1977, Penny, renting a rustic cabin, rushed into the office, and breathlessly said, "My floor's on fire. Help!"

At the first call for help, I panicked. Here we go again, another fire! God help us!

Larry and Glenn rushed down to her cabin with pails. They ran to the spigot, filled them and threw the icy cold water on the floor.

I watched Penny's cabin with my binoculars expecting to see flames shooting out and the cabin burn to the ground. I couldn't understand why we had to have so many fires. It was always winter fires, never summer. My stomach churned and my teeth clenched tight.

When Larry and Glenn finally returned, I learned that they found smoldering wood in the ashbin and they quickly doused it. After the stove cooled down, they moved it to one side leaving the stove pipe dangling from the ceiling. Several weakened and charred floor planks, where the fire had been, were cut out and new boards installed. Then they put back the stove, ready for a new fire…in the right place.

Glenn told me that he asked why the devil she built the fire in the ashbin and that no wonder the floor about caught on fire.

Larry said that Penny cried and told them she was sorry, but her friend built the fire and Penny didn't pay attention. The friend had shrunk back into a corner of the cabin. Her arms were folded around herself and tears streamed down her face. He told her nicely to be sure not to do that again, but he knew she wouldn't. He felt sorry for both the girls. Penny had been a good tenant and we had no other problems with her. She and her friend had learned a valuable lesson…build the fire in the firebox, not the ashbin that is next to the floor.

I finally learned that this time we had lucked out. I would not hold my breath, though.

Hammering Hassle (1977)

Winter finally died and we didn't have anymore fire scares. Spring began to appear on the horizon with warm days, snow started to melt and the snowmobiles were put to bed. The long-term tenants moved out and we repaired and cleaned. Spring brought smiles once again. New life and a new season brought hope for better days.

Fires always created additional work and a change in plans. Over coffee, on a spring evening, Larry told me, "We need to replace the old Groundhog cabin that burned down last Thanksgiving. Glenn and I have been discussing what would work."

"Are you two going to build it?"

"Sure. We can do it. We'll have the cement poured for the foundation and then do the rest ourselves. We can do our work and then build in the afternoons or evenings." Long hours and hard work did not bother him. "I'll do the building and Glenn will do the plumbing and electrical." I knew that the licensed friends would supervise Glenn's work and the inspections would be approved by the County.

He began sketching on a piece of paper as he talked. His college engineering classes proved worthy again. "We'll make it a duplex and each unit will have a living room, kitchen, two bedrooms and a bath. A sliding glass door off each living room will open onto a deck facing the peaks. The furnace and hot water tanks will be in a room in the middle of the building and will separate the units. See, this is kind of what it will look like." He held out his drawing. "What do you think?"

I leaned over to see. "Wow. That will be something compared to the old log cabin that burned. Looks good to me, but it's going to be a lot of work."

"We can do it. No problem." So many times I heard that statement!

The next week, Larry used his engineering skills again, drew up the plans, and then applied for a building permit. Next, came the contracting. The cement truck almost sunk in the quicksand-like mud when it poured the foundation in mid-May. Construction began when the lumber arrived. Larry got the flooring on and then nailed two-by-fours together, building each wall while flat on the ground. When ready, he and our wrangler, or Glenn, raised the walls and anchored each in place. The roof trusses were delivered and a young man had been hired to help by using ropes to haul each truss up and into place. Larry and our wrangler, Jim, were perched like monkeys guiding them and then anchored each truss to the frame. When finished, they nailed the particle boards on the trusses followed by roofing paper. Lastly, the shingles were tacked on for the final layer. Glenn did the plumbing and the electrical. Then, Larry installed the itchy insulation in the ceiling and on the walls. He came home in the evenings itching all over from the insulation.

Next, Larry nailed the wall paneling in place and installed all the trim for doors and windows. The wood flooring, vinyl, and the bath wall tile took longer. Last, he and Glenn applied the outside tongue and groove siding. The afternoons and evenings were full of the sound of pounding, banging, groaning and a few cuss words coming from the construction site.

While Larry worked on the duplex, I worked in the office. Or, I spring-cleaned some cabins and hung my freshly washed and ironed curtains, put out the dishes, pans and the utensils. Linen would come later, when a cabin was rented.

On a sunny afternoon, I tried to catch up on correspondence while Larry worked on the duplex. A young man walked in off the road and started for the pay phone. Then he stopped and called me to the lobby.

"Hey, my van's dead up at my tent and I need a jump-start. I'm going to take your Jeep and go start my van. I'll have someone bring back your Jeep. Let me have the keys." His hand reached over the counter with his palm up ready to take the keys. Not even a "please" was muttered.

"I can't let you take it and my husband isn't here to give his okay."

He glanced outside at our Jeep. "Just give me the keys, lady. I'll return it later. It's no big deal." His ponytail swished to one side.

"No way, I won't let you take it." He wasn't going to intimidate me!

He tried again, but I would not budge. Then he realized the obvious. "Hey, I'll bet the keys are in the Jeep, aren't they?" My expression must have been a give-away. "I'm going to take it and get my van going. You'll get your Jeep back later." He turned and started to walk out.

I jumped out from behind the counter and followed him. "You can't take it without permission. If you do, you're stealing and I'll call the sheriff."

He continued to walk toward the Jeep. His lanky legs took long strides.

My short legs burst into quick action and I stepped in front of him. "Don't take that Jeep!" Hands on hips, head tilted up, eyes snapping, I shouted, "You can't take it. Don't you dare!"

"Get out of my way, lady. I'm going to take it and start my van. I'll bring it back later." He tried to sidestep me.

I sidestepped with him and wouldn't let him by. Each sidestep he took, he got closer to me, but I wouldn't budge. In between yelling at him, I started to scream, "Larry, get up here. Larry, come here. Larry, Larry."

"Move lady!" We did more sidestepping and he came close enough for me to smell his foul breath and wood-smoked stringy hair.

I tilted my head up and yelled into his nostrils. "Get off this property or I'll have you arrested for trespassing. Get out of here." My temper escalated and my eyes blinked faster and faster. I shrieked again, "Larry, get up here. Larry, Larry."

As we faced off, I thought my only recourse would be to deck him. Of course, that would be ridiculous because my punches would have been easily deflected by him and he would stop me cold. If I were a man and as big as him, there would have been an all-out tangle. I continued to scream, "Larry. I need you. Larry, Larry." I never took my eyes off him while I yelled. I wanted to be prepared to move when he did.

Finally, Larry heard me and came rushing up. "What's up?" and looked from me to the hippie. He stayed alert and listened to both while holding his hammer loosely at his side. Then he said, "I'll jump start your van this time, but you better not come on this property again because I don't know what my wife will do. She can use a gun. Her aim is pretty good too and she runs people off our property." His exaggeration didn't seem too farfetched considering the way I felt right then.

The guy stammered, "I...I can use the pay phone anytime I want. It's a public phone."

"It is a public phone, but it's on private property. The phone company told me that we can keep anyone we want off our property. The only way for you to use this phone, will be to walk on air. Got it? You can just go to town now to use a phone."

That silenced and deflated the guy and he decided to just get his van started and not argue anymore. By the time Larry got back from jump-starting the van, I had calmed down, but I wondered if the guy would come back, because we had the only public phone in the valley. I'd be ready. Maybe I would use a gun, if he tried that again. Disrespect never gained my respect.

There's a Murderer Loose! (1977)

I didn't have anyone else come to get a jump-start and guests were arriving for our cabins. They were the sugar-topping for our summer season. But summer did bring fear this year.

Glenn joined the Sheriff's Department and Mountain Rescue on June 7th for an unusual search, not a rescue. An alleged killer escaped!

I must go back in time to explain. A nurse from Michigan was on a ski vacation at Snowmass, Colorado with her fiancé in 1975, just a few miles from Aspen. They were relaxing in the hotel lounge when she decided to go back to their room and get a magazine she wanted to read. She never made it to their room and she never returned to the lounge. A month later her body was found. She had been brutally murdered.

Not until 1977 was Ted Bundy, the accused killer of many young girls, captured in Utah. He was transferred to the Pitkin County Jail in Aspen to await his trial for the alleged murder of the nurse in Snowmass.

While awaiting trial, he decided he could be a better defense lawyer than the one appointed to him, so he took over his own defense. He received permission to leave the confines of the jail in the Pitkin County Courthouse in Aspen, without shackles, to use the county law library in the courthouse.

That June 7th day, he used the library and had already decided on his plan of escape. He jumped out of an open window of the courthouse and fled before anyone could catch him or be discovered as missing. Because he had not been handcuffed or in leg irons, no passersby noticed him. Then the court system realized he was missing; about 150 searchers were called to scour the town and mountains for Bundy. They had no luck.

Later that week, they discovered that Bundy had been 5 miles up our Castle Creek Road. He broke into a cabin close to the turnoff to Conundrum Valley. The cabin sat right by the road, but no one saw anything unusual. I don't recall if they said he used the propane gas range for cooking or had any heat, but he very well could have used both. Anyone driving by the cabin wouldn't think to notice. The owners had already left and locked up the cabin for the winter and Bundy did not venture outside the cabin until he left.

While on the run, for about a week, Bundy stole food from other cabins and slept in some that were abandoned or closed up for the winter such as the one on Castle Creek Road. He eventually stole a car, but was pulled over by the State Patrol because of weaving. Back in custody, he wore handcuffs and leg irons and was transferred to the Garfield County Jail in Glenwood Springs to await trial. It wasn't long and he escaped from that jail, and much later landed in Florida under an assumed name. Years later, Bundy's day finally came, but only after the loss of too many young women by his hands.

The surrounding area of Aspen and Glenwood Springs finally relaxed. Fear had been abated…at least as far as murderers on the run!

PUC License and reservations (1977)

There were no more jail breaks, but we had another change. Glenn decided, in the spring to lease out the Public Utilities Commission license for the Jeep tours. He still worked some for Sardy, plus on rescues or education, practices, or meetings with the Aspen Mountain Rescue. Larry and I had a hard time to keep up with the rest of the work and the Jeep tours were getting more and more popular.

Glenn said, "I found two guys, Dick and Lester, who are going to lease the PUC license. "They'll start the tours from here. Joanne, I told them that you'd handle the reservations for them and give them the schedule for each day."

"Well, thanks a lot. Guess I don't have enough to do here." I had not been consulted.

Larry tried to appease me. "They don't know how to do the reservations. I'll help you when I can." It would take more than an offer to help to make me feel better!

Soon, I received many calls and began to schedule the Jeep tours. Even though I was not happy with the assigned job, I wouldn't shirk my duties when my word, or someone else's word, had been given that I would do something.

Tours began at Elk Mountain Lodge, the same as always. Dick and Lester found the trips to be a full day's work. During the night hours, they relaxed at a bar in Aspen or at a friend's home. Some of their friends tried to leave messages with me in the middle of the night, but I refused. I soon put a stop to that by threatening to quit taking their reservations, if the 2:00 or 3:00 a.m. calls continued. They didn't take my threat serious. So, after a few days of no reservations...not a one...they got the message. There were no more middle of the night calls and I began reservations again.

Jeep tours ended and I received a bottle of scotch for my summer of taking Jeep Tour reservations and talking to the tourists about the tours. "One bottle of scotch for all summer! I'll tell you, I will not do it next summer." No way would my mind be changed. Larry and Glenn knew I would never give in. From then on Jeep tours with Dick and Lester would have to be handled from town...reservations and departures. No more Joanne. They could forget buying the bottle of scotch.

Conundrum Rescue (1977)

Summer moved at a fast pace and without any troubles. Our lodge and horse business flourished. It would be a good season. We had efficient wranglers, and Jim and Robins handled all situations well. At least we didn't have to worry about the horses this year…we thought.

In August, the stables scheduled a pack trip to Conundrum Hot Springs deep in a Forest Service wilderness valley high in the mountains with hot springs surrounded by 13,000- and 14,000-foot peaks. A group of eight hippie-types rented our horses for the trip and wanted a wrangler to take care of the horses and their supplies for the four days. Ray, a teenaged wrangler helper would take the pack trip. He had proven his worth in rodeos and seemed to be turning into a capable, burly cowboy.

When Ray arrived the next day in late afternoon, instead of four days later, we all wanted to hear his story. He told us that the horseback ride took longer than usual because they insisted on stopping so they could pass a marijuana joint around, giving each a "Rocky Mountain High". They were a happy group when they finally arrived at the campsite. Ray unsaddled the horses and hobbled them.

He told us, "After the camp was set up, the gals began to fix dinner. One started to cut up vegetables. She gulped her share of booze when it was passed around. The beer and marijuana had her laughing, joking, and playing around with the food. She danced around the makeshift table, holding a knife high in one hand and a carrot in the other." Ray stopped to demonstrate, in a mocking way, the girl dancing. We all laughed.

He continued, "Suddenly, she tripped over a rock, her arms came down to catch herself when she fell forward. The knife blade jammed into her upper chest about four inches deep. She crumbled and blood spilled onto the ground. Then she pulled the knife out and screamed, 'I'm dying. I'm dying!' and I almost panicked.

"The other gals began to scream when they saw her down and the blood staining the ground. The guys just looked on and said they didn't know what to do. So, I immediately made the gal stay still. I've seen plenty of blood spilled at rodeos and tried to remember what to do. I got a towel and had one of the girls press to stop the bleeding."

Ray seemed so grownup for a teenager and I think he took the time to relish the attention he received. *Guess I can't consider him just a boy anymore.*

"I tried to stay focused and not panic. She needed to get out of there and to a hospital as soon as possible. So, I told the girls to keep pressing on the wound, try to stop the bleeding and keep her warm. I got her on a sleeping bag and then covered her with another and said I'd go for help."

We knew that Ray quickly saddled his horse and raced down the 10 miles to the first house he saw. He said he was short of breath when he jumped off his mount and knocked on the door. They let him in when he asked to call the sheriff's office for a rescue. Then he called our lodge.

Because the Conundrum Hot Springs is in a wilderness area, Aspen Mountain Rescue could not take any vehicles to the site. They felt immediate medical attention would be necessary and no time for them to hike in and back out. A helicopter was quickly dispatched and hovered above while two rescuers were lowered into the camp site. They gave the girl immediate medical attention and carefully placed her in the litter strapping her in tight. The helicopter hoisted the litter up and another man, hanging out the helicopter door, guided the litter in and the chopper headed to the hospital. The two rescuers on the ground hiked out of the valley and were picked up by their team members and headed home.

Larry had gone to the hospital to see about the girl. When he came home, he said that the doctor told him the girl had been very lucky. The knife just missed all vital organs. One inch made the difference between life and death.

My head still swirled with all that happened. "So, she's okay?"

"Yeah. Maybe she'll lay off the pot and booze the next time she plays with a knife. Since she wasn't in any danger, she didn't need to remain in the hospital and they released her."

That night Ray rode back up to the site to bring the other hippies out the next day…their 4-day trip cancelled. Ray came back exhausted, but that's when he told us the story. He took care of the horses and then fell into bed and slept for 10 hours. Jim and Robins felt he deserved it. We did too.

That turned out to be the last big event for the season. Summer waned without any more accidents or other catastrophes.

Fall meant time to clear out the cabins and begin the long-term tenant troubles. Another "Dippy Hippie Season" to keep us on our toes.

After one warning and payment for extra people, word must have spread because the rest of the tenants seemed to abide by our rules. The balance of the winter sped by with no rescues, no frozen pipes, no fires and no more tenant problems. It seemed that we had gotten the hang of finding better tenants.

Maybe my prayers had been heard. Or maybe the winter gods were giving us a break. Whatever it was, I appreciated it. Winter peace!

Icy days faded and the sun became warmer enticing new growth. Spring rains brought a heavenly scent, melted the snow, and the earth began to give colorful newness to the fields and mountains. How nice to see the color after the long months of white and the skeletal aspen trees. The mountainsides displayed the glorious wildflowers, fields showed an abundance of dandelion yellow, and the aspen trees proudly showed off their new leaves. Grass grew tall and enticed the deer, elk and horses. Season changes always renewed my spirits with hope.

Chapter 22

Sale and Larry (1978)

The summer of 1978 changed our lives forever. Larry and Glenn accepted an offer on Elk Mountain Lodge and signed a contract to sell. Times had changed and it felt right for us to move on with our lives. Larry seemed to be tiring and Glenn seemed to be less interested in the business and ready to move. I would once again follow my husband wherever he went. I just had to have faith that it would all work out. It did before. We were still young and we would find other work.

After the contract was signed, we knew we had to find a new home by September. We took three days off at a time to search and then Glenn took three days off to find his new location. Tina had been accepted to the YCC, Youth Conservation Corps, at Colorado State Park near Wolcott, Colorado, and we only had Greg and Susy with us on our searches in Colorado. The rest of the time we spent back at the lodge to handle business and make arrangements for our move.

Larry and I wanted to stay in Colorado and close to the mountains, but not in the Aspen area and we wanted a lower altitude. We wanted to start a new life in completely new surroundings and would walk through that search until we came to something that struck us.

While we drove from town to town in our search, Larry began to loose more weight, drank a lot of water, and ate a lot of the fruit fresh from the harvest. He had no energy and seemed exhausted just climbing one flight of stairs, but he refused to see a doctor.

After one of our trips and much discussion, we decided on Montrose, Colorado. We drove over McClure Pass, through Delta, and on to Montrose to sign a contract on a new home. While there, Larry got worse and when we got back to the lodge, I insisted that he see a doctor. He felt miserable enough and agreed without any argument.

Larry's doctor appointment came on August 7th. After testing, the diagnosis proved to be diabetes and it was severe enough that Larry was immediately admitted to the hospital.

When he was settled in, I went to our friends, the Conners, and cried on her shoulder. I had heard that diabetes was very serious and could be a death sentence. Somehow, I would have to carry on, but I had no idea what I was going to do. Here I was with a sick husband, three children, a move to handle, and had to take care of all the business. I decided that all I could do was accept the way life was and not wish upon a star for something different. I would do what I had to do.

While at the hospital, a diabetes specialist doctor began teaching Larry and he also insisted that I listen and learn about the foods, insulin, and everything he could tell us. Larry learned how to give himself insulin shots, which he needed twice daily after the diabetes was under control. At first, the nurse gave him insulin injections every two hours until his blood sugar level was out of danger. Larry never lost his humor and always joked with the nurses and made the staff smile.

Looking back, I realized that Larry's fatigue began much earlier and here I thought he was just getting lazy. Boy! Did I ever have to eat my words. Maybe he had known deep down and that was why he seemed so agreeable to selling and leaving his beloved valley.

Later, he would also be diagnosed with hemochromotosis, which is an overload of iron in his organs and it killed his pancreas, causing the diabetes. Hemochromotosis also enlarged his heart and liver, doubling them in size and to a dangerous point. It wasn't long before another doctor ordered weekly phlebotomies to rid his body of the extra iron in all his organs. I looked at the dismal side while Larry kept an optimistic side. His humor continued.

August continued amid final lodge business, my packing and making arrangements…all while Larry remained in the hospital unable to do anything except give encouragement. The leaves on the higher mountains were just beginning to turn color, but green still remained prominent. When a slight dusting of snow melted, it left colorful sparkles flickering in a breeze and accented the hues. The beauty of the mountains and the peace before the winter gave a respite that I cherished. Oh! How those beautiful mountain views would be missed.

I packed all our belongings for the move to our new home. I loaded our station wagon with boxes and drove over McClure Pass and on to Montrose three times. The contractor of the new home we were buying agreed to let me store the boxes in the garage until closing date. Glenn loaded his pickup and brought over more. Trips were made in a day, leaving early in the morning and returning about dusk. One time, I registered the children for school at Montrose. In between packing, moving and making arrangements, I visited Larry at the hospital every day.

On August 12th, I took Tina's friend, Barb, with me and drove up to the YCC camp to bring Tina home. We returned in a downpour, but stopped at the hospital so Tina could say hello to her dad. She did not like to see him so sick and she already began grieving the loss of her friends, the horses and the mountains. Greg had made up his mind that he would accept his new home and Susy seemed to just take everything in stride. I knew I had to adjust to whatever came.

I walked down by the Homestead on August 28, 1978, and sat on my favorite boulder. I tried to permanently seal in my memory every detail of the valley. My eyes followed the creek weaving back and forth from Ashcroft and the Sawtooth Range of the Elk Mountains. I lingered my gaze on Star Peak and tried to memorize each crag and crevice.

How fast those 13 years had passed…too fast. Life had changed so much and so did Aspen and the United States. The Vietnam War was over and civil rights progressed, but still had, and has, many battles to fight. The 1960s and 70s brought one bad change in my mind…the open and loose morals. I had a hard time swallowing that change.

There definitely came one good thing with those years, however. I had been transformed from a pampered city girl to a Rocky Mountain outdoor lover. I felt I really had grown in those years and I treasured the lessons of God's nature. Larry had taught me so much as well. I knew the time for my family to move on was right, even though it meant leaving Elk Mountain Lodge and the glorious beauty and peacefulness of our valley. Then I realized that our days of the "Dippy Hippie Season" were over. I would no longer have to have the binoculars handy and I would no longer have to be like Cinderella's mean stepmother, or just a wicked old witch.

I would truly miss our summer days of repeat families who rented the cabins. Most of all, I would miss my views of the Rocky Mountains, so close with their glorious vistas and rushing streams. Also, the winter outings up to 12,000 feet would definitely be missed.

The stillness in the mountain air seemed to penetrate me and there came a hint of cold promising to freeze later. It gave me a feeling of loneliness. It had been a terrible loneliness in 1965 when I found myself left alone that winter. Now, in 1978, it became the loneliness of a loss…more of a grief.

I had to say goodbye to the mountains, our cabins and our life at Elk Mountain Lodge. Larry would not be my rock when I arrived in Montrose and I would have to learn to become that rock for our family.

I patted the logs of the Homestead cabin. "Goodbye, Homestead." Then I looked up the valley. "Goodbye, Ashcroft and Star Peak."

I began walking slowly back to the lodge. I forced myself to think of the future with hope. I knew that life always moves forward and that change comes to all. I put my faith in the Almighty to guide me and give me strength.

Leaving Larry in the hospital and moving to Montrose alone with the children caused me a great deal of sadness and fear. I had to face life alone once more, but really alone this time, with no husband to stand by me, no friends, and no relatives nearby.

The moving van came the next day and loaded our belongings. The children and I left the same day, but stopped to say goodbye to Larry before we drove over McClure Pass to our new home. Tina drove our little car while I drove the station wagon loaded with the remainder of our belongings and our little dog and cat. I would come back on September 10th to bring Larry home. Our lives would never be the same, but the memories would always remain with us.

When I drove away from Elk Mountain Lodge forever, I stiffened, looked straight ahead and gave a silent goodbye. I wondered if the new owners would have the same loving feeling for that glorious spot in the Rocky Mountains. I hoped so.

Ten miles from Aspen and our <u>Brand's</u> Elk Mountain Lodge would never be the same and it was no more.

Epilogue

After my family settled in Montrose, Colorado, Larry and I became Realtors, obtained our GRIs from Colorado University, and I became the Broker of our company. Larry was diagnosed with emphysema in 1988 and along with his diabetes and hemochromotosis, the three diseases contributed to his gradual decline in health, but he kept his humor and love for the Elk Mountains. I became the rock of the family and handled business, family, and whatever life threw next. There are more stories to tell about the adventures of property management with struggles or laughs. In 1995, we sold our business and property and retired in St. George, Utah until Larry's death in 2000. I then moved back to Colorado to be near my children and grandchildren and, also, to get my "fix" of the Rocky Mountains by getting into the high country as often as possible.

Glenn moved to Evergreen, Colorado and later to Wheat Ridge, Colorado. He was active in the Rescue Association until he died in 2008. The two other Brand brothers, George and Michael, are also deceased.

The Homestead cabin is all that remains of the Brand's Elk Mountain Lodge. Our lodge and all the other cabins and buildings we had are gone and have been replaced. The Homestead cabin has been changed and modernized. The grounds now display a huge log structure and several other modern buildings. It is a private residence and not a lodge for the public. The friendly, family-oriented Elk Mountain Lodge we knew is history.

My life has changed drastically and I am now busier than ever with volunteering, writing, painting, reading, friends, meeting people, researching, and especially enjoying my family. I enjoy my life and I treasure my memories of the days spent in the Rockies.

Joanne Brand

www.ingramcontent.com/pod-product-compliance
Lightning Source LLC
LaVergne TN
LVHW051502080426
835509LV00017B/1888